MW01065177

Adobe® Photoshop

**Adobe® Photoshop® CS2 Official
JavaScript Reference**

Adobe

Contents

---

1 | Introduction

This book is divided into two parts. Part 1 provides an introduction to scripting Adobe® Photoshop® CS2 on Mac OS® and Windows®. Part 2 is a complete reference of the objects and commands in the Adobe Photoshop CS2 JavaScript type library.

Advisory of previous publication

This book represents a subset of material included in the product CD for Adobe Photoshop CS2. If you have the product CD, you already have access to a PDF version of this material.

What's in this book

Part 1, "Photoshop Scripting Guide," introduces scripting terminology, concepts, and techniques. It has the following sections:

- "Scripting Basics" on page 5 presents the fundamentals of scripting and introduces the Photoshop CS2 Object Model.
- "Scripting Adobe Photoshop CS2" on page 27 addresses Photoshop-specific objects and components, and describes advanced techniques for scripting the Photoshop CS2 application.

Part 2, "Photoshop JavaScript Reference," provides reference details of the Photoshop object model and additional information on JavaScript-specific features. Adobe Photoshop CS2 uses ExtendScript, Adobe's extended implementation of JavaScript. See "Script Support in Adobe Photoshop CS2" for additional information. Part 2 contains the following sections:

- "Using JavaScript with Adobe Photoshop CS2" on page 61 describes scripting support in Adobe Photoshop CS2, and lists changes to the JavaScript interface since the previous release.
- "JavaScript Object Reference" on page 65 provides a complete reference for all Photoshop DOM objects and commands.
- "Using ScriptUI" on page 225 describes how to use ScriptUI, an ExtendScript component that provides a user-interface model to scripters.
- "ScriptUI Object Reference" on page 267 provides the reference details of the ScriptUI object model.
- "Using File and Folder Objects" on page 305 describes ExtendScript's platform-independent representation of files and folders.

- "File and Folder Object Reference" on page 311 provides a complete reference for the ExtendScript File and Folder classes.
- "Scripting Constants" on page 329 lists all enumerations used in the Photoshop type library.
- "ExtendScript Tools and Features" on page 347 describes ExtendScript's debugging tools and programming utilities.

There is also an appendix giving event ID codes.

Running JavaScript

Any system that runs Photoshop CS2 supports scripting. Because JavaScript performs identically on both Windows and Macintosh computers, it is considered a *cross-platform* scripting language.

You run a JavaScript from within Photoshop CS2 by storing the script in the ...Presets\Scripts folder of your Photoshop CS2 installation and then selecting the script from the **File > Scripts** menu.

Running JavaScripts from within Photoshop CS2 eliminates the scripts' ability to address other applications directly. For example, you cannot easily write a JavaScript to manage a workflow that involves Photoshop CS2 and a database-management program.

New features

The scripting interface now allows you to do any of the following:
- Specify Camera Raw options when opening a document.
- Optimize documents for the web.
- Create and format contact sheets.
- Specify options for the Batch command.
- Apply the Lens Blur filter.
- Automatically run scripts when specified events occur. For example, using a notifier object, you can associate a script with an event such as the Photoshop CS2 application opening, so that the script runs whenever the application opens.

Adobe® Photoshop® CS2

Part 1: Photoshop Scripting Guide

2 | Scripting Basics

This chapter provides a brief introduction to the basic concepts and syntax of scripting and JavaScript. If you are new to scripting, you should read this entire chapter.

If you are familiar with scripting or programming languages, you most likely will want to skip many sections in this chapter. Use the following list to locate information that is most relevant to you.

- For more information on Adobe Photoshop CS2's object model, see "Adobe Photoshop CS2's Object Model" on page 9.
- For examples of scripts created specifically for use with Adobe Photoshop CS2, see Chapter 3, "Scripting Adobe Photoshop CS2."

What is scripting?

A *script* is a series of commands that tells Adobe Photoshop CS2 to perform a set of specified actions, such as applying different filters to selections in an open document. These actions can be simple and affect only a single object, or they can be complex and affect many objects in a Adobe Photoshop CS2 document. The actions can call Adobe Photoshop CS2 alone or invoke other applications.

Scripts automate repetitive tasks and are often used as a creative tool to streamline tasks that might be too time consuming to do manually. For example, you could write a script to generate a number of localized versions of a particular image or to gather information about the various color profiles used by a collection of images.

Why use scripting?

While graphic design is characterized by creativity, some aspects of the actual work of illustration and image manipulation are anything but creative. Scripting helps creative professionals save time by automating repetitive production tasks such as resizing or reformatting documents.

Any repetitive task is a good candidate for a script. Once you can identify the steps and conditions involved in performing the task, you're ready to write a script to take care of it.

Why use scripts instead of actions?

If you've used Adobe Photoshop CS2 Actions, you're already familiar with the enormous benefits of automating repetitive tasks. Scripting allows you to extend those benefits by allowing you to add functionality that is not available for Adobe Photoshop CS2 Actions. For example, you can do the following with scripts and not with actions:

- You can add *conditional logic*, so that the script automatically makes "decisions" based on the current situation. For example, you could write a script that decides which color border to add depending on the size of the selected area in an image: "If the selected area is smaller than 2 x 4 inches, add a green border; otherwise add a red border."

- A single script can perform actions that involve multiple applications. For example, depending on the scripting language you are using, you could target both Adobe Photoshop CS2 and another Adobe Creative Suite 2 Application, such as Illustrator® CS2, in the same script.

- You can open, save, and rename files using scripts.

- You can copy scripts from one computer to another. If you were using an action and then switched computers, you'd have to recreate the action.

- Scripts provide more versatility for automatically opening files. When opening a file in an action, you must hard code the file location. In a script, you can use variables for file paths.

Note: See Adobe Photoshop CS2 Help for more information on Adobe Photoshop CS2 Actions.

Introducing objects

A script is a series of commands that tell Adobe Photoshop CS2 what to do. Basically, the commands manipulate objects.

What are objects in the context of a scripting language? When you use Adobe Photoshop CS2, you create documents, layers, channels, and design elements, and you can work with a specific area of an image by selecting the area. These things are objects. The Adobe Photoshop CS2 application is also an object.

Each type of object has its own methods.

Properties describe or characterize the object. For example:

- A layer object has a background color. It can also have a text item.

- A channel object has color properties such as red, green, and blue.

- The selected area of an image, or *selection object*, has size and shape properties.

Commands and methods describe actions you want to take on the object. For example, to print a document, you use the `Document` object's `print()` method.

Note: For more detailed information on commands and methods, see "Using methods" on page 12.

When you write a script to manipulate an object, you can use only the properties and commands or methods defined for that object. For example, a Channel object does not, obviously, have a `print()` method.

Tip: Throughout this guide, explanations of how to create a script for a task are followed by instructions for looking up in the appropriate scripting reference the specific elements used in the script. Using these instructions will help you quickly understand how to script Adobe Photoshop CS2.

Writing script statements

A scripting language, like human languages, uses sentences or *statements*, for communication. To write a script statement:

- Name an object.
- Name the property you want to change or create.
- Indicate the task you want to perform on the object's property. In JavaScript, you use a *method*.

For example, to create a new document called *myDocument*, you would write a script statement that says

```
Add a document called myDocument
```

In this example, the object is *document*, its "name" property is *myDocument*, and the method is *add*.

Syntax

Because you use JavaScript to communicate with the your computer, you must follow strict rules that the computer can understand. These rules are called the language's *syntax*.

Object model concepts

In a script statement, you refer to an object based on where the object is located in an *object model*. An object model is simply an arrangement of objects. The arrangement is called a *containment hierarchy*.

Here's a way to think about object models:

1. You live in a house, which we will think of as your `house` object.

2. The house has rooms, which we will call its `room` objects.

3. Each room has `window` and `door` objects.

Windows can be open or shut. (In other words, a `window` object has an `open` property that indicates whether or not the window is open.)

If you want to write a script that opens a window in your house, you would use the property or method that accomplishes the task. But first, you need to identify the window. This is where the object model comes in: you identify the window by stating where it is in the careful arrangement of objects contained in your house.

First of all, the window is contained by the house. But there are lots of windows, so you need to provide more detail, such as the room in the house. Again, there is probably more than one window in each room, so you'd also need to provide the wall that the window is in. Using the house object model, you would identify the window you want to open as "the window on the north wall in the living room in my house." To get the script to open that window, you'd simply add the command or method for opening it. Thus your scripting statement would look like this:

```
In my house, in the living room, the window on the north
wall: open it.
```

Similarly, you could create a script in your house model to change the color of a door to blue. In this case, you might be able to use the `door` object's `color` property instead of a command or method:

```
In my house, in the bedroom, the door to the bathroom:
blue.
```

Containment hierarchy

When we refer to an object model as a *containment hierarchy*, we mean that we identify objects in the model partially by the objects that contain them. You can picture the objects in the house model in a hierarchy, similar to a family tree, with the house on top, rooms at the next level, and the windows and doors branching from the rooms.

Applying the concept to Adobe Photoshop CS2

Now apply this object model concept to Adobe Photoshop CS2. The Adobe Photoshop CS2 application is the house, its documents are the rooms, and the layers, layersets, channels, and selected areas in your documents are the windows, doors, ceilings, and floors. You can tell Adobe Photoshop CS2 documents to add and remove objects or set or change individual object properties like color, size, and shape. You can also use commands or methods, such as opening, closing, or saving a file.

Adobe Photoshop CS2's Object Model

To create efficient scripts, you need to understand the containment hierarchy of the Adobe Photoshop CS2 object model.

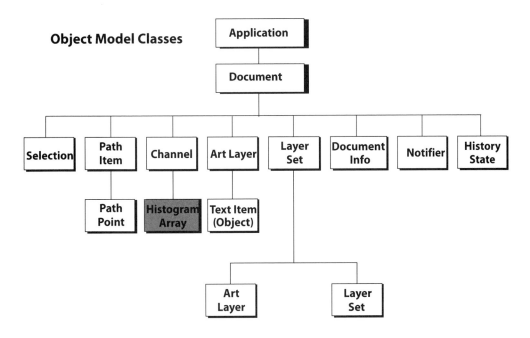

The following table provides information about each object.

Object Name	Description	To create this object without using a script:
Application	The Adobe Photoshop CS2 application.	Start the Adobe Photoshop CS2 application.
Document	The working object, in which you create layers, channels, actions, and so on. In a script, you name, open, or save a document as you would a file in the application.	In Adobe Photoshop CS2, choose **File > New** or **File > Open**.
Selection	The selected area of a layer or document.	Choose the marquee or lasso tools and drag your mouse.

Object Name	Description	To create this object without using a script:
Path Item	A drawing object, such as the outline of a shape or a straight or curved line.	Choose the path selection or pen tools and draw a path with the mouse.
Channel	Pixel information about an image's color.	Choose **Window > Channels**.
Art Layer	A layer class within a document that allows you to work on one element of an image without affecting other elements in the image.	Choose **Layer > New > Layer** or **Window > Layers**.
Layer Set	A collection of `Art Layer` objects.	Choose **Layer > New > Layer Set**.
Document Info	Metadata about a `Document` object. **Note:** Metadata is any data that helps to describe the content or characteristics of a file, such filename, creation date and time, author name, the name of the image stored in the file, etc.	Choose **File > File Info**.
Notifier	Notifies a script when an event occurs; the event then triggers the script to execute. For example, when a user clicks an **OK** button, the notifier object tells the script what to do next.	Choose **File > Scripts > Script Events Manager**.
History State	Stores a version of the document in the state the document was in each time you saved it. **Note:** You can use a `History State` object to fill a `Selection` object or to reset the document to a previous state.	Choose **Window > History**, and then choose a history state from the History palette.

Object collections

When you add an object to your script, the object is included automatically in a JavaScript collection. The objects in a single collection are identical types of objects. For example, each `Channel` object in your script belongs to a `Channels` collection; each `Art Layer` object belongs to an `Art Layers` collection.

Note: Your scripts place objects in collections even when there is only one object of that type in the entire script, that is, only one object in the collection.

When you add an object, the object is numbered automatically within its respective collection. You can identify the object in other script statements by using its collection name and assigned number.

Using the house example, when you add a room to your house, your script stores a number that identifies the room. If it's the first room you've added, your JavaScript considers the room to be *room0*.

Here's how the JavaScript handles the automatic numbering if you add a second room:

- JavaScript numbers are static; they don't shift when you add a new object to the collection. Object numbering in JavaScript indicates the order in which the objects were added to the script. Because the first room you added was considered *room0*, the next room you add is considered *room1*; if you add a third room, it is labeled *room2*.

When you add an object that is not a room, the numbering starts all over for the new object collection. For example, if you add a door, your JavaScript considers the door *door0*.

Note: You can also name objects when you add them. For example, you can name the rooms *livingRoom* and *bedRoom*. If an object has a name, you can refer to the object in your script either by name or by the collection name followed by the assigned number.

In JavaScript, you'll find object numbers very useful. For example, you might have several files in which you want to make the background layer white. You can write a script that says "Open all files in this folder and change the first layer's color to white." If you didn't have the capability of referring to the layers by number, you'd need to include in your script the names of all of the background layers in all of the files. Chances are, if you created the files using the Adobe Photoshop CS2 application rather than a script, the layers don't even have names.

Indexes or Indices

An object's number in an collection is called an *index*.

Referring to an object in a collection

A collection name is the plural version of the object type name. For example, a collection of `Document` objects is called *documents*. In JavaScript, you can use the collection name and the index to refer to an object.

The following code samples demonstrate the correct syntax for using an object's index when referring to the object.

Tip: Remember that JavaScript indexes begin with 0. Beginning your count with 0 might seem confusing, but as you learn about scripting, you'll find that using 0 gives you added capabilities for getting your scripts to do what you want.

The collection name is followed by the index in square brackets with no space between the object name and the brackets.

```
documents[0]
```

Object references

Because scripts use a containment hierarchy, you can think of an object reference as being similar to the path to a file.

You can use an object's name or index to refer to the object. (See "Indexes or Indices" on page 11.)

The following code sample demonstrates the syntax for referring to an `artLayer` object named *Profile*, which was the first layer added to the `layerSet` object named *Silhouettes*, which in turn was the first layer added to the current document:

Object index reference:

```
app.documents[1].layerSets[0].layers[0]
```

Object name reference:

```
appRef.document("MyDocument").layerSet("Silhouettes").la
yer("Profile")
```

You can also combine the two types of syntax:

```
appRef.activeDocument.layerSet("Silhouettes").layers[0]
```

Note: When you refer to an object by its assigned name you use the object classname, which is singular (`document` or `layerSet` or `layer`). When you use a numeric index to refer to an object, you use the collection name, which is plural (`documents` or `layerSets` or `layers`).

Using methods

Methods are directions you add to a script to perform tasks or obtain results. For example, you could use the `open()` method to open a specified file.

Note: You can use only the methods or commands associated with that object type. For example, you can use the `open()` method on a `Document` object but not on a `Selection` object which, obviously, cannot be opened.

Before using a method on a JavaScript object, look up the method in the Methods table for the object type in the scripting reference later in this book.

For example, you could look up the `Document` object in the "Interface" chapter, and then find the object's Methods table.

Methods and arguments

You insert methods at the end of a JavaScript statement. You must place a period before the method name to separate it from the rest of the statement.

A method in JavaScript must be followed by parentheses, as in the following statement:

```
app.documents[0].print()
```

Some methods require additional data, called *arguments*, within the parentheses. Other methods have optional arguments. The following statement uses the `add()` method to add a bitmap document named *myDocument* that is 4000 pixels wide and 5000 pixels tall and has a resolution of 72 pixels per inch:

Note: Even though the `Document` object in the following script statements is given a name (*myDocument*), you use the object collection name when you add the object. See "Referring to an object in a collection" on page 11 for more information on object collections. See "Object references" on page 12 for information on object collection names versus object names in a singular form.

```
app.documents.add(4000, 5000, 72, "myDocument",
DocumentMode.BITMAP)
```

Using variables

A *variable* is a container for data you use in your script.

Why use variables?

There are several reasons for using variables rather than entering values directly in the script.

- Variables make your script easier to update or change. For example, if your script creates several 4 x 2 inch documents and later you want to change the documents' size to 4 x 3 inches, you could simply change the value of the variable `docHeight` from *2* to *3* at the beginning of your script and the entire script would be updated automatically.

  If you had used the direct value *2 inches* to enter the height for each new document, updating the document sizes would be much more tedious. You would need find and change each statement throughout the script that creates a document.

- Variables make your scripts reusable in a wider variety of situations. As a script executes, it can assign data to the variables that reflects the state of the current document and selection, and then make decisions based on the content of the variables.

Data contained in variables

The data that a variable contains is the variable's *value*. To assign a value to a variable, you use an *assignment statement*. A variable's value can be a number, a *string* (a word or phrase or other list of characters enclosed in quotes), an object reference, a mathematical expression, another variable, or a list (including collections, elements, and arrays).

See "Using operators" on page 22 for information on using mathematical expressions or other variables as values. See "Using object properties" on page 16 for information about arrays.

Assignment statements require specific syntax in each scripting language. See "Creating variables and assigning values" on page 14 for details.

Creating variables and assigning values

This section demonstrates how to create two variables named *thisNumber* and *thisString*, and then assign the following values:

Variable	Value
thisNumber	10
thisString	"Hello World"

Note: When you assign a string value to a variable, you must enclose the value in straight, double quotes (""). The quotes tell the script to use the value as it appears without interpreting or processing it. For example, 2 is a number value; "2" is a string value. The script can add, subtract, or perform other operations with a number value. It can only display a string value.

The var keyword declares (that is, creates) variables in JavaScript. The following example uses separate statements to declare and assign a value to the variable thisNumber; the variable thisString is assigned and declared in a single statement.

```
var thisNumber
thisNumber = 10
var thisString = "Hello, World"
```

To assign a reference to an object in JavaScript, you use the same syntax as other JavaScript assignment statements:

```
var docRef = app.activeDocument
```

JavaScript value types

You can use the following types of values for variables.

Note: For now, don't worry about the value types you don't understand.

Value Type	Description	Examples
String	A series of text characters that appear inside (straight) quotation marks	"Hello" "123 Main St." " "
Number	Any number not inside double quotes	3.7 15000
Boolean	Logical true or false	true
Null	Something that points to nothing	
Object	Properties and methods belonging to an object or array	activeDocument Documents(1).artLayers(2)
Function	Value returned by a function	See "Using subroutines, handlers, and functions" on page 25.
Undefined	Devoid of any value	undefined

Naming variables

It's a good idea to use descriptive names for your variables—such as firstPage or corporateLogo, rather than names only you would understand and that you might not recognize when you look at your script a year after you write it, such as x or c. You can also give your variable names a standard prefix so that they'll stand out from the objects, commands, and keywords of your scripting system. For example, you could use the prefix "doc" at the beginning of any variables that contain Document objects, or "layer" to identify variables that contain Art Layer objects.

- Variable names must be a single word (no spaces). Many people use internal capitalization (such as myFirstPage) or underscore characters (my_first_page) to create more readable names.

- Variable names cannot begin with a number or contain punctuation or quotation marks.

  You can use underscore characters (_), but not as the first character in the name.

- Variable names in JavaScript are case sensitive. ThisString is not the same as thisstring or thisString.

Using object properties

Properties describe an object. For example, a `Document` object's height and width properties describe the document's size.

To access and modify a property of an object, you name the object and then name the property.

In JavaScript, you name the object, type a period (.), and then name the property, using the equals sign (=) to set the property value.

```
var layerRef = artLayers.add()
layerRef.kind = LayerKind.TEXT
```

Note: The `kind` property in JavaScript uses a *constant* value indicated by the uppercase formatting. In JavaScript, you must use constant values exactly as they appear in the scripting language reference. To find constant values, refer to the "Constants" chapter in the scripting reference later in this book. For more information, see "Understanding and finding constants" on page 16.

Understanding and finding constants

Constants are a type of value that defines a property. Using the example of the `kind` property of an `Art Layer` object, you can define only specific kinds that Adobe Photoshop CS2 allows.

In JavaScript, you must use constants exactly as they are defined—with the exact spelling and capitalization.

Note: Throughout this document, actual values of enumerations are given using the following format:

```
newLayerRef.Kind = 2 '2 indicates psLayerKind --> 2
(psTextLayer)
```

The single quote (') before the explanation creates a *comment* and prevents the text to the right of the single quote (') from being read by the scripting engine. For more information, see "Documenting scripts" on page 18 for more information on comments.

A constant is indicated as a hypertext link in the Value Type column of the Properties table in the scripting language reference in Part 2 of this book. When you click the link, you can view the list of possible values for the property.

For example, look up the `Art Layer` object in the "Interface" chapter. In the Properties table, look up `kind`. The Value Type column for `kind` contains a link. Click the link to view the values you can use to define the `kind` property.

Note: Different objects can use the same property with different constant values. The constant values for the `Channel` object's `kind` property are different than the constant values for the `Art Layer` object's `kind` property.

Understanding object classes and inheritance

In Adobe Photoshop CS2, every type of object—document, layer, etc.—belongs to its own class, each with its own set of properties and behaviors.

Object classes can also "inherit," or share, the properties of a parent, or superclass. When a class inherits properties, that class is called a *child* or *subclass* of the class from which it inherits properties. In Adobe Photoshop CS2, `Art Layer` objects, for example, inherit from the `Layer` class.

Classes can have properties that aren't shared with their superclass. Using an example from the house object, both window objects and door objects might inherit an "opened" property from the parent `Opening` class, but a window could have a `numberOfPanes` property which the `Opening` class could not have.

In Adobe Photoshop CS2 for example, `Art Layer` objects have the property `grouped` which is not inherited from the `Layer` class.

When you use the scripting language reference later in this book, the term *inherited from* indicates that the object class you are looking at is a child class of the parent class named in the definition.

Using arrays

In JavaScript, arrays are similar to collections; however, arrays are not created automatically.

You can think of an array as a list of values for a single variable. For example, the following JavaScript array lists 4 values for the variable `myFiles`:

```
var myFiles = new Array ()
myFiles[0] = "clouds.bmp"
myFiles[1] = "clouds.gif"
myFiles[2] = "clouds.jpg"
myFiles[3] = "clouds.pdf"
```

Notice that each value is numbered. To use a value in a statement, you must include the number. The following statement opens the file `clouds.gif`:

```
open(myFiles[1])
```

Documenting scripts

You can document the details of your script by including *comments* throughout the script. Because of the way they are formatted, comments are ignored by the scripting system as the script executes.

Comments help clarify (to humans, including yourself) what your script does. It is generally considered good programming practice to document each bit of logic in your script.

You use comments to:

- Help you remember the purpose of a section of your script.
- Help you remember to include all the components you planned for your script. Unless you are an experienced programmer, you can review your script by reading through the comments more easily than you can by reading the code.
- Help others understand your script. It's possible that other people in your organization will need to use, update, or debug your script.

Comment syntax

You can create the following types of comments:

- Single-line: An entire line is a comment and therefore ignored when your script runs.
- End-of-line: The line begins with executable code, then becomes a comment which is ignored when the script runs.
- Multi-line: An entire block of text, which runs more than a single line in your script, is a comment.

In JavaScript, use the double forward slash to comment a single or partial line:

```
// This comments until the end of the line
var thisString = "Hello, World" // this comments until
the end of the line as well
```

Enclose multi-line comments in the following notation /* */.

```
/* This entire
block of text
is a comment*/
```

Note: Generally, your scripts are easier to read if you format all comments as single-line comments because the comment status of the line is indicated at the beginning of the line.

In some cases, individual script lines are too long to fit on a single line in your script editor window. When an individual statement is too long to fit on a

---

Adobe® Photoshop® CS2 Official JavaScript Reference

single line, the next line simply wraps to the following line. However, to make your script easier to read, you can use the space bar or Tab to indent the continuation line.

Note: You can put more than one JavaScript statement on a single line if you separate the statements with a semicolon (;). However, your scripts are easier to read if you start a new line for each statement. Here is an example of putting two statements on a single line:

```
var thisNumber= 10; var thisString= "Hello, Word"
```

Creating a sample Hello World script

It's time to put the scripting concepts you've just learned into practice. Traditionally, the first thing to accomplish in any programming environment is the display of a "Hello World" message.

➤ **Our Hello World scripts will do the following:**

1. Open the Adobe Photoshop CS2 application.

2. Create a new `Document` object.
    When we create the document, we will also create a variable named `docRef` and then assign a reference to the document as the value of `docRef`. The document will be 4 inches wide and 2 inches high.

3. Create an `Art Layer` object.
    In our script, we will create a variable named `artLayerRef` and then assign a reference to the `Art Layer` object as the value of `artLayerRef`.

4. Define `artLayerRef` as a text item.

5. Set the contents of the text item to "Hello World".

Note: We will also include comments throughout the scripts. In fact, because this is our first script, we will use comments to excess.

These steps mirror a specific path in the containment hierarchy, as illustrated below.

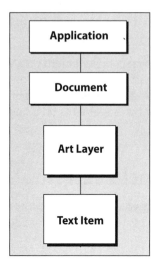

Creating and running a JavaScript

Follow these steps to create and run a JavaScript that displays the text *Hello World!* in a Adobe Photoshop CS2 document.

Because you will be actually using Adobe Photoshop CS2 to run your JavaScripts, it is not necessary to include code that opens Adobe Photoshop CS2 at the beginning of the script.

Note: Adobe has created the Extend Script scripting language to augment JavaScript for use with Adobe Photoshop CS2. You can use the Extend Script command #target to target the Adobe Photoshop CS2 application and create the ability to open JavaScripts that manipulate Adobe Photoshop CS2 from anywhere in your file system. See "Chapter 8, "ScriptUI Object Reference," in Part 2 of this book for more information.

➤ **To create and run your first Adobe Photoshop CS2 JavaScript:**

1. Type the following script:

    Note: Entering comments is optional.

    ```
    // Hello Word Script
    // Remember current unit settings and then set units to
    // the value expected by this script
    var originalUnit = preferences.rulerUnits
    preferences.rulerUnits = Units.INCHES
    ```

```
// Create a new 4x4 inch document and assign it to a
variable
var docRef = app.documents.add( 4, 4 )

// Create a new art layer containing text
var artLayerRef = docRef.artLayers.add()
artLayerRef.kind = LayerKind.TEXT

// Set the contents of the text layer.
var textItemRef = artLayerRef.textItem
textItemRef.contents = "Hello, World"

// Release references
docRef = null
artLayerRef = null
textItemRef = null

// Restore original ruler unit setting
app.preferences.rulerUnits = originalUnit
```

2. Save file as a text file with a `.jsx` file name extension in the Presets > Scripts folder in your Adobe Adobe Photoshop CS2 directory.

   Note: You must place your JavaScripts in the Presets > Scripts folder in order to make the scripts accessible from the **File > Scripts** menu in Adobe Photoshop CS2. The scripts do not appear on the **File > Scripts** menu until you restart the application.

   Note: Adobe Photoshop CS2 also supports JavaScript files that use a `.js` extension.

3. Do either of the following:
   - If Adobe Photoshop CS2 is already open, choose **File > Scripts > Browse**, and then navigate to the Presets > Scripts folder and choose your script.
   - Start or restart Adobe Photoshop CS2, and then choose **File > Scripts**, and then select your script from the **Scripts** menu.

What's next

The remainder of this chapter provides information about general scripting tips and techniques. Experienced JavaScript programmers might want to skip to Chapter 3, "Scripting Adobe Photoshop CS2," for specifics on scripting Adobe Photoshop CS2.

Using operators

Operators perform operations on variables or values and return a result. In the following table, the examples use the following variables:

- `thisNumber =10`
- `thisString = "Pride"`

Operator	Operation	Example	Result
+	add	`thisNumber + 2`	12
-	subtract	`thisNumber - 2`	8
*	multiply	`thisNumber * 2`	20
/	divide	`thisNumber/2`	5
=	assign	`thisNumber = 10`	10
+	concatenate[a]	`thisString + " and Prejudice"`	Pride and Prejudice

a. Concatenation operations combine two strings. Note that a space has been added at the beginning of the string " and Prejudice"; without the space following the first enclosing quote, the result would be: Prideand Prejudice

Comparison operators

You can use a different type of operator to perform comparisons such as equal to, not equal to, greater than, or less than. These are called *comparison operators*. Consult a scripting language guide, such as the guides listed in this document's "Bibliography" on page 26, for information on comparison operators.

Using conditional statements

Conditional statements give your scripts a way to evaluate something and then act according to the result. For example, you might want your script to detect the blend mode of a layer or the name or date of a history state.

Most conditional statements contain the word `if`, or the words `if` and `then`.

The following example checks whether any documents are open; if no documents are open, the script displays a dialog box that contains the message "No Adobe Photoshop CS2 documents are open!" If one or more documents are open, then no dialog is displayed.

```
//create a variable named docCount,
//then get its value using
//the length property of the documents (collection)
object*/
```

```
var docCount = documents.length
if (docCount == 0)
{
    alert("No Adobe Photoshop CS2 documents are open!")
}
```

Loops

Loops are control structures that repeat a process until the script achieves a specific goal, status, or condition.

Simple loops

The simplest loops repeat a series of script operations a set number of times. Although you'll find more substantial uses for loops, the following script uses a variable named counter to demonstrate how to display a dialog box that contains the number 1, then displays another dialog box that contains the number 2, and then displays a third dialog box that contains 3.

In JavaScript, this type of loop is called a *for* loop.

Note: In the following script, the variable that contains the counter is named *i*. This represents an exception to the rule of thumb for good naming practices for variables. However, *i* is a traditional counter variable name and most script writers recognize its meaning, especially when *i* is used in a loop. See "Naming variables" on page 15 for details on variable naming practices.

```
var i
for (i =1; i < 4; i=i + 1)
{
    alert(i)
}
```

The condition in the for loop contains three statements (separated by semicolons):

- i = 1 — Set the value of i to 1.
- i<4 — If i is less than 4, execute the statement in brackets; if i is equal to or more than 4, stop and don't do anything else with this loop.
- i=i + 1 — After executing the statement in the brackets, add 1 to the value of i.

  Note: The equation i=i + 1 can be abbreviated to i++.

More complex loops

A more complicated type of loop includes conditional logic, so that it performs a task while or until some condition is true. Conditional statements in a script can include the words *while*, *until*, or *if* — just like in English.

For example, you could make the conditional statement "I'll use scripts only *if* they make my life easier." Another way to say this is, "I'll use scripts only on the condition that they make my life easier."

Similarly, in the sentence, "I'll write scripts only *while* I'm at work," the condition is *being at work*. The same condition is worded with a slight difference in the following sentence: "I'll write scripts only *until* I leave work."

➤ **The following scripts use *while* loops to do the following:**

1. Display a "Quit?" dialog box.

    The dialog box contains two possible responses: an *OK* button and a *Cancel* button.

2. When the user clicks *Cancel* (for "Don't quit."), the script displays the dialog box again.

3. When the user clicks *OK* (for "Please quit!"), the script displays a different dialog box that asks whether the user really wants to quit.

4. When the user clicks *Cancel* in the new dialog box, the second dialog appears again.

5. When the user clicks *OK*, the loop ends and the dialog boxes quit appearing.

    ```
    //create a variable named flag and make its value false
    var flag = false

    //create the loop and the condition
    while (flag == false)
    {
       /*create a confirm dialog with the text Quit?
       and two response buttons
       change the value of flag to the selected response*/
       flag = confirm("Quit?")
    }

    //change the value of flag back to false
    var flag = false
    do
    ```

```
{
    flag = confirm("Are you sure?")
}
while (flag == false)
```

Using subroutines, handlers, and functions

Subroutines are scripting modules you can refer to from within your script. They allow you to re-use parts of scripts. If you find yourself typing or pasting the same lines of code into several different places in a script, you've identified a good candidate for a subroutine.

Note: Subroutines can also be called *handlers*, *functions*, or *routines*; these terms can have slight differences in different scripting languages. JavaScript generally uses the term *function*.

You can pass one or more values to a subroutine or function; you can receive one or more values in return. For example, you could pass a single measurement value (such as inches) to a function and ask the function to return the equivalent value in a different measurement system (such as centimeters). Or you could ask a function to return the geometric center point of an object from its geometric bounds.

The following script presents a form with one command button. When a user clicks the button, a dialog box with the message "Are you sure?" appears.

```
/*create a variable and assign its value as the return
value
of the function named DoConfirm*/
var theResult = DoConfirm( "Are you sure?" )

//display an alert box with the assigned value as its
message
alert(theResult)

//define DoConfirm
function DoConfirm(message)
{
    var result = confirm(message)
    return result
}
```

Troubleshooting and error handling

JavaScript debugging is described in detail in the scripting reference later in this book.

You can add *error handling* code to your script to respond to conditions other than those you expect it to encounter. For instance, imagine that you've written a script that formats the current text selection. What should the script do if the current selection turns out not to be text at all, but a path item?

The following example shows how you can stop a script from executing when a specific file cannot be found. This example stores a reference to the document named `MyDocument` in a variable named `docRef`. If a document named `MyDocument` does not exist in the current document, the script displays a message.

```
try
{
    for (i = 0; i < app.documents.length; ++i)
    {
        var myName = app.documents[i].name;
        alert(myName)
    }
}
catch(someError)
{
    alert( "JavaScript error occurred. Message = " +
            someError.description)
}
```

Bibliography

For further information and instruction in using the JavaScript scripting language, see these documents and resources:

- "JavaScript: The Definitive Guide," David Flanagan, O'Reily Media Inc, 2002. ISBN 0-596-00048-0.
- "JavaScript Bible," Danny Goodman, Hungry Minds Inc, 2001. ISBN 0-7645-4718-6.
- "Adobe Scripting," Chandler McWilliams, Wiley Publishing, Inc., 2003. ISBN 0-7645-2455-0.
- "JavaScript for the World Wide Web, Fifth Edition: Visual QuickStart Guide." Tom Negrino and Dori Smith, Peachpit, 2003. ISBN 0-321-19439-X.

3 | Scripting Adobe Photoshop CS2

This chapter demonstrates several techniques for creating scripts to use specifically with Adobe Photoshop CS2.

More importantly, you will learn how to use the Adobe Photoshop CS2 scripting references to find the objects, classes, properties, methods, and even some values (called *constants* or *enumerations*) you can use to create JavaScripts for Adobe Photoshop CS2.

Tip: Throughout this chapter, the explanation of how to create a script is followed by instructions for locating information about the specific elements used in the script. Using these instructions will help you quickly understand how to script Adobe Photoshop CS2.

Viewing Photoshop CS2 objects, commands, and methods

In JavaScript, all properties and methods of the application are accessible without any qualification. You can reference the application as part of the containment hierarchy or leave it out, whichever makes your scripts easier for you to read. The following statements are equivalent:

```
var docRef = app.documents[1]
```

and

```
var docRef=documents[1]
```

Note: JavaScript samples throughout this guide do not reference the `Application` object.

Creating new objects in a script

To create a new document in the Adobe Photoshop CS2 application, you select **File > New**. To create other types of objects within a document, such as a layer, channel, or path, you use the Window menu or choose the *New* icon on the appropriate palette. This section demonstrates how to accomplish these same tasks in a script.

To create an object in a script, you name the type of object you want to create and then use the `add()` method.

As you can see in the Adobe Photoshop CS2 Object Model, the `Document` object contains all other objects except the `Application` object. Therefore,

---

you must reference the `Document` object when adding objects other than `Document` objects to your script.

In JavaScript, you can use the `add()` method only with the collection name. The `add()` method is not valid with objects other than collection objects.

The JavaScript statement to create a document is:

```
documents.add()
```

and *not*:

```
document.add()
```

Note: You can include an `Application` object reference if you wish. The following statement is equivalent to the previous example:

```
app.documents.add()
```

To add an `ArtLayer` object, you must reference the `Document` object that will contain the layer.

```
documents(0).artLayers.add()
```

The `add()` method is associated with the JavaScript `Documents` object but not with the `Document` object (see Part 2 of this book).

Similarly, the `ArtLayer` object does not have an `add()` method; the `ArtLayers` object does.

Note: The `Layers` collection object does not include an `add()` method. For more information, look up the `Layers` object in the scripting reference in Part 2.

Setting the active object

To work on a an object in the Adobe Photoshop CS2 application, you must make the object the front-most, or *active* object. For example, to work in a layer, you must first bring the layer to the front.

In scripting, the same rule applies. If your script creates two or more documents, the commands and methods in your script are executed on the active document. Therefore, to ensure that your commands are acting on the correct document, it is good programming practice to designate the active document before executing any commands or methods in the script.

To set an active object, use the `active`*Object* property of the parent object (such as `activeDocument` or `activeLayer`).

Note: The parent object is the object that contains the specified object. For example, the application is the parent of the document; a document is the parent of a layer, selection, or channel.

For example, if you search for `activeDocument` in the scripting reference (Part 2), you will find it is a property of the `Application` object; if you search for `activeLayer` or `activeHistoryState`, you will find they are properties of the `Document` object.

For sample scripts that set active objects, see the following sections.

- Setting the active document
- Setting the active layer
- Setting the active channels

Setting the active document

The following example demonstrates how to set the active document.

```
// Create 2 documents
var docRef = app.documents.add( 4, 4)
var otherDocRef = app.documents.add (4,6)

//make docRef the active document
app.activeDocument = docRef
//here you would include command statements
//that perform actions on the active document. Then, you
could
//make a different document the active document

//use the activeDocument property of the Application
object to
//bring otherDocRef front-most as the new active document
app.activeDocument = otherDocRef
```

Setting the active layer

The following example demonstrates how to use the `current layer` (`ActiveLayer/activeLayer`) property of the `Document` object to set the active layer.

```
docRef.activeLayer = docRef.layers["Layer 1"]
```

Look up the `activeLayer` property in the Properties table of the `Document` object in "Chapter 5, "JavaScript Object Reference" in Part 2 of this book.

Setting the active channels

More than one channel can be active at a time.

Set the active channels to the first and third channel using a channel array:

```
theChannels = new Array(docRef.channels[0],
docRef.channels[2])
docRef.activeChannels = theChannels
```

Alternatively, select all component channels by using the componentChannels property of the Document object:

```
app.activeDocument.activeChannels =
    activeDocument.componentChannels
```

Opening a document

You use the open() method of the Application object to open an existing document. You must specify the document name (that is, the path to the file that contains the document) with the method.

Specifying file formats to open

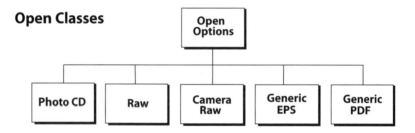

Because Adobe Photoshop CS2 supports many different file formats, the open() method lets you specify the format of the document you are opening. If you do not specify the format, Adobe Photoshop CS2 will infer the type of file for you. The following example opens a document using its default type:

```
var fileRef = new File("//MyFile")
var docRef = app.open (fileRef)
```

Notice that you must create a File object and then pass a reference to the object to the open() command.

For the document types on the following list, you can set options to specify how the document will be opened, such as the height and width of the window in which the document is opened, which page to open to in a multi-page file, etc.

- PhotoCD
- CameraRaw

- RawFormat
- Adobe PDF
- EPS

To find out which options you can set for each of file type, look up the properties for the *OpenOptions* objects that begin with the file format name. For example, look up `PhotoCDOpenOptions` or `EPSOpenOptions` in the scripting reference (Part 2).

The following example demonstrates how to open a generic (multi-page/multi-image) PDF document with the following specifications:

- The document will open in a window that is 100 pixels high and 200 pixels wide.
- The document will open in RGB mode with a resolution of 72 pixels/inch.
- Antialiasing will be used to minimize the jagged appearance of the edges of images in the document.
- The document will open to page 3.
- The document's original shape will change to conform to the height and width properties if the original shape is not twice as wide as it is tall.

```
// Set the ruler units to pixels
var originalRulerUnits = app.preferences.rulerUnits
app.preferences.rulerUnits = Units.PIXELS
// Get a reference to the file that we want to open
var fileRef = new File( C:\\PDFFiles\MyFile.pdf )

// Create a PDF option object
var pdfOpenOptions = new PDFOpenOptions
pdfOpenOptions.antiAlias = true
pdfOpenOptions.height = 100
pdfOpenOptions.width = 200
pdfOpenOptions.mode = OpenDocumentMode.RGB
pdfOpenOptions.resolution = 72
pdfOpenOptions.page = 3
pdfOpenOptions.constrainProportions = false

// open the file
app.open( fileRef, pdfOpenOptions )

// restore unit settings
app.preferences.rulerUnits = originalRulerUnits
```

Saving a document

Options for saving documents in Adobe Photoshop CS2 are illustrated below. To find out which properties you can specify for a specific file format save option, look up the object that begins with the file format name. For example, to find out about properties for saving an `.eps` file, look up `EPSSaveOptions` in Part 2 of this book.

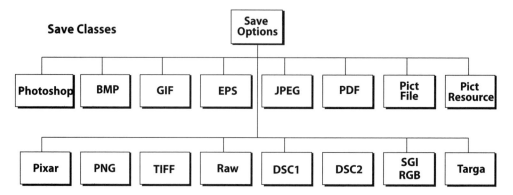

Save Classes

Save Options: Photoshop, BMP, GIF, EPS, JPEG, PDF, Pict File, Pict Resource, Pixar, PNG, TIFF, Raw, DSC1, DSC2, SGI RGB, Targa

Note: It is important to note that the `Open` and `Save` formats are not identical. See "Opening a document" on page 30 for comparison.

Note: The following optional formats are available only when installed explicitly:

- Alias PIX
- Electric Image
- SGI RGB
- Wavefront RLA
- SoftImage

The following script saves a document as a `.jpeg` file:

```
jpgFile = new File( "/Temp001.jpeg" )
jpgSaveOptions = new JPEGSaveOptions()
jpgSaveOptions.embedColorProfile = true
jpgSaveOptions.formatOptions =
FormatOptions.STANDARDBASELINE
jpgSaveOptions.matte = MatteType.NONE
jpgSaveOptions.quality = 1
app.activeDocument.saveAs(jpgFile, jpgSaveOptions, true,
    Extension.LOWERCASE)
```

Setting application preferences

Your script can set application preferences such as color picker, file-saving options, guide-grid-slice settings, and so on.

Note: The properties in the `Preferences` object correlate to the Adobe Photoshop CS2 Preferences dialog options, which you display by choosing **Photoshop > Preferences** on Mac OS or **Edit > Preferences** in Windows versions of Adobe Photoshop CS2. For explanations of individual preferences, please refer to Adobe Photoshop CS2 Help.

The Preferences object is a property of the `Application` object.

```
preferences.rulerUnits =Units.INCHES
preferences.typeUnits = TypeUnits.PIXELS
```

In the scripting reference, look up the `Preferences` object to view all of the settings properties you can use. Additionally, look up the `Application` object > `preferences` property.

Suppressing dialog boxes

It is important to be able to control dialog boxes properly from a script. If a dialog appears while a script is executed, it stops until a user dismisses the dialog box. This is normally fine in an interactive script that expects a user to be sitting at the machine. But if a script runs in an unsupervised (batch) mode, you do not want dialogs to be displayed, stopping your script.

You use the `displayDialogs` property of the `Application` object to control whether or not dialog boxes are displayed.

Note: Using dialog boxes in your script is roughly equivalent to using stops in a Adobe Photoshop CS2 action.

To set dialog preferences, you use the `displayDialogs` property of the `Application` object.

```
displayDialogs = DialogModes.NO
```

In the scripting reference, Part 2 of this book, look up the `Application` object property `displayDialogs`, and then look up the constant `DialogModes` in the "Constants" chapter.

Working with the Adobe Photoshop CS2 Object Model

This section contains information about using the objects in the Adobe Photoshop CS2 Object Model. For information on object models, see "Object model concepts" on page 7 and "Adobe Photoshop CS2's Object Model" on page 9.

Using the Application object

This section describes how and when to use the `Application` object in a script. It also describes how to use some properties of the `Application` object.

You use the properties and methods of the `Application` object to work with Adobe Photoshop CS2 functionality and objects such as the following:

- Global Adobe Photoshop CS2 settings or preferences, such as unit values or color settings. See "Setting application preferences" on page 32.
- Documents—You can add or open documents and set the active document. See "Opening a document" on page 30 and "Setting the active object" on page 28.
- Actions—You can execute actions created either via scripting or using the Actions palette in the Adobe Photoshop CS2 application.

You can use Application object properties to get information such as the following:

- A list of fonts installed on the system:
  - `var fontstInstalled = app.fonts`
- The amount of unused memory available to Adobe Photoshop CS2.
- The location of the Presets folder.

  Note: See "Creating and running a JavaScript" on page 20 for information on the Presets folder.

Using the Document object

The `Document` object can represent any open document in Adobe Photoshop CS2. You can think of a `Document` object as a file; you can also think of it as a canvas. You work with the `Document` object to do the following:

- Access script objects contained in the `Document` object, such as `ArtLayer` or `Channel` objects. See "Containment hierarchy" on page 8 and "Adobe Photoshop CS2's Object Model" on page 9 for more information.
- Manipulate a specific `Document` object. For example, you could crop, rotate or flip the canvas, resize the image or canvas, and trim the image. See "Manipulating a Document object" on page 35 for a demonstration.
- Get the active layer. See "Setting the active layer" on page 29.
- Save the current document. See "Saving a document" on page 31.
- Copy and paste within the active document or between different documents. See "Understanding clipboard interaction" on page 46.

Manipulating a Document object

The following example demonstrates how to do the following:

- Change the size of the image to 4 inches wide and 4 inches high.
- Change the size of the document window (or canvas) to 5 inches high and 6 inches wide.
- Trim the top and bottom of the image.
- Crop the image.
- Flip the entire window.

Note: The following examples assume the ruler units have been set to inches. See "Setting application preferences" on page 32 for information on ruler units.

```
//this sample script assumes the ruler units have been
set to inches
docRef.resizeImage( 4,4 )
docRef.resizeCanvas( 4,4 )
docRef.trim(TrimType.TOPLEFT, true, false, true, false)

//the crop command uses unit values
//change the ruler units to pixels
app.preferences.rulerUnits =Units.PIXELS
docRef.crop (new Array(10,20,40,50), 45, 20, 20, 72)
docRef.flipCanvas(Direction.HORIZONTAL)
```

Working with layer objects

The Adobe Photoshop CS2 object model contains two types of layer objects:

- `ArtLayer` objects, which can contain image contents and are basically equivalent to Layers in the Adobe Photoshop CS2 application.

  Note: An `ArtLayer` object can also contain text if you use the `kind` property to set the `ArtLayer` object's type to text layer.

- `Layer Set` objects, which can contain zero or more `ArtLayer` objects.

When you create a layer you must specify whether you are creating an `ArtLayer` or a `Layer Set` object.

Note: Both the `ArtLayer` and `LayerSet` objects have corresponding collection objects, `ArtLayers` and `LayerSets`, which have an `add()` method. You can reference, but not add, `ArtLayer` and `LayerSet` objects using the `Layers` collection object, because, unlike other collection objects, it does not have an `add()` method.

Creating an ArtLayer object

The following example demonstrates how to create an `ArtLayer` object filled with red at the beginning of the current document.

```
// Create a new art layer at the beginning of the current
document
var layerRef = app.activeDocument.artLayers.add()
layerRef.name = "MyBlendLayer"
layerRef.blendMode = BlendMode.NORMAL

// Select all so we can apply a fill to the selection
app.activeDocument.selection.selectAll

// Create a color to be used with the fill command
var colorRef = new SolidColor
colorRef.rgb.red = 255
colorRef.rgb.green = 100
colorRef.rgb.blue = 0

// Now apply fill to the current selection
app.activeDocument.selection.fill(colorRef)
```

The following example shows how to create a `Layer Set` object after the creating the first `ArtLayer` object in the current document:

```
// Get a reference to the first layer in the document
var layerRef = app.activeDocument.layers[0]

// Create a new LayerSet (it will be created at the
beginning of the // document)
var newLayerSetRef = app.activeDocument.layerSets.add()

// Move the new layer to after the first layer
newLayerSetRef.move(layerRef,
ElementPlacement.PLACEAFTER)
```

Referencing ArtLayer objects

When you create a layer in the Adobe Photoshop CS2 application (rather than a script), the layer is added to the Layers palette and given a number. These numbers act as layer names and do not correspond to the index numbers of `ArtLayer` objects you create in a script.

Your JavaScript will always consider the layer at the top of the list in the Layers palette as the first layer in the index. For example, if your document has four layers, the Adobe Photoshop CS2 application names them Background Layer, Layer 1, Layer 2, and Layer 3. Normally, Layer 3 would be at the top of the list in the Layers palette because you added it last. If your script is working on this open document and uses the syntax `layers[0].select()` to tell Adobe Photoshop CS2 to select a layer, Layer 3 will be selected. If you then you drag the Background layer to the top of the list in the Layers palette and run the script again, the Background layer is selected.

You can use the following syntax to refer to the layers by the names given them by the Application:

```
layers["Layer 3"].select() //using the collection name
and square brackets for the collection
```

Working with layer set objects

Existing layers can be moved into layer sets. The following example shows how to create a `Layer Set` object, duplicate an existing `ArtLayer` object, and move the duplicate object into the layer set.

In JavaScript you must duplicate and place the layer.

```
var layerSetRef = docRef.layerSets.add()
var layerRef =
docRef.artLayers[0].duplicate(layerSetRef,
    ElementPlacement.PLACEATEND)
layerRef.moveToEnd (layerSetRef)
```

Linking Layer Objects

Scripting also supports linking and unlinking layers. You link layers together so that you can move or transform the layers in a single statement.

```
var layerRef1 = docRef.artLayers.add()
var layerRef2 = docRef.artLayers.add()
layerRef1.link(layerRef2)
```

Look up `link()` in the Methods table of the `ArtLayer` object in Part 2 of this book. Additionally, look up `add()` in the Methods table of the `ArtLayers` object.

Applying styles to layers

Note: This procedure corresponds directly to dragging a style from the Adobe Photoshop CS2 Styles palette to a layer.

Your script can apply styles to an `ArtLayer` object. To apply a style in a script, you use the `applyStyle()` method with the style's name as an argument enclosed in straight double quotes.

Note: The layer style names are case sensitive.

Please refer to Adobe Photoshop CS2 Help for a list of styles and for more information about styles and the Styles palette.

The following example sets the Puzzle layer style to the layer named "L1."

```
docRef.artLayers["L1"].applyStyle("Puzzle (Image)")
```

Look up `applyStyle()` in the Methods table of the `ArtLayer` object in Part 2 of this book.

Using the Text Item object

You can change an existing `ArtLayer` object to a text layer, that is, a `Text Item` object, if the layer is empty. Conversely you can change a `Text Item` object to an `ArtLayer` object. This "reverse" procedure rasterizes the text in the layer object.

The `Text Item` object is a property of the `ArtLayer` object. However, to create a new text layer, you must create a new `ArtLayer` object and then set the art layer's `kind` property to `LayerKind.TEXT`.

To set or manipulate text in a text layer, you use the `textItem` object, which is also a property of the `ArtLayer` object.

Creating a Text Item object

The following examples create an `ArtLayer` object and then use the `kind` property to convert it to a text layer.

```
var newLayerRef = docRef.artLayers.add()
newLayerRef.kind = LayerKind.TEXT
```

See "Adobe Photoshop CS2's Object Model" on page 9 for information on the relationship between `ArtLayer` objects and `TextItem` objects.

Also, look up the `kind` and `TextItem` properties of the `ArtLayer` object in Part 2 of this book.

Determining a layer's kind

The following example uses an `if` statement to check whether an existing layer is a text layer.

```
if (newLayerRef.kind == LayerKind.TEXT)
```

Adding and manipulating text in a text item object

The following example adds and right-justify text in a text layer.

```
var textItemRef = artLayers["my text"].textItem
textItemRef.contents = "Hello, World!"
docRef.artLayers["my text"].textItemRef.justification =
   Justification.RIGHT
```

Note: The `text item` object has a `kind` property, which can be set to either `TextType.POINTTEXT` or `TextType.PARAGRAPHTEXT`. When a new `text item` is created, its `kind` property is automatically set to `point text`.

The `text item` properties `height`, `width`, and `leading` are valid only when the text item's `kind` property is set to `paragraph text`.

To familiarize yourself with this objects, properties, and methods, look up the `TextItem` property of the `ArtLayer` object in Part 2 of this book. To find the properties and methods you can use with a text layer, look up the `TextItem` object.

Working with Selection objects

You create a `Selection` object to allow your scripts to act only on a specific, selected section of your document or a layer within a document. For example, you can apply effects to a selection or copy the current selection to the clipboard.

The `Selection` object is a property of the `Document` object. In Part 2 of this book, look up selection in the Properties table for the `Document` object. Also, look up the `select` in the Methods table for the `Selection` object.

Creating and defining a selection

To create a selection, you use the `select()` method of the `Selection` object.

You define a `Selection` object by specifying the coordinates on the screen that describe the selection's corners. Since your document is a 2-dimensional object, you specify coordinates using the x-axis and y-axis as follows:

- You use the x-axis to specify the horizontal position on the canvas.
- You use the y-axis to specify the vertical position on the canvas.

The origin point in Adobe Photoshop CS2, that is, x-axis = 0 and y-axis = 0, is the upper left corner of the screen. The opposite corner, the lower right, is the extreme point of the canvas. For example, if your canvas is 1000 x 1000 pixels, then the coordinate for the lower right corner is x-axis = 1000 and y-axis = 1000.

You specify coordinate points that describe the shape you want to select as an array, which then becomes the argument or parameter value for the `select()` method.

The following example assumes that the ruler units have been set to pixels and create a selection by:

---

1. Creating a variable to hold a new document that is 500 x 500 pixels in size.

2. Creating a variable to hold the coordinates that describe the selected area (that is, the `Selection` object).

3. Adding an array as the selection variable's value.

4. Using the `Document` object's `selection` property, and the `Selection` object's `select()` method to select an area. The area's coordinates are the selection variable's values.

```
var docRef = app.documents.add(500, 500)
var shapeRef = [
    [0,0],
    [0,100],
    [100,100],
    [100,0]
]
docRef.selection.select(shapeRef)
```

Stroking the selection border

The following example uses the `stroke()` method of the `Selection` object to stroke the boundaries around the current selection and set the stroke color and width.

Note: The transparency parameter cannot be used for background layers.

```
app.activeDocument.selection.stroke (strokeColor, 2,
    StrokeLocation.OUTSIDE, ColorBlendMode.VIVIDLIGHT,
    75, false)
```

Inverting selections

You can use the `invert()` method of the Selection object to a selection so you can work on the rest of the document, layer or channel while protecting the selection.

```
selRef.invert()
```

Expanding, contracting, and feathering selections

You can change the size of a selected area using the expand, contract, and feather commands.

The values are passed in the ruler units stored in Adobe Photoshop CS2 preferences and can be changed by your scripts. If your ruler units are set to pixels, then the following example will expand, contract, and feather by 5 pixels. See section "Setting application preferences" on page 32 for examples of how to change ruler units.

```
var selRef = app.activeDocument.selection
selRef.expand( 5 )
selRef.contract( 5 )
selRef.feather( 5 )
```

Filling a selection

You can fill a selection either with a color or a history state.

To fill with a color:

```
var fillColor = new SolidColor()
fillColor.rgb.red = 255
fillColor.rgb.green = 0
fillColor.rgb.blue = 0
app.activeDocument.selection.fill( fillColor,
ColorBlendMode.VIVIDLIGHT,
   25, false)
```

To fill the current selection with the tenth item in the history state:

Note: See "Using history state objects" on page 42 for information on `History State` objects.

```
selRef.fill(app.activeDocument.historyStates[9])
```

Loading and storing selections

You can store `Selection` objects in, or load them from, `Channel` objects. The following examples use the `store()` method of the `Selection` object to store the current selection in a channel named `My Channel` and extend the selection with any selection that is currently in that channel.

```
selRef.store(docRef.channels["My Channel"],
SelectionType.EXTEND)
```

To restore a selection that has been saved to a `Channel` object, use the `load()` method.

```
selRef.load (docRef.channels["My Channel"],
SelectionType.EXTEND)
```

See section "Understanding clipboard interaction" on page 46 for examples on how to copy, cut and paste selections.

Working with Channel objects

The `Channel` object gives you access to much of the available functionality on Adobe Photoshop CS2 channels. You can create, delete, and duplicate channels or retrieve a channel's histogram and change its kind. See "Creating new objects in a script" on page 27 for information on creating a `Channel` object in your script.

You can set or get (that is, find out about) a `Channel` object's type using the `kind` property. See "Understanding and finding constants" on page 16 for script samples that demonstrate how to create a masked area channel.

Changing channel types

You can change the `kind` of a any channel except component channels. The following example demonstrates how to change a masked area channel to a selected area channel:

Note: Component channels are related to the document mode. Refer to Adobe Photoshop CS2 Help for information on channels, channel types, and document modes.

```
channelRef.kind = ChannelType.SELECTEDAREA
```

Using the DocumentInfo object

In Adobe Photoshop CS2, you can associate information with a document by choosing **File > File Info**.

To accomplish this task in a script, you use the `DocumentInfo` object. The following example demonstrates how to use the `DocumentInfo` object to set the copyrighted status and owner URL of a document.

```
docInfoRef = docRef.info
docInfoRef.copyrighted = CopyrightedType.COPYRIGHTEDWORK
docInfoRef.ownerUrl = "http://www.adobe.com"
```

For information about other types of information (properties) you can associate with a document, look up the Properties table for the `DocumentInfo` object in Part 2 of this book.

Using history state objects

Adobe Photoshop CS2 keeps a history of the actions that affect documents. Each time you save a document in the Adobe Photoshop CS2 application, you create a *history state*; you can access a document's history states from the History palette by selecting **Window > History**.

In a script, you can access a `Document` object's history states using the `HistoryStates` object, which is a property of the `Document` object. You can use a `HistoryStates` object to reset a document to a previous state or to fill a `Selection` object.

The following example reverts the document contained in the variable `docRef` back to the form and properties it had when it was first saved. Using history states in this fashion gives you the ability to undo modifications to the document.

```
docRef.activeHistoryState = docRef.historyStates[0]
```

Note: Reverting back to a previous history state does not remove any latter states from the history collection. Use the `Purge` command to remove latter states from the `History States` collection as shown below:

```
app.purge(PurgeTarget.HISTORYCACHES)
```

The example below saves the current state, applies a filter, and then reverts back to the saved history state.

```
savedState = docRef.activeHistoryState
docRef.applyMotionBlur( 20, 20 )
docRef.activeHistoryState = savedState
```

Using Notifier objects

You use the `Notifier` object to tie an event to a script. For example, if you would like Adobe Photoshop CS2 to automatically create a new document when you open the application, you could tie a script that creates a `Document` object to an `Open Application` event.

Note: This type of script corresponds to selecting *Start Application* in the Script Events Manager (**File > Scripts > Script Events Manager**) in the Adobe Photoshop CS2 application. Please refer to Adobe Photoshop CS2 Help for information on using the Script Events Manager.

Using the PathItem object

To add a `PathItem` object, you create an array of `PathPointInfo` objects, which specify the coordinates of the corners or anchor points of your path. Additionally, you can create an array of `SubPathInfo` objects to contain the `PathPoint` arrays.

The following script creates a `PathItem` object that is a straight line.

```
//line #1--it's a straight line so the coordinates
//for anchor, left, and right
//for each point have the same coordinates
var lineArray = new Array()
    lineArray[0] = new PathPointInfo
    lineArray[0].kind = PointKind.CORNERPOINT
    lineArray[0].anchor = Array(100, 100)
```

```
lineArray[0].leftDirection = lineArray[0].anchor
lineArray[0].rightDirection = lineArray[0].anchor

lineArray[1] = new PathPointInfo
lineArray[1].kind = PointKind.CORNERPOINT
lineArray[1].anchor = Array(150, 200)
lineArray[1].leftDirection = lineArray[1].anchor
lineArray[1].rightDirection = lineArray[1].anchor

var lineSubPathArray = new Array()
    lineSubPathArray[0] = new SubPathInfo()
    lineSubPathArray[0].operation =
ShapeOperation.SHAPEXOR
    lineSubPathArray[0].closed = false
    lineSubPathArray[0].entireSubPath = lineArray
```

Working with color objects

Your scripts can use the same range of colors that are available from the Adobe Photoshop CS2 user interface. Each color model has its own set of properties. For example, the RGB color class contains three properties: red, blue, and green. To set a color in this class, you indicate values for each of the three properties.

The SolidColor class contains a property for each color model. To use this object, you first create an instance of a SolidColor object, then set appropriate color model properties for the object. After a color model has been assigned to a SolidColor object, the SolidColor object cannot be reassigned to a different color model.

The following example demonstrates how to set a color using the CMYK color class.

```
//create a solid color array
var solidColorRef = new SolidColor()
solidColorRef.cmyk.cyan = 20
solidColorRef.cmyk.magenta = 90
solidColorRef.cmyk.yellow = 50
solidColorRef.cmyk.black = 50

foregroundColor = solidColorRef
```

Solid color classes

The solid color classes available in Adobe Photoshop CS2 are illustrated below.

Color Classes

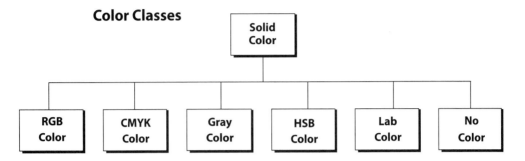

Using hex values

You can express RGB colors as hex (or *hexadecimal*) values. A hex value contains three pairs of numbers which represent red, blue, and green (in that order).

In JavaScript, the RGBColor object has a string property called HexValue/hexValue.

Getting and converting colors

The following example converts an RGB color to its CMYK equivalent. This example uses the foregroundColor property of the Application object to get the original color to be converted.

```
var someColor = foregroundColor.cmyk
```

Look up the following in Part 2 of this book:

- cmyk in the Properties table of the SolidColor object
- foregroundColor in the Properties table of the Application object

Comparing colors

Using the isEqual() method, you can compare colors. The following statement returns true if the foreground color is visually equal to background color.

```
if (app.foregroundColor.isEqual(backgroundColor))
```

Getting a web safe color

To convert a color to a web-safe color, use the `nearestWebColor` property of the `SolidColor` object.

```
var webSafeColor = new RGBColor()
webSafeColor = app.foregroundColor.nearestWebColor
```

Working with filters

To apply a filter, you use a specific filter method. For example, to apply a Gaussian blur filter, you use the `applyGaussianBlur()` method. All filter methods belong to the `ArtLayer` object.

Note: Please refer to Adobe Photoshop CS2 Help for information about the effects produced by individual filter types.

The following example applies the Gaussian blur filter to the active layer.

```
docRef.activeLayer.applyGaussianBlur(5)
```

Note: In Part 2 of this book, look up `applyGaussianBlur()` method and other methods whose name includes *filter* in the Methods table of the `artLayer` object.

Other filters

If the filter type that you want to use on your layer is not part of the scripting interface, you can use the Action Manager from a JavaScript to run a filter. See Part 2 of this book for information on using the Action Manager.

Understanding clipboard interaction

The clipboard methods in Adobe Photoshop CS2 operate on `ArtLayer` and `Selection` objects. The methods can be used to operate on objects within a single document, or to move information between documents.

The clipboard methods of the `ArtLayer` and `Selection` objects are:

- `copy()`
- `copy(merge parameter value)`
- `paste()`
- `paste(intoSelection parameter value)`
- `cut()`

Note: For information on copy, copy merged, paste, paste into, and cut functions, see Adobe Photoshop CS2 Help.

Using the Copy and Paste methods

The following example copies the contents an the background layer to the clipboard, creates a new document, and then pastes the clipboard contents to the new document. The scripts assume that there is a document already open in Adobe Photoshop CS2 and that the document has a background layer.

Note: If your script creates a new document in which you paste the clipboard contents, be sure the document uses the same ruler units as the original document. See "Setting application preferences" on page 32 for information.

```
//make firstDocument the active document
var docRef = app.activeDocument
docRef.artLayers["Background"].copy()

var newDocRef = app.documents.add(8, 6, 72, "New Doc")
newDocRef.paste()
```

Using the Copy Merged method

You can also perform a merged copy to copy of all visible layers in the selected area. In JavaScript, you must use the `ArtLayer` or `Selection` object's `copy()` method with the `merge` parameter. To perform the merged copy, you must enter, or *pass*, the value `true`, as in the following example.

```
docRef.selection.copy(true)
```

Look up the `copy()` method in the Methods table for the `ArtLayer` and `Selection` objects in Part 2 of this book.

Working with units

Adobe Photoshop CS2 provides two rulers for documents. You can set the measurement units for the rulers in your script. The rulers are:

- A graphics ruler used for most graphical layout measurements or operations on a document where height, width, or position are specified.

  You set measurement unit types for the graphics ruler using the `rulerUnits` property.

- A type ruler, which is active when using the type tool

  You set measurement unit types for the type ruler using the `typeUnits` property.

Note: These settings correspond to those found in the Adobe Photoshop CS2 preference dialog under **Photoshop >Preferences >**

Units & Rulers on Mac OS or **Edit >Preferences > Units & Rulers** in Windows.

Unit values

All languages support plain numbers for unit values. These values are treated as being of the type currently specified for the appropriate ruler.

To ensure that your scripts produce the expected results you should check and set the ruler units to the type appropriate for your script. After executing a script the original values of the rule settings should be restored if changed in the script. See "Setting ruler and type units in a script" on page 49 for directions on setting unit values.

Please refer to Adobe Photoshop CS2 Help for information about available unit value types.

Special unit value types

The unit values used by Adobe Photoshop CS2 are length units, representing values of linear measurement. Support is also included for pixel and percent unit values. These two unit value types are not, strictly speaking, length values but are included because they are used extensively by Adobe Photoshop CS2 for many operations and values.

Using unit values in calculations

To use a unit value in a calculation it is necessary to first convert the value to a number (unit value cannot be used directly in calculations). To multiply an inch value write:

```
set newValue to (inchValue as number) * someValue
```

Note: Because Adobe Photoshop CS2 is a pixel-oriented application you may not always get back the same value as you pass in when setting a value. For example, if `ruler units` is set to mm units, and you create a document that is 30 x 30, the value returned for the height or width will be 30.056 if your document resolution is set to 72 ppi. The scripting interface assumes settings are measured by ppi.

Unit value usage

The following tables list the properties of the classes/objects that are defined to use unit values. Unit values for these properties, unless otherwise indicated in the table, are based the graphics ruler setting.

To use this table, look up the property in the object's Properties table in Part 2 of this book.

Class/Object	JavaScript Properties
Document	height width
EPS open options	height width
PDF open options	height width
lens flare open options	height width
offset filter	horizontalOffset verticalOffset
Text Item	baselineShift* firstLineIndent* height hyphenationZone* leading* leftIndent* position rightIndent* spaceBefore* spaceAfter* width

* Unit values based on type ruler setting.

The following list contains the methods that use unit values as parameters or arguments. In some cases the parameters are required. The methods are preceded by the object to which they belong. Look up the method in the Methods table of the object in the "Interface" chapter in Part 2 of this book.

- `document.crop(bounds, height, width)`
- `document.resizeCanvas(height, width)`
- `document.resizeImage(height, width)`
- `selection.contract(by)`
- `selection.expand(by)`
- `selection.feather(by)`
- `selection.selectBorder(width)`
- `selection.translate(deltaX, deltaY)`
- `selection.translateBoundary(deltaX, deltaY)`

Setting ruler and type units in a script

The unit type settings of the two Adobe Photoshop CS2 rulers control how numbers are interpreted when dealing with properties and parameters that support unit values. Be sure to set the ruler units as needed at the beginning of your scripts and save and restore the original ruler settings when your script has completed.

In JavaScript `ruler units` and `type units` are properties of the `Preferences`, accessed through the `Application` object's preferences property as shown below.

```
app.preferences.rulerUnits = Units.INCHES
app.preferences.typeUnits = TypeUnits.PIXELS
app.preferences.pointSize = PointType.POSTSCRIPT
```

Note: Remember to reset the unit settings back to the original values at the end of a script. See "Working with document preferences" on page 51 for an example of how to do this.

Sample workflow automation JavaScripts

The following sample workflow automation JavaScripts are provided with Adobe Photoshop CS2 and demonstrate various kinds of scripting usage. The scripts are located in the `Presets/Scripts` folder in your application directory. See "Creating and running a JavaScript" on page 20 for information on the `Presets/Scripts` folder.

Script name	Description
`Layer Comps to Files.jsx`	Saves layer comps as files.
`Layer Comps to PDF.jsx`	Saves layer comps as a PDF presentation.
`Layer Comps to WPG.jsx`	Saves layer comps as a Web photo gallery.
`Export Layers to Files.jsx`	Exports each document in the document to a separate file.
`Script Events Manager.jsx`	Enables and disables notifier objects.
`Image Processor.jsx`	Processes camera raw images in various file formats.

Advanced scripting

This section demonstrates how to use the information contained in the previous sections of this chapter to create scripts that do the following:

- Configure document preferences.
- Apply color to text items. In this section, you will also learn how to do the following:
  - Create a reference to an existing document.

- Create a layer object and make the layer a text layer.
- Rasterize text so that *wrap* and *blur* processing can be applied to words. In these sections you will also learn how to do the following:
  - Select and work with a specific area of a layer by creating a selection object.
  - Apply wave and motion blur filters to selected text.

Note: When you finish the lesson in each of the following sections, save the script you have created in the lesson. Each lesson builds upon the script created in the previous lesson.

Working with document preferences

The sample scripts in this section activate a Adobe Photoshop CS2 Application object and then save the default configuration settings into variables so that they can be restored later when the script completes. These are the default configurations you most probably set up in the Preferences dialog when you initially installed and configured Adobe Photoshop CS2.

Note: To view or set the Preferences on Mac OS, choose **Photoshop >Preferences> Units & Rulers**; in Windows choose **Edit >Preferences> Units & Rulers**.

Next, the scripts set the following preferences to the following values:

Preference	Set to	Description
rulers	inches	Uses inches as the unit of measurement for graphics.
units	pixels	Uses pixels as the unit of measurement for text (type).
dialog modes	never	Suppresses the display of dialog boxes so that your script executes without the user being asked for input (such as clicking an OK button) at various stages of the process. **Note:** Dialog modes is not an option in the Adobe Photoshop CS2 application.

Next, variables are declared that store document dimensions in inches and document resolution in pixels. A display resolution is declared and the text "Hello, World!" is assigned to a string variable.

Finally, an `if` statement checks whether a `Document` object has been created and then creates a new `Document` object if none exists.

➤ **To work with document preferences:**

1. Create the following script.

   Note: See "Creating and running a JavaScript" on page 20 for details on creating a JavaScript.

   ```
   //create and assign variables for default preferences
   startRulerUnits = app.preferences.rulerUnits
   startTypeUnits = app.preferences.typeUnits
   startDisplayDialogs = app.displayDialogs

   //change settings
   app.preferences.rulerUnits = Units.INCHES
   app.preferences.typeUnits = TypeUnits.PIXELS
   app.displayDialogs = DialogModes.NO

   //create and assign variables for document settings
   docWidthInInches = 4
   docHeightInInches = 2
   resolution = 72

   //use the length property of the documents object to
   //find out if any documents are open
   //if none are found, add a document
   if (app.documents.length == 0)
      app.documents.add(docWidthInInches,
   docHeightInInches, resolution)

      //restore beginning preferences
      app.preferences.rulerunits = startRulerUnits
      app.preferences.typeunits = startTypeUnits
      app.displayDialogs = startDisplayDialogs
   ```

2. Name the script `HelloWorldDoc.jsx` and save it in the Scripts folder.

3. Open Adobe Photoshop CS2 and choose **File > Scripts > HelloWorldDoc** to run the script.

4. Choose **Edit > Preferences > Units & Rulers** to verify that your preferences have been returned to your original settings.

5. After viewing the document in Adobe Photoshop CS2, close the document without saving it.

6. To prepare the script for the next section, comment the statements that restore the beginning preferences by adding slashes as follows:

   ```
   //app.preferences.rulerunits = startRulerUnits
   //app.preferences.typeunits = startTypeUnits
   ```

7. Save the script.

Applying color to a text item

In this section, we will add a layer to the `HelloWorldDoc` script, then change the layer to a text object that displays the text *Hello, World!* in red.

Before you begin, do the following:

- Quit Adobe Photoshop CS2.
- Open the script file `HelloWorldDoc` in your script editor application.

➤ To create and specify details in a text item:

1. Type the following code into the `HelloWorldDoc` script immediately before the commented statements that restore original preferences.

```
//create a reference to the active document
docRef = app.activeDocument

//create a variable named textColor
//create a SolidColor object whose color is red
//assign the object to textColor
textColor = new SolidColor
textColor.rgb.red = 255
textColor.rgb.green = 0
textColor.rgb.blue = 0

helloWorldText = "Hello, World!"

//create a variable named newTextLayer
//use the add() method of the artLayers class to create a
//layer object assign the object to newTextLayer
newTextLayer = docRef.artLayers.add()

//use the kind property of the artLayer class to make the
//layer a text layer
newTextLayer.kind = LayerKind.TEXT

newTextLayer.textItem.contents = helloWorldText
newTextLayer.textItem.position = Array(0.75, 1)
newTextLayer.textItem.size = 36
newTextLayer.textItem.color = textColor
```

2. Save the script, and then open Adobe Photoshop CS2 and select the script from the Scripts menu (choose **File > Script > HelloWorldDoc**). Be patient while Adobe Photoshop CS2 executes your commands one by one.

3. After viewing the document in Adobe Photoshop CS2, close Adobe Photoshop CS2 without saving the document.

Note: Look up the following classes in the "Object Reference" chapter of Part 2 of this book to see if you understand how you used them in this script:

- SolidColor
- ArtLayer. Notice that the LayerKind.TEXT value of the kind property uses the LayerKind constant. Constants are always depicted in uppercase letters in Adobe Photoshop CS2 JavaScripts.

Applying a wave filter

In this section we'll apply a wave filter to the word *Hello* in our document. This entails the following steps:

- Set the document width and height to pixels and then rasterize the text object in the Text Layer.

Note: Because text is a vector graphic and a wave filter cannot be applied to vector graphics, we must first convert the image to a bitmap. Rasterizing converts mathematically defined vector artwork to pixels. For more information on rasterizing, refer to Adobe Photoshop CS2 Help.

- Select the area of the layer to which we want to apply the wave filter.

    Note: See "Defining the area of a selection object" on page 54 in order to understand the code within the script that accomplishes this task.

- Apply a wave filter to the selection.

    Note: The wave is a truncated sine curve.

Defining the area of a selection object

To define the area of a selection object, we will create an array of coordinates, or points specified in pixels within the document. The array indicates the coordinates that define the outside corners of a rectangular area that begins at the top left corner of the document and extends half way across the document.

Note: You can define any number of points for a selected area. The number of coordinates determines the shape of the selection. The last coordinate defined must be the same as the first so that the area.

Note: See "Adobe Photoshop CS2's Object Model" on page 9 for information on selection objects and other Adobe Photoshop CS2 objects.

The array values in order are:

- Upper left corner of the selection: `0,0`
  - `0` indicates the left-most column in the document.
  - `0` indicates the top row in the document.
- Upper right corner of the selection: `theDocWidthInPixels / 2, 0`
  - `theDocWidthInPixels / 2` indicates the column in the middle of the document; that is, the column whose coordinate is the total number of columns in the document divided by 2.

  Note: The value of `theDocWidthInPixels` is the total number of pixels that defines the document's horizontal dimension. Columns are arranged horizontally.

  - `0` indicates the top row in the document.
- Lower right corner: `theDocWidthInPixels / 2, theDocHeightInPixels`
  - `theDocWidthInPixels / 2` indicates the middle of the document.
  - `theDocHeightInPixels` indicates the bottom row in the document; that is row whose coordinate is the total number of rows in the document.

  Note: The value of `theDocHeightInPixels` is the total number of pixels that determine the vertical dimension of the document. Rows are stacked vertically.

- Lower left corner: `theDocWidthInPixels / 2, 0`
  - `theDocWidthInPixels / 2`
  - `0`
- Upper left corner of the selection: `0,0`

➤ To select an area and apply a wave filter to it:

1. Type the following code into the script file `HelloWorldDoc` just above the commented statements that restore original preferences:

```
//create new variables to contain doc width and height
//convert inches to pixels by multiplying the number of
inches by
//the resolution (which equals number of pixels per inch)
docWidthInPixels = docWidthInInches * resolution
docHeightInPixels = docHeightInInches * resolution
//use the rasterize method of the artLayer class
newTextLayer.rasterize(RasterizeType.TEXTCONTENTS)

//create a variable to contain the coordinate values
//for the selection object
```

```
selRegion = Array(Array(0, 0),
    Array(docWidthInPixels / 2, 0),
    Array(docWidthInPixels / 2, docHeightInPixels),
    Array(0, docHeightInPixels),
    Array(0, 0))

//use the select method of the selection object
//to create an object and give it the selRegion values
//as coordinates
docRef.selection.select(selRegion)

//
newTextLayer.applyWave(1, 1, 100, 5, 10, 100, 100,
    WaveType.SINE, UndefinedAreas.WRAPAROUND, 0)
```

2. Save the script, and then open Adobe Photoshop CS2 and select the script from the Scripts menu (choose **File > Script > HelloWorldDoc**).

3. After viewing the document in Adobe Photoshop CS2, close Adobe Photoshop CS2 without saving the document.

Note: Look up the following classes in the *Adobe JavaScript Scripting Reference* "Object Reference" chapter to see if you understand how you used them in this script:

- `ArtLayer`
  - `Rasterize()` method. Notice that the `RasterizeType.TEXTCONTENTS` argument uses the `RasterizeType` constant. Constants are always depicted in uppercase letters in Adobe Photoshop CS2 JavaScripts.
  - `applyWave()` method

Applying a motionblur filter

In this section, we will apply a different filter to the other half of our document.

Additionally, because this is the last exercise in this that deals with our Hello World document, we will uncomment the statements that reset our original application preferences for rulers and units.

➤ **To apply a motionblur filter to HelloWorldDoc:**

1. Type the following code into the script file `HelloWorldDoc` just above the commented statements that restore original preferences.

```
//change the value of selRegion to the other half of the
document
selRegion = Array(Array(docWidthInPixels / 2, 0),
   Array(docWidthInPixels, 0),
   Array(docWidthInPixels, docHeightInPixels),
   Array(docWidthInPixels / 2, docHeightInPixels),
   Array(docWidthInPixels / 2, 0))

docRef.selection.select(selRegion)

newTextLayer.applyMotionBlur(45, 5)

docRef.selection.deselect()
```

2. Delete the slashes from the commented statements above the end tell statement as follows:

```
app.preferences.rulerUnits = startRulerUnits
app.preferences.typeUnits = startTypeUnits
```

3. Save the script, and then open Adobe Photoshop CS2 and select the script from the Scripts menu (choose **File > Script > HelloWorldDoc**).

Note: Look up the `ArtLayer` class `applyMotionBlur()` method in the "Object Reference" chapter of Part 2 of this book to see if you understand how you used it in this script:

Adobe® Photoshop® CS2

Part 2: Photoshop JavaScript Reference

4 | Using JavaScript with Adobe Photoshop CS2

This chapter explains the basics of using JavaScript in Adobe Photoshop CS2.

Script Support in Adobe Photoshop CS2

The Scripts menu supports JavaScript scripts for Windows®.

For a file to be recognized by Photoshop as a valid script file it must have the correct file name extension:

Script Type	File Type	Extension	Platform
AppleScript	compiled script OSAS file	`.scpt` (none)	Mac OS®
JavaScript ExtendScript	text	`.js` `.jsx`	Mac OS & Windows
VBScript	text	`.vbs`	Windows
Visual Basic	executable	`.exe`	Windows

JavaScript support

All of the Adobe Creative Suite 2 applications, including Adobe Photoshop CS2, use ExtendScript, Adobe's extended implementation of JavaScript. ExtendScript files are distinguished by the `.jsx` extension. ExtendScript offers all standard JavaScript features, plus additional features and utilities, such as:

- A debugging environment (the ExtendScript Toolkit)
- A localization utility
- Tools that allow you to combine scripts and direct them to particular applications
- Platform-independent file and folder representation

For details of these and additional features, see "Using File and Folder Objects" on page 305 and "ExtendScript Tools and Features" on page 347.

Executing scripts

Adobe Photoshop CS2's interface includes a Scripts menu (**File > Scripts**) which provides quick and easy access to your JavaScripts. Scripts can be listed directly as menu items that run when you select them, or you can navigate to and run any JavaScript in your file system.

If Adobe Photoshop CS2 encounters an error during script execution, it displays the error message.

Installing scripts

To install a JavaScript in the Scripts menu, place it in the Scripts folder (**Photoshop CS2 > Presets > Scripts**). The names of the scripts in the Scripts folder, without the file name extension, will be displayed in the Scripts menu. Any number of scripts may be installed in the Scripts menu.

Scripts added to the Scripts folder while Adobe Photoshop CS2 is running will not appear in the Scripts menu until the next time you launch the application.

You may use sub-folders in the Scripts folder to help organize the scripts in the Scripts menu. Each subfolder will be displayed as a separate submenu containing the scripts in that subfolder.

Executing other scripts

The **Browse** item at the end of the **Scripts** menu (**File > Scripts > Browse**) allows you to execute scripts which are not installed in the Scripts folder. You can also use Browse to select scripts installed in the Scripts folder after the application was last launched.

Selecting **Browse** displays a file browser dialog which allows you to select a script file for execution. Only `.js` or `.jsx` files are displayed in the browse dialog. When you select a script file, it is executed the same way as an installed script.

Startup scripts

On startup, Adobe Photoshop CS2 executes all `.jsx` files that it finds in the startup folders.

- On Windows, the startup folder for user-defined scripts is:

  `%APPDATA%\Adobe\StartupScripts`

- On Mac OS, the startup folder for user-defined scripts is:

  `~/Library/Application Support/Adobe/StartupScripts/`

If your script is in this main startup folder, it is also executed by all other Adobe Creative Suite 2 applications at startup. If such a script is meant to be executed only by Adobe Photoshop CS2, it must include code such as the following:

```
if ( BridgeTalk.appName == "photoshop" ) {
    //continue executing script
}
```

For additional details, see "Script Locations and Checking Application Installation" on page 387.

Changes since earlier versions

The following changes have been made to the JavaScript object model and language support in Adobe Photoshop CS2:

- The following classes have been added to the JavaScript interface:
  - `CameraRawOpenOptions`, which you use to specify options when opening a document in Camera Raw format.
  - `ExportOptionsSaveForWeb`, which you use to optimize documents for the Web.
  - `ContactSheetOptions`, which you use to create and format contact sheets.
  - `BatchOptions`, which you use to specify options for the Batch command.
  - `LensBlurOptions`, which you use to specify options when applying the Lens Blur filter to a layer.
  - `Notifier` and `Notifiers`, which you use to associate a script with an event so that the script executes when the event occurs. For example, you can create a `notifier` object to associate a script with the Photoshop CS2 application opening; whenever the application opens, the script runs.
- Support for interapplication communication among Creative Suite 2 applications through exported ExtendScript functions and interapplication messaging. For details, see the *Adobe® Bridge Official JavaScript Reference for Windows and Macintosh*.
- Support for the ExtendScript Toolkit and other ExtendScript features and utilities. See "ExtendScript Tools and Features" on page 347.

Changes in ScriptUI

The ScriptUI component of JavaScript has been updated and extended in this release, and some features are incompatible with the CS version.

- In CS you could define an `onClick` event handler function for a `StaticText` element, and the function would be invoked when you click on the text. This is not supported in CS2.

- In Photoshop CS, if a ScriptUI dialog contained one or more `edittext` control elements, keyboard focus was automatically assigned to the first-created `edittext` field. For example, when Photoshop CS runs the following script, focus is assigned to w.name, and the content of that control (the string 'Jane Doe') is highlighted.

```
var w = new Window ('dialog', 'Sample dialog',
    [0, 0, 180, 110]);
w.add ('statictext', [15, 15, 65, 35], 'Name:');
w.name = w.add ('edittext', [70, 15, 165, 35], '
    Jane Doe');
w.add ('statictext', [15, 45, 65, 65], 'Address:');
w.addr = w.add ('edittext', [70, 45, 165, 65],
    'Notes');
w.ok = w.add ('button', [40, 75, 140, 95], 'OK', {
name:'ok' });
w.center ();
var ok = w.show () == 1;
```

In Photoshop CS2, the keyboard focus is not automatically assigned to any control element. The script must specify which control, if any, should have the focus, by setting its `active` property to `true`. For example, you must change the previous script as follows to explicitly assign focus to the w.name field:

```
var w = new Window ('dialog', 'Sample dialog',
    [0, 0, 180, 110]);
w.add ('statictext', [15, 15, 65, 35], 'Name:');
w.name = w.add ('edittext', [70, 15, 165, 35],
    'Jane Doe');
w.name.active = true;
w.add ('statictext', [15, 45, 65, 65], 'Address:');
w.addr = w.add ('edittext', [70, 45, 165, 65],
    'Notes');
w.ok = w.add ('button', [40, 75, 140, 95], 'OK', {
name:'ok' });
w.center ();
var ok = w.show () == 1;
```

5 | JavaScript Object Reference

The objects of the JavaScript type library for Adobe® Photoshop® CS2 are presented alphabetically and in tabular format in this chapter.

Object properties and methods are described in separate tables for each object. See "Working with the Properties tables" on page 65 and "Working with the Methods tables" on page 65 for information on how to use these tables.

Sample code for several object model classes is given to help illustrate the syntax as well as usage of the object class.

Working with the Properties tables

The Properties table for an object lists the following:

- The properties you can use with the object
- The value type for each property

  When the value type is a constant or another object, the value is a hypertext link to the constant's or object's listing, as in the following Properties table sample.

- The property's input status: read-only or read-write
- A description that explains what the property is

  Descriptions are omitted for self-explanatory properties.

Property	Value Type	What it is
displayDialogs	DialogModes (page 333)	Read-write. Controls whether or not Adobe Photoshop CS2 displays dialog boxes.

Working with the Methods tables

The Methods table for an object lists the following:

- The method name
- Parameter(s)

  When a parameter type or return value is a constant or another object, the value is a hypertext link to the constant's or object's listing. In the following Methods table sample, the parameter type

ActionDescriptor is an object; the parameter type DialogModes is a constant; the return value ActionDescriptor is also an object.

Appeasements can be required or optional. Optional parameters are indicated in the table by square brackets ([ ]). See "Working with method parameters" on page 66 for information on using parameters.

- Return value type(s)
- A description, if applicable

Method	Parameter Type	Returns	What it does
executeAction (eventID [, descriptor] [, displayDialogs])	number (long) ActionDescriptor (page 67) DialogModes (page 333)	ActionDescriptor	Plays an ActionManager event.

Working with method parameters

Optional parameters are surrounded by square brackets ([ ]). In the following Methods table sample, the parameters descriptor and displayDialogs are optional and the parameter eventID is not. See

Therefore, if you use the executeAction() method for the object associated with the sample Methods table above, you *must* include an eventID value in the parentheses following the method name. The eventID value must be a number, as indicated by the number (long) in the table's Parameter Type column.

If you use an optional parameter, you must separate the parameters with a comma, as indicated by the comma that precedes each optional parameter in the table.

Also, if you use an optional parameter, you must enter the values in the order they are listed in the table so that the JavaScript compiler knows which value you are entering. To skip an optional parameter, insert an extra comma to act as a placeholder.

The following sample provides values for an eventID and a displayDialog, but skips the descriptor parameter (represented by the empty value between two commas). The statement executes action #4233 and allows only error type dialog boxes to be displayed.

```
app.executeAction(4233,,error)
```

ActionDescriptor

A record of key-value pairs for actions, such as those included on the Adobe Photoshop CS2 Actions menu.

Note: The `ActionDescriptor` class is part of the Action Manager functionality. See Chapter 6, "Action Manager."

Properties

Property	Value Type	What it is
count	number (long)	Read-only. The number of keys contained in the descriptor.
typename	string	Read-only. The class name of the referenced `actionDescriptor` object.

Methods

Method	Parameter Type	Returns	What it does
clear ()			Clears the descriptor.
erase (key)	number (long)		Erases a key from the descriptor.
fromStream (value)	string		Creates a descriptor from a stream of bytes; for reading from disk.
getBoolean (key)	number (long)	boolean	Gets the value of a key of type boolean.
getClass (key)	number (long)	number (long)	Gets the value of a key of type class.
getData (key)	number (long)	string	Gets raw byte data as a string value.
getDouble (key)	number (long)	number (double)	Gets the value of a key of type double.
getEnumerationType (key)	number (long)	number (long)	Gets the enumeration type of a key.
getEnumerationValue (key)	number (long)	number (long)	Gets the enumeration value of a key.
getInteger (key)	number (long)	number (long)	Gets the value of a key of type integer.

Method	Parameter Type	Returns	What it does (Continued)
getKey (index)	number (long)	number (long)	Gets the ID of the Nth key.
getList (key)	number (long)	ActionList (page 70)	Gets the value of a key of type list.
getObjectType (key)	number (long)	number (long)	Gets the class ID of an object in a key of type object.
getObjectValue (key)	number (long)	ActionDescriptor (page 67)	Gets the value of a key of type object.
getPath (key)	number (long)	file	Gets the value of a key of type Alias.
getReference (key)	number (long)	ActionReference (page 73)	Gets the value of a key of type ActionReference (page 73).
getString (key)	number (long)	string	Gets the value of a key of type string.
getType (key)	number (long)	DescValueType (page 333)	Gets the type of a key.
getUnitDoubleType (key)	number (long)	number (long)	Gets the unit type of a key of type UnitDouble.
getUnitDoubleValue (key)	number (long)	number (double)	Gets the value of a key of type UnitDouble.
hasKey (key)	number (long)	boolean	Checks whether the descriptor contains the provided key.
isEqual (otherDesc)	ActionDescriptor (page 67)	boolean	Determines whether the descriptor is the same as another descriptor.
putBoolean (key, value)	number (long) boolean		Sets the value for a key whose type is boolean.
putClass (key, value)	number (long) number (long)		Sets the value for a key whose type is class.
putData (key, value)	number (long) string	string	Puts raw byte data as a string value.
putDouble (key, value)	number (long) number (double)		Sets the value for a key whose type is double.

Method	Parameter Type	Returns	What it does (Continued)
putEnumerated (key, enumType, value)	`number (long)` `number (long)` `number (long)`		Sets the enumeration type and value for a key. See Chapter 11, "Scripting Constants," for information on enumerated types.
putInteger (key, value)	`number (long)` `number (long)`		Sets the value for a key whose type is integer.

putList
(key,
value)
	`number (long)`
	`ActionList`
	(page 70)
			Sets the value for a key whose type is an `ActionList` object.

putObject
(key,
classID,
value)
	`number (long)`
	`number (long)`
	`ActionDescripto`
	`r` (page 67)
			Sets the value for a key whose type is an Action Descriptor.

putPath (key, value)	`number (long)` `file`		Sets the value for a key whose type is path.

putReference
(key,
value)
	`number (long)`
	`ActionReference`
	(page 73)
			Sets the value for a key whose type is an object reference.

putString (key, value)	`number (long)` `string`		Sets the value for a key whose type is string.

putUnitDouble
(key,
unitID,
value)
	`number (long)`
	`number (long)`
	`number (double)`
			Sets the value for a key whose type is a unit value formatted as a double.

toStream		`string`	Gets the entire descriptor as a stream of bytes; for writing from disk.

ActionList

The list of commands that comprise an Action (such as an Action created using the Actions palette in the Adobe Photoshop CS2 application).

Note: The `ActionList` object is part of the Action Manager functionality. Properties. For details on using the Action Manager, see Chapter 6, "Action Manager."

Property	Value Type	What it is
count	number (long)	Read-only. The number of commands that comprise the action.
typename	string	Read-only. The class name of the referenced `ActionList` object.

Methods

With the exception of the `clear()` method, you use the methods of this object to either get the value of a specific type of data in the list or set (put) the value type.

Method	Parameter Type	Returns	What it does
clear ()			Clears the list.
getBoolean (index)	number (long)	boolean	Gets the value of a list item of type boolean.
getClass (index)	number (long)	number (long)	Gets the value of a list item of type class.
getData (index)	number (long)	string	Gets raw byte data as a string value.
getDouble (index)	number (long)	number (double)	Gets the value of a list item of type double.
getEnumerationType (index)	number (long)	number (long)	Gets the enumeration type of a list item.
getEnumerationValue (index)	number (long)	number (long)	Gets the enumeration value of a list item.
getInteger (index)	number (long)	number (long)	Gets the value of a list item of type integer.
getList (index)	number (long)	ActionList (page 70)	Gets the value of a list item of type list.

Method	Parameter Type	Returns	What it does (Continued)
getObjectType (index)	number (long)	number (long)	Gets the class ID of a list item of type object.
getObjectValue (index)	number (long)	ActionDescriptor (page 67)	Gets the value of a list item of type object.
getPath (index)	number (long)	file	Gets the value of a list item of type Alias.
getReference (index)	number (long)	ActionReference (page 73)	Gets the value of a list item of type ActionReference.
getString (index)	number (long)	string	Gets the value of a list item of type string.
getType (index)	number (long)	DescValueType (page 333)	Gets the type of a list item.
getUnitDoubleType (index)	number (long)	number (long)	Gets the unit value type of a list item of type Double.
getUnitDoubleValue (index)	number (long)	number (double)	Gets the unit value of a list item of type double.
putBoolean (value)	boolean		Sets the value to either true or false.
putClass (value)	number (long)		Sets the class or data type.
putData (value)	string		Puts raw byte data as a string value.
putDouble (value)	number (double)		Sets the value type as a double.
putEnumerated (enumType, value)	number (long) number (long)		Sets the value type as an enumerated, or constant, value. Both the type of constant and the actual value are required in the following format: *constantType.VALUE* See Chapter 11, "Scripting Constants," for information on constant value types and values.
putInteger (value)	number (long)		Sets the value of a list item of type integer.
putList (value)	ActionList (page 70)		Sets the value of a list item of type list or array.

Method	Parameter Type	Returns	What it does (Continued)
putObject (classID, value)	number (long) ActionDescriptor (page 67)		Sets the value of a list item of type object.
putPath (value)	file		Sets the value of a list item of type path.
putReference (value)	ActionReference (page 73)		Sets the value of a list item whose type a reference to an object created in the script.
putString (value)	string		Sets the value of a list item of type string.
putUnitDouble (classID, value)	number (long) number (double)		Sets the value of a list item of type unit value represented as a double.

ActionReference

Contains data describing a referenced Action.

Note: The `ActionReference` object is part of the Action Manager functionality. For details on using the Action Manager, see Chapter 6, "Action Manager."

Properties

Property	Value type	What it does
typename	string	Read-only. The class name of the referenced Action object.

Methods

Method	Parameter Type	Returns	What it does
getContainer ()		ActionReference (page 73)	Gets the container object in the containment hierarchy for the object.
getDesiredClass ()		number (long)	Gets a number representing the class of the object.
getEnumeratedType ()		number (long)	Gets the enumeration type. See Chapter 11, "Scripting Constants," for information on enumeration types and values.
getEnumeratedValue ()		number (long)	Gets the enumeration value.
getForm ()		ReferenceFormType (page 341)	Gets the form of an ActionReference (page 73).
getIdentifier ()		number (long)	Gets the identifier value for a reference whose form is identifier.
getIndex ()		number (long)	Gets the index value for a reference in a list or array.
getName ()		string	Gets the name of a reference.
getOffset ()		number (long)	Gets the offset of the object's index value.
getProperty ()		number (long)	Gets the property ID value.
putClass (desiredClass)	number (long)		Sets the class type of the object. The class name is required.

Method	Parameter Type	Returns	What it does (Continued)
putEnumerated (desiredClass, enumType, value)	number (long) number (long) number (long)		Sets the object's type to "Enumerated." The class type, enumeration type and actual enumeration value are required in the following format: *classtype.enumerationType.VALUE*
putIdentifier (desiredClass, value)	number (long) number (long)		Sets the value of the identifier.
putIndex (desiredClass, value)	number (long) number (long)		Sets the object's index value in a list.
putName (desiredClass, value)	number (long) string		Sets the object's name.
putOffset (desiredClass, value)	number (long) number (long)		Sets the object's offset from the current object.
putProperty (desiredClass, value)	number (long) number (long)		Sets the value of the object's property.

Application

The Adobe Adobe Photoshop CS2 application object, which contains all other Adobe Photoshop CS2 objects.

Note: Because you open JavaScripts through the application itself, you do not need to use the `Application` object as part of the containment hierarchy that describes an object.

However, if you choose to include the `Application` object in your code, you must use the pre-defined global object name `app`, rather than the class name `Application`, in a script, as in the following sample:

```
var docRef = app.documents.add(800, 600, 72, "docRef",
NewDocumentMode.RGB)
```

The following sample uses the `Application` object incorrectly:

```
var docRef = Application.documents.add(800, 600, 72,
"docRef", NewDocumentMode.RGB)
```

However, the most common way to add an element in your code is to omit references to the `Application` object altogether, as in the following sample:

```
var docRef = documents.add(800, 600, 72, "docRef",
NewDocumentMode.RGB)
```

Properties

Property	Value Type	What it is
activeDocument	Document (page 115)	Read-write. The frontmost document. (Setting this property is equivalent to clicking an open document in the Adobe Photoshop CS2 application to bring it to the front of the screen.)
backgroundColor	SolidColor (page 203)	Read-write. The color mode for the document's background color.
colorSettings	String	Read-write. The name of selected color setting's set.
displayDialogs	DialogModes (page 333)	Read-write. The dialog mode for the document, which indicates whether or not Adobe Photoshop CS2 displays dialogs when the script runs.
documents	Documents (page 129)	Read-only. The collection of open documents.
fonts	TextFonts (page 209)	Read-only. The fonts installed on this system.

Property	Value Type	What it is (Continued)
foregroundColor	SolidColor (page 203)	Read-write. The default foreground color (used to paint, fill, and stroke selections).
freeMemory	number (double)	Read-only. The amount of unused memory available to Adobe Photoshop CS2.
locale	string	Read-only. The language location of the application.
macintoshFileTypes	array of strings	Read-only. A list of file image types Adobe Photoshop CS2 can open.
name	string	Read-only. The application's name.
notifiers	Notifiers (page 165)	Read-only. The collection of notifiers currently configured (in the Scripts Events Manager menu in the Adobe Photoshop CS2 application).
notifiersEnabled	boolean	Read-write. Indication of whether all notifiers are enabled or disabled.
path	file	Read-only. The full path to the location of the Adobe Photoshop CS2 application.
playbackDisplayDialogs	DialogModes (page 333)	Read-write. The dialog mode for playback mode, which indicates whether or not Adobe Photoshop CS2 displays dialogs in playback mode.
playbackParameters	ActionDescriptor (page 67)	Read-write. The playback options, which indicate the speed at which Adobe Photoshop CS2 plays actions.
preferences	Preferences (page 187)	Read-only. The application preference settings (equivalent to selecting **Edit > Preferences** in the Adobe Photoshop CS2 application in Windows or **Photoshop > Preferences** in Mac OS).
preferencesFolder	alias	Read-only. The full path to the Preferences folder.
scriptingVersion	string	Read-only. The version of the Scripting interface.
typename	string	Read-only. The class name of the referenced app object.
version	string	Read-only. The version of Adobe Photoshop application you are running.
windowsFileTypes	array of strings	Read-only. A list of file image extensions Adobe Photoshop CS2 can open.

Methods

Method	Parameter Type	Returns	What it does

`batch`
  (inputFiles,
  action,
  from
  [, options])
	array of files
	string
	string
	BatchOptions (page 96)
		string	Runs the batch automation routine (similar to the `Batch` command, or **File > Automate > Batch** in the Adobe Photoshop CS2 application).
			Note: The `inputFiles` parameter specifies the source for the files to be manipulated by the Batch command.

`beep` ()			Causes a "beep" sound.
`bringToFront`			Makes Adobe Photoshop CS2 the active (front-most) application.
`charIDToTypeID` (charID)	string	number (long)	Converts from a four character code (character ID) to a runtime ID.

`doAction`
  (action,
  from)
	string
	string
			Plays an action from the Actions palette.

`executeAction`
  (eventID
  [, descriptor]
  [,
displayDialogs])
	number (long)
	ActionDescriptor (page 67)
	DialogModes (page 333)
		ActionDescriptor	Plays an `ActionManager` event.

`executeActionGet` (reference)	ActionReference (page 73)	ActionDescriptor (page 67)	Obtains an `ActionDescriptor`.
`load` (document)	file		Loads the support document from the specified location.

`makeContactSheet`
  (inputFiles
  [, options])
	array of files
	ContactSheetOptions (page 111)
		string	Creates a contact sheet from the specified files.

Method	Parameter Type	Returns	What it does
makePDFPresentation (inputFiles outputFiles [, options])	array of files file PresentationOptions (page 192)	string	Creates an Adobe PDF presentation file from the specified input files.
makePhotoGallery (inputFolder outputFolder [, options])	file file GalleryOptions (page 139)	string	Creates a web photo gallery from the files in the specified input folder.
makePhotomerge (inputFiles)	array of files	string	Merges multiple files into one; user interaction required.
makePicturePackage (inputFiles [, options])	array of files PicturePackageOptions (page 184)	string	Creates a picture package from the specified input files.
open (document [, as])	file object object (open options) **Note:** See individual file type open options, such as CameraRawOpen Options (page 100) or EPSOpenOptions (page 130), etc.	Document (page 115)	Opens the specified document as the optionally specified file type.
purge (target)	PurgeTarget (page 340)		Purges one or more caches.
stringIDToTypeID (stringID)	string	number (long)	Converts from a string ID to a runtime ID.
typeIDToCharID (typeID)	number (number (long))	string	Converts from a runtime ID to a character ID.
typeIDToStringID (typeID)	number (number (long))	string	Converts from a runtime ID to a string ID.

First Sample Script

The following script invokes an alert box to display Properties important to an application such as version number, the path to the application, the amount of memory available, and the number of documents open.

colors set for the document presently open. If no document is open, the script opens a new document for the user.

The script (with no document open) produces a progression of three dialogs.

Application.jsx

```
//Create a Welcome message
// Use the name and version properties of the application
// Object to append the application's name and version
// to the Welcome message
// use "\r" to insert a carriage return
// use the combination operator += to append info to the
message
var message = "Welcome to " + app.name;
message += " version " + app.version + "\r\r";

// find out where Adobe Photoshop CS2 is installed
// and add the path to the message
// add the optional parameter fsName to the path property
// to display the file system name in the most
// common format
message += "I'm installed in " + app.path.fsName + "\r\r"

// see how much memory Adobe Photoshop CS2
// has to play with
message += "You have this much memory available for Adobe
Photoshop CS2: " + app.freeMemory + ""\r\r"

// use the length property of the documents object to
// see how many documents are open
var documentsOpen = app.documents.length
message += "You currently have " + documentsOpen + "
document(s) open.\r\r"

// display the message to the user
alert(message)

// answer will be true for a "Yes" answer and
// false for a "No" answer
var answer = confirm("Do you want me to set the foreground
and background to my favorite colors?")

// set the colors
```

```
if (answer) {
   // I don't have a favorite color.
   // Why did I ask you may wonder?
   app.foregroundColor.rgb.red = Math.random() * 255
   app.foregroundColor.rgb.green = Math.random() * 255
   app.foregroundColor.rgb.blue = Math.random() * 255

   app.backgroundColor.rgb.red = Math.random() * 255
   app.backgroundColor.rgb.green = Math.random() * 255
   app.backgroundColor.rgb.blue = Math.random() * 255
}

// Open a document
if (app.documentsOpen == 0) {

   // use the application's path and the offset
   // to the samples folder
   var sampleDocToOpen = File(app.path +
   "/Samples/Eagle.psd")

   // compose a message with the name of the file
   message = "Would you like me to open a sample for you?
   ("message += sampleDocToOpen.fsName
   message += ")"

   // ask the user another question
   answer = confirm(message)

   // open the document accordingly
   if (answer) {
      open(sampleDocToOpen)
   }
}
```

Second Sample Script

The following script presents a progression of images as an Adobe PDF slide show.

PDFPresentation.jsx

```
// use all the files in the Samples folder
var inputFolder = new Folder(app.path + "/Samples/")

// see if we have something interesting
if (inputFolder != null) {

        // get all the files found in this folder
        // that are Adobe Photoshop CS2 (.psd format)
        var inputFiles = inputFolder.getFiles("*.psd")

        // output to the desktop
        var outputFile =
            File("~/Desktop/JavaScriptPresentation.pdf")

        // there are defaults but I like to set
        // the options myself
        var options = new PresentationOptions
        options.presentation = true
        options.view = true
        options.autoAdvance = true
        options.interval = 5
        options.loop = true
        options.transition = TransitionType.RANDOM

        // create the presentation
        makePDFPresentation(inputFiles, outputFile,
            options)
}
```

Note: To run this code on non-English platforms, substitute the following path for the `outputFile` variable:

```
var outputFile =
    File("~/JavaScriptPresentation.pdf")
```

ArtLayer

An object within a document that contains the visual elements of the image (equivalent to a layer in the Adobe Photoshop CS2 application).

Note: Most likely, you will use variables to refer to `ArtLayer` objects in your script. However, if you choose not to use a variable, be aware that, because the `ArtLayer` class is also a property of the Document (page 115) object, you use the object name, `artLayer`, rather than the class name, `ArtLayer`, in your code.

The following example uses correct syntax to refer to an `ArtLayer` object by name and then assign its `allLocked` property value:

```
documents(0).artLayer("my layer").allLocked = true
```

The following example, which uses an uppercase *A* in the object name, is incorrect:

```
documents(0).ArtLayer("my layer").allLocked = true
```

Properties

Property	Value Type	What it is
`allLocked`	`boolean`	Read-write. Indicates whether to completely lock the layer's contents and settings.
`blendMode`	`BlendMode` (page 330)	Read-write. The layer's blending mode.
`bounds`	`Array(UnitValue)`	Read-only. An array of coordinates that describes the bounding rectangle of the layer.
`fillOpacity`	`number (double)`	Read-write. The interior opacity of the layer (between 0.0 and 100.0).
`grouped`	`boolean`	Read-write. Indication of whether to group this layer with the layer beneath it.
`isBackgroundLayer`	`boolean`	Read-write. Indicates whether the layer is a background layer or normal layer. **Note:** A document can have only one background layer.

Property	Value Type	What it is (Continued)
kind	LayerKind (page 337)	Read-write. Sets the layer's kind (such as 'text layer') for an empty layer. **Note:** Valid only when the layer is empty and when isBackgroundLayer is false. See "isBackgroundLayer" on page 82. **Note:** You can use the kind property to make a background layer a normal layer; however, to make a layer a background layer, you must set isBackgroundLayer to true.
linkedLayers	array of layers	Read-only. The layers linked to this layer. **Note:** See "link" on page 89.
name	string	Read-write. The layer's name.
opacity	number (double)	Read-write. The master opacity of the layer (0.0 - 100.0).
parent	object (Document) (page 115)	Read-only. The object's container.
pixelsLocked	boolean	Read-write. Indicates whether the pixels in the layer's image can be edited using the paintbrush tool.
positionLocked	boolean	Read-write. Indicates whether the pixels in the layer's image can be moved within the layer.
textItem	TextItem (page 210)	Read-only. The text item that is associated with the layer. **Note:** Valid only when kind = LayerKind.TEXT. See "kind" on page 83.
transparentPixelsLocked	boolean	Read-write. Indicates whether editing is confined to the opaque portions of the layer.
typename	string	Read-only. The class name of the referenced artLayer object.
visible	boolean	Read-write. Indicates whether the layer is visible.

Methods

Method	Parameter Type	Returns	What it does
adjustBrightnessContrast (brightness, contrast)	number (number (long)) number (number (long))		Adjusts the brightness (-100 - 100) and contrast (-100 - 100).
adjustColorBalance ([shadows] [, midtones] [, highlights] [, preserveLuminosity])	array of integers array of integers array of integers boolean		Adjusts the color balance of the layer's component channels. For shadows, midtones, and highlights, the array must include three values (-100 - 100), which represent cyan or red, magenta or green, and yellow or blue, when the document mode is CMYK or RGB. **Note:** See mode in the Properties table of the Document (page 115) object.
adjustCurves (curveShape)	array of points (Array (Array(x, y)))		Adjusts the tonal range of the selected channel using up to fourteen points.

adjustLevels
(inputRangeStart,
  inputRangeEnd,
  inputRangeGamma,
  outputRangeStart,
  outputRangeEnd)
	number (long)
	number (long)
	number (double)
	number (long)
	number (long)
			Adjusts the levels of the selected channels (inputRangeStart: 0 - 253; inputRangeEnd: (inputRangeStart + 2) - 255; inputRangeGamma: 0.10 - 9.99; outputRangeStart: 0 - 253; outputRangeEnd: (outputRangeStart + 2) - 255.

applyAddNoise
(amount,
  distribution,
  monochromatic)
	number (double)
	NoiseDistribution
	(page 337)
	boolean
			Applies the Add Noise filter (amount: 0.1% - 400%).

applyAverage ()			Applies the Average filter.
applyBlur ()			Applies the Blur filter.
applyBlurMore ()			Applies the Blur More filter.

Method	Parameter Type	Returns	What it does (Continued)
applyClouds ()			Applies the Clouds filter.
applyCustomFilter (characteristics, scale, offset)	array of twenty-five numbers (long) number (long) number (long)		Applies a custom filter. **Note:** Required parameter values define the filter. Refer to Adobe Photoshop CS2 Help for specific instructions.
applyDeInterlace (eliminateFields, createFields)	EliminateFields (page 334) CreateFields (page 332)		Applies the De-Interlace filter.
applyDespeckle ()			Applies the Despeckle filter.
applyDifferenceClouds ()			Applies the Difference Clouds filter.
applyDiffuseGlow (graininess, glowAmount, clearAmount)	number (long) number (long) number (long)		Applies the Diffuse Glow filter (graininess: 0 - 10; glowAmount: 0 - 20; clearAmount: 0 - 20).
applyDisplace (horizontalScale, verticalScale, displacement, undefinedareas, displacementMapFiles)	number (long) number (long) DisplacementMapType (page 333) UndefinedAreas (page 344) file		Applies the Displace filter using the specified horizontal and vertical scale (-999 - 999), mapping type, treatment of undistorted areas, and path to the distortion image map.
applyDustAndScratches (radius, threshold)	number (long) number (long)		Applies the Dust & Scratches filter (radius: 1 - 100; threshold: 0 - 255).
applyGaussianBlur (radius)	number (double)		Applies the Gaussian Blur filter within the specified radius (in pixels) (0.1 - 250.0).
applyGlassEffect (distortion, smoothness, scaling [, invert] [, texture] [, textureFile])	number (long) number (long) number (long) boolean TextureType (page 343) file		Applies the Glass filter (distortion: 0 - 20; smoothness: 1 - 15; scaling (in percent): 50 - 200).

Method	Parameter Type	Returns	What it does (Continued)
applyHighPass (radius)	number (double)		Applies the High Pass filter within the specified radius (in pixels) (0.1 - 250.0).
applyLensBlur ([options])	LensBlurOptions (page 162)		Applies the Lens Blur filter.
applyLensFlare (brightness, flareCenter, lensType)	number (long) Array(UnitValue) LensType (page 337)		Applies the Lens Flare filter with the specified brightness (0 - 300%), the x and y coordinates (unit value) of the flare center, and the lens type.
applyMaximum (radius)	number (double)		Applies the Maximum filter within the specified radius (in pixels) (1 - 100).
applyMedianNoise (radius)	number (double)		Applies the Median Noise filter within the specified radius (in pixels) (1 - 100).
applyMinimum (radius)	number (double)		Applies the Minimum filter within the specified radius (in pixels) (1 - 100).
applyMotionBlur (angle, radius)	number (long) number (double)		Applies the Motion Blur filter (angle: -360 - 360; radius: 1 - 999).
applyNTSC ()			Applies the NTSC colors filter.
applyOceanRipple (size, magnitude)	number (long) number (long)		Applies the Ocean Ripple filter in the specified size (1 - 15) and magnitude (0 - 20).
applyOffset (horizontal, vertical, undefinedAreas)	UnitValue UnitValue OffsetUndefinedAreas (page 337)		Moves the layer the specified amount horizontally and vertically (min/max amounts depend on layer size), leaving an undefined area at the layer's original location.
applyPinch (amount)	number (long)		Applies the Pinch filter in the specified amount (as a percentage) (-100 - 100).
applyPolarCoordinates (conversion)	PolarConversionType (page 340)		Applies the Polar Coordinates filter.

Method	Parameter Type	Returns	What it does (Continued)
applyRadialBlur (amount, blurMethod, blurQuality)	number (long) RadialBlurMethod (page 341) RadialBlurQuality (page 341)		Applies the Radial Blur filter in the specified amount (1 - 100) using either a spin or zoom effect and the specified quality.
applyRipple (amount, size)	number (long) RippleSize (page 341)		Applies the Ripple filter in the specified amount (-999 to 999) throughout the image and in the specified size.
applySharpen ()			Applies the Sharpen filter.
applySharpenEdges ()			Applies the Sharpen Edges filter.
applySharpenMore ()			Applies the Sharpen More filter.
applyShear (curve, undefinedAreas)	array of points (Array (Array(x, y))) UndefinedAreas (page 344)		Applies the Shear filter (curve: 2 - 255 points).
applySmartBlur (radius, threshold, blurQuality, mode)	number (double) number (double) SmartBlurQuality (page 343) SmartBlurMode (page 343)		Applies the smart blur filter (radius: 0.1 - 100.0; threshold: 0.1 - 100.0).
applySpherize (amount, mode)	number (long) SpherizeMode (page 343)		Applies the Spherize filter in the specified amount (as percentage) (-100 - 100).
applyStyle (styleName)	string		Applies the specified style to the layer. **Note:** You must use a style from the Styles list in the Layer Style dialog.
applyTextureFill (textureFile)	file		Applies the Texture Fill filter.
applyTwirl (angle)	number (long)		Applies the Twirl filter at the specified angle (-999 - 999).

Method	Parameter Type	Returns	What it does (Continued)

`applyUnSharpMask`
  (amount,
    radius,
    threshold)
	number (double)
	number (double)
	number (long)
			Applies the Unsharp Mask filter (amount: 1 - 500 as percent; radius: 0.1 - 250.00; threshold: 0 - 255).

`applyWave`
  (generatorNumber,
    minimumWavelength,
    maximumWavelength,
    minimumAmplitude,
    maximumAmplitude,
    horizontalScale,
    verticalScale,
    waveType,
    undefinedAreas,
    randomSeed)
	number (long)
	number (long)
	number (long)
	number (long)
	number (long)
	number (long)
	number (long)
	WaveType (page 345)
	UndefinedAreas (page 344)
	number (long)
			Applies the Wave filter (generatorNumber: **1 - 999;** minimumWavelength: **1 - 998;** maximumWavelength: **2** - minimumWavelength + 1; minimumAmplitude: **1 - 998;** maximumAmplitude: **2** - minimumAmplitude + 1; horizontalScale: **1% - 100%;** verticalScale: **1% - 100%**).

`applyZigZag`
  (amount,
    ridges,
    style)
	number (long)
	number (long)
	ZigZagType (page 346)
			Applies the Zigzag filter (amount: -100 - 100; ridges: 0 - 20).

`autoContrast` ()			Adjusts the contrast of the selected channels automatically.
`autoLevels` ()			Adjusts the levels of the selected channels using the auto levels option.
`clear` ()			Cuts the layer without moving it to the clipboard.
`copy` ([merge])	boolean		Copies the layer to the clipboard. When the optional argument is set to true, a merged copy is performed (that is, all visible layers are copied to the clipboard).
`cut` ()			Cuts the layer to the clipboard.
`desaturate` ()			Converts a color image to a grayscale image in the current color mode by assigning equal values of each component color to each pixel.

`duplicate`
  ([relativeObject]
  [, insertionLocation])
	object (Layer)
	ElementPlacement (page 334)
		object (Layer)	Creates a duplicate of the object on the screen.

Method	Parameter Type	Returns	What it does (Continued)
equalize ()			Redistributes the brightness values of pixels in an image to more evenly represent the entire range of brightness levels within the image.
invert ()			Inverts the colors in the layer by converting the brightness value of each pixel in the channels to the inverse value on the 256-step color-values scale.
link (with)	object (Layer)		Links the layer with the specified layer.
merge ()		ArtLayer (page 82)	Merges the layer down, removing the layer from the document; returns a reference to the art layer that this layer is merged into.
mixChannels (outputChannels [, monochrome])	array of array of numbers (double) boolean		Modifies a targeted (output) color channel using a mix of the existing color channels in the image. (outputChannels = An array of channel specifications. For each component channel, specify a list of adjustment values (-200 - 200) followed by a 'constant' value (-200 - 200).) **Note:** When monochrome = true, the maximum number of channel value specifications is 1. **Note:** Valid only when document.mode = DocumentMode.RGB or document.mode = DocumentMode.CMYK. **Note:** RGB arrays must include four doubles. CMYK arrays must include five doubles.

Method	Parameter Type	Returns	What it does (Continued)
move (relativeObject, insertionLocation)	object (artLayer or layerSet) ElementPlacement (page 334)		Moves the layer relative to the object specified in parameters. **Note:** For art layers, only the constant values ElementPlacement. PLACEBEFORE and ElementPlacement. PLACEATEND are valid. For layer sets, only the constant values ElementPlacement. PLACEBEFORE and ElementPlacement. INSIDE are valid.
photoFilter ([fillColor] [, density] [, preserveLuminosity])	SolidColor (page 203) number (long) boolean		Adjusts the layer's color balance and temperature as if a color filter had been applied (density: 1% - 100%).
posterize (levels)	number (long)		Specifies the number of tonal levels (2 - 255) for each channel and then maps pixels to the closest matching level.
rasterize (target)	RasterizeType (page 341)		Converts the targeted contents in the layer into a flat, raster image.
remove ()			Deletes the object.
resize ([horizontal] [, vertical] [, anchor])	number (double) number (double) AnchorPosition (page 329)		Resizes the layer to the specified dimensions (as a percentage of its current size) and places it in the specified position.
rotate (angle [, anchor])	number (double) AnchorPosition (page 329)		Rotates rotates the layer around the specified anchor point (default: AnchorPosition. MIDDLECENTER).

Method	Parameter Type	Returns	What it does (Continued)

selectiveColor
(selectionMethod
  [, reds]
  [, yellows]
  [, greens]
  [, cyans]
  [, blues]
  [, magentas]
  [, whites]
  [, neutrals]
  [, blacks])
	AdjustmentReference
	(page 329)
	array of numbers
	(long)
	array of numbers
	(long)
	array of numbers
	(long)
	array of numbers
	(long)
	array of numbers
	(long)
	array of numbers
	(long)
	array of numbers
	(long)
	array of numbers
	(long)
	array of numbers
	(long)
	array of numbers
	(long)
			Modifies the amount of a process color in a specified primary color without affecting the other primary colors.
			
			Note: Each color array must have four components.

shadowHighlight
([shadowAmount]
  [, shadowWidth]
  [, shadowRadius]
  [, highlightAmount]
  [, highlightWidth]
  [, highlightRadius]
  [, colorCorrection]
  [, midtoneContrast]
  [, blackClip]
  [, whiteClip])
	number (long)
	number (long)
	number (long)
	number (long)
	number (long)
	number (long)
	number (long)
	number (long)
	number (double)
	number (double)
			Adjusts the range of tones in the image's shadows and highlights (shadowAmount: 0 - 100 as percent; shadowWidth: 0 - 100 as percent; shadowRadius: 0 - 2500 in pixels; highlightAmount: 0 - 100 as percent; highlightWidth: 0 - 100 as percent; highlightRadius: 0 - 2500 in pixels; colorCorrection: -100 - 100; midtoneContrast: -100 - 100; blackClip: 0.000 - 50.000; whiteClip: 0.000 - 50.000).

threshold (level)	number (long)		Converts grayscale or color images to high-contrast, B/W images by converting pixels lighter than the specified threshold to white and pixels darker than the threshold to black (level: 1 - 255).
translate ([deltaX] [, deltaY])	UnitValue UnitValue		Moves the layer the specified amount (in pixels) relative to its current position.
unlink ()			Unlinks the layer.

Sample Script

The following script creates art layers to display a duck and a sand dune in an overlying checkerboard pattern. An alert box prompts the user to press **OK**. A multi-layered collage then displays.

ArtLayer.jsx

```javascript
// Save the current preferences
var startRulerUnits = app.preferences.rulerUnits
var startTypeUnits = app.preferences.typeUnits
var startDisplayDialogs = app.displayDialogs

// Set Adobe Photoshop CS2 to use pixels and
// display no dialogs
app.preferences.rulerUnits = Units.PIXELS
app.preferences.typeUnits = TypeUnits.PIXELS
app.displayDialogs = DialogModes.NO

//Close all the open documents
 while (app.documents.length) {
    app.activeDocument.close()
}

// Create a new document to merge all the samples into
var mergedDoc = app.documents.add(1000, 1000, 72, "Merged
Samples", NewDocumentMode.RGB, DocumentFill.TRANSPARENT,
1)

// Use the path to the application and
// append the samples folder
var samplesFolder = Folder(app.path + "/Samples/")

//Get all the files in the folder
var fileList = samplesFolder.getFiles()

// open each file
for (var i = 0; i < fileList.length; i++) {
    // The fileList is folders and files so open only files
    if (fileList[i] instanceof File) {
        open(fileList[i])

        // use the document name for the layer name
        // in the merged document
        var docName = app.activeDocument.name

        // flatten the document so we get everything
        // and then copy
        app.activeDocument.flatten()
```

```
            app.activeDocument.selection.selectAll()
            app.activeDocument.selection.copy()

            // don't save anything we did

app.activeDocument.close(SaveOptions.DONOTSAVECHANGES)

            // make a random selection on the document
            // to paste into by dividing
            // the document up in 4 quadrants and pasting
            // into one of them by selecting that area
            var topLeftH = Math.floor(Math.random() * 2)
            var topLeftV = Math.floor(Math.random() * 2)
            var docH = app.activeDocument.width.value / 2
            var docV = app.activeDocument.height.value / 2
            var selRegion = Array(Array(topLeftH * docH,
                    topLeftV * docV),
                Array(topLeftH * docH + docH,
                    topLeftV * docV),
                Array(topLeftH * docH + docH,
                    topLeftV * docV + docV),
                Array(topLeftH * docH, topLeftV * docV +
                    docV),
                Array(topLeftH * docH, topLeftV * docV))
            app.activeDocument.selection.select(selRegion)
            app.activeDocument.paste()

            // change the layer name and opacity
            app.activeDocument.activeLayer.name = docName
            app.activeDocument.activeLayer.fillOpacity = 50
    }
}

// sort the layers by name
for (var x = 0; x < app.activeDocument.layers.length;
x++) {
    for (var y = 0; y < app.activeDocument.layers.length -
1 - x; y++) {
            // Compare in a non-case sensitive way
            var doc1 = app.activeDocument.layers[y].name
            var doc2 = app.activeDocument.layers[y +
                1].name
            if (doc1.toUpperCase() > doc2.toUpperCase()) {

app.activeDocument.layers[y].move(
app.activeDocument.layers[y+1],
                ElementPlacement.PLACEAFTER)
        }
```

```
      }
}

// Reset the application preferences
app.preferences.rulerUnits = startRulerUnits
app.preferences.typeUnits = startTypeUnits
app.displayDialogs = startDisplayDialogs
```

ArtLayers

The collection of `artLayer` objects in the document.

Note: Because the `ArtLayers` class is a property of the Document (page 115) object, you use the object name, `artLayers`, rather than the class name, `ArtLayers`, in your code. For example:

```
var layerRef = docRef.artLayers.add()
```

The following sample uses the `ArtLayers` object incorrectly:

```
var layerRef = docRef.ArtLayers.add()
```

Properties

Property	Value Type	What it is
length	number (long)	Read-only. The number of elements in the `artLayers` collection.
parent	object (document)	Read-only. The object's container.
typename	string	Read-only. The class name of the referenced `artLayers` object.

Methods

Method	Parameter Type	Returns	What it does
index (itemKey)	number	ArtLayer (page 82)	Gets an element from the `artLayers` collection.
add ()		ArtLayer (page 82)	Creates a new `artLayer` in the document.
getByName (name)	string	ArtLayer (page 82)	Gets the first element in the `artLayers` collection with the provided name.
removeAll ()		Nothing	Removes all elements from the `artLayers` collection.

BatchOptions

Options to specify when running a Batch command.

Note: You specify the batch source folder as the `inputFiles` parameter of the `batch()` method, which is a method of the `Application` class. See "batch" on page 77. JavaScript supports only folders as sources for batch commands.

Properties

Property	Value type	What it is
destination	BatchDestinationType (page 329)	Read-write. The type of destination for the processed files (default: `BatchDestinationType.NODESTINATION`).
destinationFolder	file	Read-write. The folder location for the processed files. **Note:** Valid only when destination = `BatchDestinationType.FOLDER`. See "destination" on page 96.
errorFile	file	Read-write. The file in which to log errors encountered. **Note:** To display errors on the screen (and stop batch processing when errors occur) leave blank.
fileNaming	Array (FileNamingType options) (page 334)	Read-write. A list of file naming options (maximum: 6). **Note:** Valid only when destination = `BatchDestinationType.FOLDER`. See "destination" on page 96.
macintoshCompatible	boolean	Read-write. Indication of whether to make the final file names Macintosh compatible (default: `true`). **Note:** Valid only when destination = `BatchDestinationType.FOLDER`. See "destination" on page 96.
overrideOpen	boolean	Read-write. Indication of whether to override action open commands (default: `false`).

Property	Value type	What it is (Continued)
overrideSave	boolean	Read-write. Indication of whether to override save as action steps with the specified destination (default: `false`). **Note:** Valid only when `destination = BatchDestinationType.FOLDER` or `destination = BatchDestinationType.SAVEANDCLOSE`. See "destination" on page 96.
startingSerial	number (long)	Read-write. The starting serial number to use in naming files (default: `1`). **Note:** Valid only when `destination = BatchDestinationType.FOLDER`. See "destination" on page 96.
suppressOpen	boolean	Read-write. Indication of whether to suppress the file open options dialogs (default: `false`).
suppressProfile	boolean	Read-write. Indication of whether to suppress the color profile warnings (default: `false`).
typename	string	Read-only. The class name of the referenced `batchOptions` object.
unixCompatible	boolean	Read-write. Indication of whether to make the final file name Unix compatible (default: `true`). **Note:** Valid only when `destination = BatchDestinationType.FOLDER`. See "destination" on page 96.
windowsCompatible	boolean	Read-write. Indication of whether to make the final file names Windows compatible (default: `true`). **Note:** Valid only when `destination = BatchDestinationType.FOLDER`. See "destination" on page 96.

BitmapConversionOptions

Options to be specified when converting an image to Bitmap mode.

Note: Convert color images to grayscale before converting the image to bitmap mode. See "desaturate" on page 88 (in the Methods table of the `ArtLayer` object).

Properties

Property	Value Type	What it is
angle	number (double)	Read-write. The angle (in degrees) at which to orient individual dots (-180 - 180). See "shape" on page 98. **Note:** Valid only when method = `BitmapConversionType.HALFTONESCREEN`. See "method" on page 98.
frequency	number (double)	Read-write. The number of printer dots (per inch) to use (1.0 - 999.99). **Note:** Valid only when method = `BitmapConversionType.HALFTONESCREEN`. See "method" on page 98.
method	BitmapConversionType (page 329)	Read-write. The conversion method to use (default: `BitmapConversionType.DIFFUSIONDITHER`).
patternName	string	Read-write. The name of the pattern to use. **Note:** Valid only when method = `BitmapConversionType.CUSTOMPATTERN`. See "method" on page 98.
resolution	number (double)	Read-write. The output resolution in pixels per inch (default: 72.0).
shape	BitmapHalfToneType (page 329)	Read-write. The dot shape to use. **Note:** Valid only when method = `BitmapConversionType.HALFTONESCREEN`. See "method" on page 98.
typename	string	Read-only. The class name of the referenced `bitmapConversionOptions` object.

BMPSaveOptions

Options that can be specified when saving a document in BMP format.

Properties

Property	Value Type	What it is
alphaChannels	boolean	Read-write. Indication of whether to save the alpha channels.
depth	BMPDepthType (page 330)	Read-write. The number of bits per channel.
flipRowOrder	boolean	Read-write. Indication of whether to write the image from top to bottom (default: false). **Note:** Available only when osType = OperatingSystem.WINDOWS. See "osType" on page 99.
osType	OperatingSystem (page 338)	Read-write. The target OS. (default: OperatingSystem.WINDOWS).
rleCompression	boolean	Read-write. Indication of whether to use RLE compression. **Note:** Available only when osType = OperatingSystem.WINDOWS. See "osType" on page 99.
typename	string	Read-only. The class name of the referenced BMPSaveOptions object.

CameraRawOpenOptions

Options that can be specified when opening a document in Camera Raw format.

Properties

Property	Value type	What it is
bitsPerChannel	BitsPerChannelType (page 330)	Read-write. The number of bits per channel.
blueHue	number (long)	Read-write. The blue hue of the shot (-100 - 100).
blueSaturation	number (long)	Read-write. The blue saturation of the shot (-100 - 100).
brightness	number (long)	Read-write. The brightness of the shot (0 - 150).
chromaticAberrationBY	number (long)	Read-write. The chromatic aberration B/Y of the shot (-100 - 100).
chromaticAberrationRC	number (long)	Read-write. The chromatic aberration R/C of the shot (-100 - 100).
colorNoiseReduction	number (long)	Read-write. The color noise reduction of the shot (0 - 100).
colorSpace	ColorSpaceType (page 332)	Read-write. The colorspace for the image.
contrast	number (long)	Read-write. The contrast of the shot (-50 - 100).
exposure	number (double)	Read-write. The exposure of the shot (4.0 - 4.0).
greenHue	number (long)	Read-write. The green hue of the shot (-100 - 100).
greenSaturation	number (long)	Read-write. The green saturation of the shot (-100 - 100).
luminanceSmoothing	number (long)	Read-write. The luminance smoothing of the shot (0 - 100).
redHue	number (long)	Read-write. The red hue of the shot (-100 - 100).
redSaturation	number (long)	Read-write. The red saturation of the shot (-100 - 100).
resolution	number (double)	Read-write. The resolution of the document in pixels per inch (1 - 999).

Property	Value type	What it is (Continued)
saturation	number (long)	Read-write. The saturation of the shot (-100 - 100).
settings	CameraRAWSettingsTyp e (page 330)	Read-write. The global settings for all Camera RAW options.
shadows	number (long)	Read-write. The shadows of the shot (0 - 100).
shadowTint	number (long)	Read-write. The shadow tint of the shot (-100 - 100).
sharpness	number (long)	Read-write. The sharpness of the shot (0 - 100).
size	CameraRAWSize (page 331)	Read-write. The size of the new document.
temperature	number (long)	Read-write. The temperature of the shot (2000 - 50000).
tint	number (long)	Read-write. The tint of the shot (-150 - 150).
typename	string	Read-only. The class name of the referenced cameraRawOpenOptions object.
vignettingAmount	number (long)	Read-write. The vignetting amount of the shot (-100 - 100).
vignettingMidpoint	number (long)	Read-write. The vignetting mid point of the shot (-100 - 100).
whiteBalance	WhiteBalanceType (page 346)	Read-write. The white balance options for the image.

Channel

Object that stores information about a color element in the image, analogous to a plate in the printing process that applies a single color. The document's color mode determines the number of default channels; for example, an RGB document has four default channels:

- A composite channel: RGB
- Three component channels: red, green, blue

A channel can also be an alpha channel, which stores selections as masks, or a spot channel, which stores spot colors.

Note: Most likely, you will use variables to refer to `Channel` objects in your script. However, if you choose not to use a variable, be aware that, because the `Channel` class is also a property of the Document (page 115) object, you use the object name, `channel`, rather than the class name, `Channel`, in your code.

The following example uses correct syntax to refer to a `Channel` object by name and then assign its `opacity` property value:

```
documents(0).channel("my channelr").opacity = 22
```

The following example, which uses an uppercase *C* in the object name, is incorrect:

```
documents(0).Channel("my channelr").opacity = 22
```

Properties

Property	Value Type	What it is
color	SolidColor (page 203)	Read-write. The color of the channel. **Note:** Not valid when `type = ChannelType.COMPONENT`.
histogram	array of 256 numbers (long)	Read-only. A histogram of the color of the channel. **Note:** Not valid when `type = ChannelType.COMPONENT`. For component channel histogram values, use the `histogram` property of the `document` object instead. See "histogram" on page 102.
kind	ChannelType (page 331)	Read-write. The channel type.
name	string	Read-write. The channel's name.
opacity	number (double)	Read-write. The opacity to use for alpha channels or the solidity to use for spot channels (0 - 100). **Note:** Valid only when `type = ChannelType.MASKEDAREA` or `type = ChannelType.SELECTEDAREA`.
parent	object (document)	Read-only. The object's container.

Property	Value Type	What it is (Continued)
typename	string	Read-only. The class name of the referenced `channel` object.
visible	boolean	Read-write. Indicates whether the channel is visible.

Methods

Method	Parameter Type	Returns	What it does
duplicate ([targetDocument])	Document (page 115)	Channel (page 102)	Duplicates the channel.
merge ()			Merges a spot channel into the component channels.
delete ()			Deletes the channel.

Channels

The collection of `channel` objects in the document. See `Channel` (page 102).

Note: Because the `Channels` class is also a property of the Document (page 115) object, you use the object name, `channels`, rather than the class name, `Channels`, in your code. For example:

```
var channelRef = docRef.channels.add()
```

The following sample uses the `ArtLayer` object incorrectly:

```
var channelRef = docRef.Channels.add()
```

Properties

Property	Value Type	What it is
length	number (long)	Read-only. The number of elements in the `channels` collection.
parent	object (document)	Read-only. The `channels` object's container.
typename	string	Read-only. The class name of the referenced `channels` object.

Methods

Method	Parameter Type	Returns	What it does
index (itemKey)	number	Channel (page 102)	Gets an element from the `channels` collection.
add ()		Channel (page 102)	Creates a new `channel` object.
getByName (name)	string	Channel (page 102)	Gets the first element in the `channels` collection with the provided name.
removeAll ()			Removes all `channel` objects from the `channels` collection.

Sample Script

The following script produces a strobe effect, as a progression of dialogs display.

Note: This script contains a switch construction that uses a `break` statement. The `break` statement requires an ending semicolon (:), as in the following sample:

```
break;
```

Histogram.jsx

```
// Save the current preferences
var startRulerUnits = app.preferences.rulerUnits
var startTypeUnits = app.preferences.typeUnits
var startDisplayDialogs = app.displayDialogs

// Set Adobe Photoshop CS2 to use pixels
// and display no dialogs
app.preferences.rulerUnits = Units.PIXELS
app.preferences.typeUnits = TypeUnits.PIXELS
app.displayDialogs = DialogModes.NO

// if there are no documents open then
// try to open a sample file
if (app.documents.length == 0) {
   open(File(app.path + "/Samples/Eagle.psd"))
}

// get a reference to the working document
var docRef = app.activeDocument

// create the output file
// first figure out which kind of line feeds we need
if ($.os.search(/windows/i) != -1) {
   fileLineFeed = "windows"
} else {
   fileLineFeed = "macintosh"
}

// create the output file accordingly
fileOut = new File("~/Desktop/Histogram.log")
fileOut.lineFeed = fileLineFeed
fileOut.open("w", "TEXT", "????")

// write out a header
fileOut.write("Histogram report for " + docRef.name)

// find out how many pixels I have
var totalCount = docRef.width.value * docRef.height.value

// more info to the out file
fileOut.write(" with a total pixel count of " +
totalCount + "\n")

// channel indexer
var channelIndex = 0
```

```
// remember which channels are currently active
var activeChannels = app.activeDocument.activeChannels

// document histogram only works in these modes
if (docRef.mode == DocumentMode.RGB ||
    docRef.mode == DocumentMode.INDEXEDCOLOR ||
    docRef.mode == DocumentMode.CMYK) {

    // activate the main channels so we can get
    // the documents histogram
    TurnOnDocumentHistogramChannels(docRef)

    // Output the documents histogram
    OutputHistogram(docRef.histogram, "Luminosity",
        fileOut)
}

// local reference to work from
var myChannels = docRef.channels

// loop through each channel and output the histogram
for (var channelIndex = 0; channelIndex <
myChannels.length; channelIndex++) {

    // the channel has to be visible to get a histogram
    myChannels[channelIndex].visible= true

    // turn off all the other channels
    for (var secondaryIndex = 0;
            secondaryIndex < myChannels.length;
            secondaryIndex++) {
        if (channelIndex != secondaryIndex) {
            myChannels[secondaryIndex].visible= false
        }
    }

    // Use the function to dump the histogram
    OutputHistogram(myChannels[channelIndex].histogram,
        myChannels[channelIndex].name, fileOut)
}

// close down the output file
fileOut.close()

// reset the active channels
docRef.activeChannels = activeChannels

// Reset the application preferences
app.preferences.rulerUnits = startRulerUnits
app.preferences.typeUnits = startTypeUnits
```

```
app.displayDialogs = startDisplayDialogs

// Utility function that takes a histogram and name
// and dumps to the output file
function OutputHistogram(inHistogram, inHistogramName,
inOutFile) {

   // find ouch which count has the largest number
   // I scale everything to this number for the output
   var largestCount = 0

   // a simple indexer I can reuse
   var histogramIndex = 0

   // see how many samples we have total
   var histogramCount = 0

   // search through all and find the largest single item
   for (histogramIndex = 0;
           histogramIndex < inHistogram.length;
           histogramIndex++) {
       histogramCount += inHistogram[histogramIndex]
       if (inHistogram[histogramIndex] > largestCount)
           largestCount = inHistogram[histogramIndex]
   }

   // These should match
   if (histogramCount != totalCount) {
       alert("Something bad is happening!")
   }

   // see how much each "X" is going to count as
   var pixelsPerX = largestCount / 100

   // output this data to the file
   inOutFile.write("One X = " + pixelsPerX + " pixels.\n")

   // output the name of this histogram
   inOutFile.write(inHistogramName + "\n")

   // loop through all the items and output in the
following format
   // 001
   // 002
   for (histogramIndex = 0;
           histogramIndex < inHistogram.length;
           histogramIndex++) {
```

```
            // I need an extra "0" for this line item
            // to keep everything in line
            if (histogramIndex < 10)
               inOutFile.write("0")

            // I need an extra "0" for this line item
            // to keep everything in line
            if (histogramIndex < 100)
               inOutFile.write("0")

            // output the index to file
            inOutFile.write(histogramIndex)

            // some spacing to make it look nice
            inOutFile.write(" ")

            // figure out how many X's I need
            var outputX =
             inHistogram[histogramIndex] / largestCount * 100

            // output the X's
            for (var a = 0; a < outputX; a++)
               inOutFile.write("X")

            inOutFile.write("\n")
      }

   inOutFile.write("\n")
}

// Function to active all the channels according
// to the documents mode
// Takes a document reference for input
function TurnOnDocumentHistogramChannels(inDocument) {

   // see how many channels we need to activate
   var visibleChannelCount = 0

   // based on the mode of the document
   switch (inDocument.mode) {

         case DocumentMode.BITMAP:
         case DocumentMode.GRAYSCALE:
         case DocumentMode.INDEXEDCOLOR:
            visibleChannelCount = 1
            break;

         case DocumentMode.DUOTONE:
            visibleChannelCount = 2
```

```
                break;

            case DocumentMode.RGB:
            case DocumentMode.LAB:
                visibleChannelCount = 3
                break;

            case DocumentMode.CMYK:
                visibleChannelCount = 4
                break;

            case DocumentMode.DUOTONE:
                visibleChannelCount = 4
                break;

            case DocumentMode.MULTICHANNEL:
            default:
                visibleChannelCount =
inDocument.channels.length + 1
                break;
    }

    // now get the channels to activate into a local array
    var aChannelArray = new Array()

    // index for the active channels array
    var aChannelIndex = 0

    for(var channelIndex = 0;
                channelIndex < inDocument.channels.length;
                channelIndex++) {
            if (channelIndex < visibleChannelCount) {
            aChannelArray[aChannelIndex++] =
                inDocument.channels[channelIndex]
        }
    }

    // now activate them
    inDocument.activeChannels = aChannelArray

}
```

CMYKColor

The definition of a CMYK color.

Properties

Property	Value Type	What it is
black	number (double)	Read-write. The black color value (as percent) (0.0 - 100.0).
cyan	number (double)	Read-write. The cyan color value (as percent) (0.0 - 100.0).
magenta	number (double)	Read-write. The magenta color value (as percent) (0.0 - 100.0).
typename	string	Read-only. The class name of the referenced CMYKColor object.
yellow	number (double)	Read-write. The yellow color value (as percent) (0.0 - 100.0).

ContactSheetOptions

Options that can be specified for a contact sheet.

Properties

Property	Value Type	What it is
acrossFirst	boolean	Read-write. Indication of whether to place the images horizontally (left to right, then top to bottom) first (default: true).
bestFit	boolean	Read-write. Indication of whether to rotate images for the best fit (default: false).
caption	boolean	Read-write. Indication of whether to use the filename as a caption for the image (default: true).
columnCount	number (long)	Read-write. The number of columns to include (1 - 100; default: 5).
flatten	boolean	Read-write. Indication of whether to flatten all layers in the final document (default: true).
font	GalleryFontType (page 335)	Read-write. The font used for the caption (default: GalleryFontType.ARIAL).
fontSize	number (long)	Read-write. The font size to use for the caption (default: 12).
height	number (long)	Read-write. The height (in pixels) of the resulting document (100 - 2900; default: 720).
horizontal	number (long)	Read-write. The horizontal spacing (in pixels) between images (0 - 29000; default: 1).
mode	NewDocumentMode (page 337)	Read-write. The document color mode (default: NewDocumentMode.RGB).
resolution	number (double)	Read-write. The resolution of the document in pixels per inch (35 - 1200; default: 72.0).
rowCount	number (long)	Read-write. The number of rows to use (1 - 100; default: 6).
typename	string	Read-only. The class name of the referenced contactSheetOptions object.
useAutoSpacing	boolean	Read-write. Indication of whether to auto space the images (default: true).

Property	Value Type	What it is (Continued)
vertical	number (long)	Read-write. The vertical spacing (in pixels) between images (0 - 29000; default: 1). **Note:** Valid only when useAutoSpacing = false.
width	number (long)	Read-write. The width (in pixels) of the resulting document (100 - 2900; default: 576).

DCS1_SaveOptions

Options that can be specified when saving a CMYK document in DCS1 format.

Properties

Property	Value Type	What it is
dCS	DCSType (page 332)	Read-write. (default: DCSType.COLORCOMPOSITE).
embedColorProfile	boolean	Read-write. Indication of whether to embed the color profile in the document.
encoding	SaveEncoding (page 342)	Read-write. The type of encoding to use for document (default: SaveEncoding.BINARY).
halftoneScreen	boolean	Read-write. Indication of whether to include halftone screen (default: false).
interpolation	boolean	Read-write. Indication of use image interpolation (default: false).
preview	Preview (page 340)	Read-write. The type of preview (default: Preview.MACOSEIGHTBIT).
transferFunction	boolean	Read-write. Indication of whether to include the Transfer functions to compensate for dot gain between the image and film (default: false).
typename	string	Read-only. The class name of the referenced DCS1_SaveOptions object.
vectorData	boolean	Read-write. Indication of whether to include vector data. **Note:** Valid only if the document includes vector data (un-rasterized text).

DCS2_SaveOptions

Options that can be specified when saving a CMYK document in DCS2 format.

Properties

Property	Value Type	What it is
dCS	DCSType (page 332)	Read-write. The type of composite file to create (default: DCSType.NOCOMPOSITE).
embedColorProfile	boolean	Read-write. Indication of whether to embed the color profile in the document.
encoding	SaveEncoding (page 342)	Read-write. The type of encoding to use (default: SaveEncoding.BINARY).
halftoneScreen	boolean	Read-write. Indication of whether to include the halftone screen (default: false).
interpolation	boolean	Read-write. Indication of whether to use image interpolation (default: false).
multiFileDCS	boolean	Read-write. Indication of whether to save color channels as multiple files or a single file (default: false).
preview	Preview (page 340)	Read-write. The preview type (default: Preview.MACOSEIGHTBIT).
spotColors	boolean	Read-write. Indication of whether to save spot colors.
transferFunction	boolean	Read-write. Indication of whether to include the Transfer functions to compensate for dot gain between the image and film (default: false).
typename	string	Read-only. The class name of the referenced DCS2_SaveOptions object.
vectorData	boolean	Read-write. Indication of whether to include vector data. **Note:** Valid only if the document includes vector data (un-rasterized text).

Document

The active containment object for layers and all other objects in the script; the basic canvas for the file.

Note: In Adobe Photoshop CS2, a document can also be referred to as an image or a canvas.

- The term *image* refers to the entire document and its contents. You can trim or crop an image. You resize an image using the `resizeImage()` method.

- The term *canvas* refers to the space in which the document sits on the screen. You can rotate or flip the canvas. You resize the canvas using the `resizeCanvas()` method.

Note: Most likely, you will use variables to refer to Document objects in your script. However, if you choose not to use a variable, be aware that, because the Document class is also a property of the Application (page 75) object, you use the object name, document, rather than the class name, Document, in your code.

The following example uses correct syntax to refer to a Document object by name and then assign its colorProfileType property value:

```
document("my document").colorProfileType =
ColorProfile.CUSTOM
```

The following example, which uses an uppercase *D* in the object name, is incorrect:

```
Document("my document").colorProfileType =
ColorProfile.CUSTOM
```

Properties

Property	Value Type	What it is
activeChannels	Array (Channel objects) (page 102)	Read-write. The selected channels.
activeHistoryBrushSource	HistoryState (page 147)	Read-write. The history state to use with the history brush.
activeHistoryState	HistoryState (page 147)	Read-write. The selected HistoryState object.
activeLayer	object (layer)	Read-write. The selected layer.
artLayers	ArtLayers (page 95)	Read-only. The artLayers collection.
backgroundLayer	ArtLayer (page 95)	Read-only. Indicates whether the layer is a background layer.

Property	Value Type	What it is (Continued)
`bitsPerChannel`	`BitsPerChannelType` (page 330)	Read-write. The number of bits per channel.
`channels`	`Channels` (page 104)	Read-write. The `channels` collection.
`colorProfileName`	`string`	Read-write. The name of the color profile. **Note:** Valid only when `colorProfileType = ColorProfile.CUSTOM` or `colorProfileType = ColorProfile.WORKING`. See "colorProfileType" on page 116.
`colorProfileType`	`ColorProfile` (page 332)	Read-write. The type of color model that defines the document's working space.
`componentChannels`	`Array (Channel objects)` (page 102)	Read-only. A list of the component color channels.
`fullName`	`file`	Read-only. The full path name of the document.
`height`	`UnitValue`	Read-only. The height of the document (unit value).
`histogram`	`array of 256 numbers (long)`	Read-only. A histogram showing the number of pixels at each color intensity level for the composite channel. **Note:** Valid only when `mode = DocumentMode.RGB;` `mode = DocumentMode.CMYK;` or `mode = DocumentMode.INDEXEDCOLOR`. See "mode" on page 116.
`historyStates`	`HistoryStates` (page 148)	Read-only. The `HistoryStates` collection.
`info`	`DocumentInfo` (page 124)	Read-only. Metadata about the document.
`layerComps`	`LayerComp` (page 153)	Read-only. The `LayerComps` collection.
`layers`	`Layers` (page 156)	Read-only. The `Layers` collection.
`layerSets`	`LayerSets` (page 159)	Read-only. The `LayerSets` collection.
`managed`	`boolean`	Read-only. Indicates whether the document a is workgroup document.
`mode`	`DocumentMode` (page 333)	Read-only. The color profile.
`name`	`string`	Read-only. The document's name.

Property	Value Type	What it is (Continued)
parent	`Application` (page 75)	Read-only. The `Document` object's container.
path	`file`	Read-only. The path to the document.
pathItems	`PathItems` (page 172)	Read-only. The `PathItems` collection.
pixelAspectRatio	`number (double)`	Read-write. The (custom) pixel aspect ratio to use (0.100 - 10.000).
quickMaskMode	`boolean`	Read-write. Indicates whether the document is in Quick Mask mode.
resolution	`number (double)`	Read-only. The document's resolution (in pixels per inch).
saved	`boolean`	Read-only. Indicates whether the document has been saved since the last change.
selection	`Selection` (page 196)	Read-only. The selected area of the document.
typename	`string`	Read-only. The class name of the `Document` object.
width	`UnitValue`	Read-only. The width of the document (unit value).
xmpMetadata	`xmpMetadata` (page 220)	Read-only. Camera raw settings for the image. **Note:** Valid only for documents opened in Camera Raw format.

Methods

Method	Parameter Type	Returns	What it does
changeMode (destinationMode [, options])	ChangeMode (page 331) object (BitmapConversionOptions , page 98, or IndexedConversionOptions, page 150)		Changes the color profile.
close ([saving])	SaveOptions (page 342)		Closes the document. If any changes have been made, the script presents an alert with three options: save, do not save, prompt to save. The optional parameter specifies a selection in the alert box (default: SaveOptions. PROMPTTOSAVECHANGES).
convertProfile (destinationProfile, intent [,blackPointCompensation] [, dither])	string Intent (page 336) boolean boolean		Changes the color profile. **Note:** The destination Profile parameter must be either a string that names the color mode or Working RGB, Working CMYK, Working Gray, Lab Color (meaning one of the working color spaces or Lab color).
crop (bounds [, angle] [, width] [, height])	Array(UnitValue) number (double) UnitValue UnitValue		Crops the document. The first parameter is an array of four coordinates that mark the portion remaining after cropping, in the following order: left, top, right, bottom.
duplicate ()		Document (page 115)	Creates a duplicate of the document object.

Adobe® Photoshop® CS2 Official JavaScript Reference

Method	Parameter Type	Returns	What it does
exportDocument (exportIn [, exportAs] [, options])	file ExportType (page 334) ExportOptionsIllustrator (page 132)		Exports the document.
flatten ()			Flattens all layers.
flipCanvas (direction)	Direction (page 333)		Flips the image within the canvas in the specified direction.
importAnnotations (file)	file		Imports annotations into the document.
mergeVisibleLayers1 ()			Flattens all visible layers in the document.
paste ([intoSelection])	boolean	ArtLayer	Pastes the contents of the clipboard into the document. If the optional argument is set to true and a selection is active, the contents are pasted into the selection.
print ([postScriptEncoding] [, sourceSpace] [, printSpace] [, intent] [blackPointCompensation])	PrintEncoding (page 340) SourceSpaceType (page 343) string Intent (page 336) boolean		Prints the document. **Note:** printSpace specifies the color space for the printer. Valid values are nothing (that is, the same as the source); or Working RGB, Working CMYK, Working Gray, Lab Color (meaning one of the working color spaces or Lab color); or a string specifying a specific colorspace (default: nothing).

Method	Parameter Type	Returns	What it does
rasterizeAllLayers ()			Rasterizes all layers.
resizeCanvas ([width] [, height] [, anchor])	UnitValue UnitValue AnchorPosition (page 329)		Changes the size of the canvas to display more or less of the image but does not change the image size. See "resizeImage" on page 120.
resizeImage ([width] [, height] [, resolution] [, resampleMethod])	UnitValue UnitValue number (double) ResampleMethod (page 341)		Changes the size of the image.
revealAll ()			Expands the document to show clipped sections.
rotateCanvas (angle)	number (double)		Rotates the canvas (including the image) in clockwise direction.
save ()			Saves the document.
saveAs (saveIn [, options] [, asCopy] [, extensionType])	file object (corresponding SaveOptions object*) boolean Extension (page 334) * Examples: BMPSaveOptions (page 99) DCS2_SaveOptions (page 114) JPEGSaveOptions (page 151) TiffSaveOptions (page 219) etc.		Saves the document with specified save options.
splitChannels ()		Array (Document objects) (page 115)	Splits the document channels into separate images.

Method	Parameter Type	Returns	What it does
trap (width)	number (long)		Applies trapping to a CMYK document. **Note:** Valid only when *document*.mode = DocumentMode.CMYK. See "mode" on page 116.
trim ([type] [, top] [, left] [, bottom] [, right])	TrimType (page 344) boolean boolean boolean boolean		Trims the transparent area around the image on the specified sides of the canvas. **Note:** Default is true for all Boolean values.

Sample Script

The following script creates a document that contains two images (an eagle and a duck) obtained from the Adobe Photoshop CS2 Samples folder and employs the following steps:

- Determines which image is larger.
- Resizes the smaller image to match the larger image.
- Creates a merged document twice as high as either image in order to hold both images.
- Selects part of the document to and pastes the eagle into the selection.
- Inverts the selection and pastes the duckinto the lower part of the document.
- Positions the eagle over the duck.

Document.jsx

```
// Save the current preferences
var startRulerUnits = app.preferences.rulerUnits
var startTypeUnits = app.preferences.typeUnits
var startDisplayDialogs = app.displayDialogs

// Set Adobe Photoshop CS2 to use pixels and
// display no dialogs
app.preferences.rulerUnits = Units.PIXELS
app.preferences.typeUnits = TypeUnits.PIXELS
app.displayDialogs = DialogModes.NO
```

```
// first close all the open documents
while (app.documents.length) {
   app.activeDocument.close()
}

// Open the eagle and duck files from the samples folder
var eagleDoc = open(File(app.path +
"/Samples/Eagle.psd"))
var duckDoc = open(File(app.path + "/Samples/Ducky.tif"))

// Find out which document is larger
// Resize the smaller document the to the larger
// document's size. The resize requires
// the document be the active/front document
if ((eagleDoc.width.value * eagleDoc.height.value) >
(duckDoc.width.value * duckDoc.height.value)) {
   app.activeDocument = duckDoc
   duckDoc.resize(eagleDoc.width, eagleDoc.height)
} else {
   app.activeDocument = eagleDoc
   eagleDoc.resizeImage(duckDoc.width, duckDoc.height)
}

// Create a new document twice as high as two files
var mergedDoc = app.documents.add(duckDoc.width,
duckDoc.height * 2, duckDoc.resolution, "EagleOverDuck")

// Copy the eagle to the top; make it the active document
// so we can manipulate it
app.activeDocument = eagleDoc
eagleDoc.activeLayer.copy()

//Paste the eagle to the merged document, making the
merged document active
app.activeDocument = mergedDoc

// Select a square area at the top of the new document
var selRegion = Array(Array(0, 0),
                 Array(mergedDoc.width.value, 0),
                 Array(mergedDoc.width.value,
mergedDoc.height.value / 2),
                 Array(0, mergedDoc.height.value / 2),
                 Array(0, 0))
// Create the selection
mergedDoc.selection.select(selRegion)

//Paste in the eagle
mergedDoc.paste()
```

```
// do the same thing for the duck
app.activeDocument = duckDoc
duckDoc.activeLayer.copy()

app.activeDocument = mergedDoc
mergedDoc.selection.select(selRegion)

// Inverting the selection so the bottom of the document
// is now selected
mergedDoc.selection.invert()

// Paste the duck
mergedDoc.paste()

// get rid of our originals without modifying them
duckDoc.close(SaveOptions.DONOTSAVECHANGES)
eagleDoc.close(SaveOptions.DONOTSAVECHANGES)

// Reset the application preferences
app.preferences.rulerUnits = startRulerUnits
app.preferences.typeUnits = startTypeUnits
app.displayDialogs = startDisplayDialogs
```

DocumentInfo

Metadata about a `document` object. These values can be set by selecting **File > File Info** in the Adobe Photoshop CS2 application.

Note: You use the object name `info`, rather than the class name `DocumentInfo`, in a script, as in the following sample, which sets the `author`, `caption`, and `copyrighted` properties:

```
var docRef = open(fileList[i])
// set the file info
docRef.info.author = "Mr. Adobe programmer"
docRef.info.caption = "Adobe Photo shoot"
docRef.info.copyrighted =
CopyrightedType.COPYRIGHTEDWORK
```

The following sample uses the `DocumentInfo` object incorrectly:

```
docRef.DocumentInfo.author = "Mr. Adobe programmer"
docRef.DocumentInfo.caption = "Adobe Photo shoot"
docRef.DocumentInfo.copyrighted =
CopyrightedType.COPYRIGHTEDWORK
```

Properties

Property	Value Type	What it is
author	string	Read-write.
authorPosition	string	Read-write.
caption	string	Read-write.
captionWriter	string	Read-write.
category	string	Read-write.
city	string	Read-write.
copyrighted	CopyrightedType (page 332)	Read-write. The copyrighted status.
copyrightNotice	string	Read-write.
country	string	Read-write.
creationDate	string	Read-write.
credit	string	Read-write.
exif	Array of arrays: Array(Array (tag, tag data)), ...)	Read-only. Camera data that includes camera settings used when the image was taken. Sample array values are: tag = "camera"; tag value = "Cannon".
headline	string	Read-write.

Property	Value Type	What it is (Continued)
`instructions`	`string`	Read-write.
`jobName`	`string`	Read-write.
`keywords`	`Array (strings)`	Read-write. A list of keywords that can identify the document or its contents.
`ownerUrl`	`string`	Read-write.
`parent`	`object (Document)` (page 115)	Read-only. The `info` object's container.
`provinceState`	`string`	Read-write.
`source`	`string`	Read-write.
`supplementalCategories`	`Array (strings)`	Read-write.
`title`	`string`	Read-write.
`transmissionReference`	`string`	Read-write.
`typename`	`string`	Read-only. The class name of the referenced `info` object.
`urgency`	`Urgency` (page 345)	Read-write.

Sample Script

The following script sets document info (metadata) for all of the files in a specified folder and then saves the modified files as low-quality JPEG images in a new folder without changing the originals.

- Ask the user to specify the folder that contains the original files and the output folder for the JPEG images, and then check that the folders exist.
- Open each file and use the `documentInfo` object properties to tag it with the following metadata:
  - author: Mr. Adobe programmer
  - caption: Adobe Photo shoot
  - captionWriter: Mr. Adobe programmer
  - city: San Jose
  - copyrightNotice: Copyright (c) Adobe programmer Photography
  - copyrighted status: Copyrighted Work
  - country: USA
  - state: CA
- Save the new documents in JPEG format with a low quality setting.

DocumentInfo.jsx

```
// Save the current preferences
var startDisplayDialogs = app.displayDialogs

// Set Adobe Photoshop CS2 to use pixels and
// display no dialogs
app.displayDialogs = DialogModes.NO

// ask the user for the input folder
var inputFolder = Folder.selectDialog("Select a folder to
tag")

// ask the user for the output folder
var outputFolder = Folder.selectDialog("Select a folder
for the output files")

// see if we got something interesting from the dialog
if (inputFolder != null && outputFolder != null) {

    // get all the files found in this folder
    var fileList = inputFolder.getFiles()

    // save the outputs in JPEG
    var jpegOptions = new JPEGSaveOptions()

    // set the jpeg quality really low
    // so the files are small
    jpegOptions.quality = 1

    // open each one in turn
    for (var i = 0; i < fileList.length; i++) {

            // The fileList includes both folders and files
            // so open only files
            if (fileList[i] instanceof File &&
fileList[i].hidden == false) {

                    // get a reference to the new document
                    var docRef = open(fileList[i])

                    // tag all of the documents with
                    // photo shoot information
                    docRef.info.author = "Mr. Adobe programmer"
                    docRef.info.caption = "Adobe Photo shoot"
                    docRef.info.captionWriter =
                        "Mr. Adobe programmer"
                    docRef.info.city = "San Jose"
```

```
docRef.info.copyrightNotice =
    "Copyright (c) Adobe programmer
    Photography"
docRef.info.copyrighted =
    CopyrightedType.COPYRIGHTEDWORK
docRef.info.country = "USA"
docRef.info.provinceState = "CA"

// change the date to a Adobe Photoshop CS2
// date format "YYYYMMDD"
var theDate = new Date()

// the year is from 1900 ????
var theYear = (theDate.getYear() +
    1900).toString()

// convert the month from 0..12 to 00..12
var theMonth =
    theDate.getMonth().toString()

if (theDate.getMonth() < 10) {
    theMonth = "0" + theMonth
}

// convert the day from 0..31 to 00.31
var theDay = theDate.getDate().toString()

if (theDate.getDate() < 10) {
    theDay = "0" + theDay
}

// stick them all together
docRef.info.creationDate = theYear +
    theMonth + theDay

// flatten because we are saving to JPEG
docRef.flatten()

// go to 8 bit because we are saving to JPEG
docRef.bitsPerChannel =
    BitsPerChannelType.EIGHT

// save and close
docRef.saveAs(new File(outputFolder +
    "/Output" + i + ".jpg"),
    jpegOptions)
```

```
                    // don't modify the original
                    docRef.close(SaveOptions.DONOTSAVECHANGES)
        }
    }
}

// Reset the application preferences
app.displayDialogs = startDisplayDialogs
```

Documents

The collection of open `document` objects. See `Document` (page 115) for information on the `document` object.

Note: Because the `Documents` class is a property of the `Application` (page 75) object, you use the object name, `documents`, rather than the class name, `Documents`, in your code, as in the following example:

```
documents.add(800, 500, 72, "myDocument",
NewDocumentMode.RGB)
```

The following example, which uses an uppercase *D* in the object name, is incorrect:

```
Documents.add(800, 500, 72, "myDocument",
NewDocumentMode.RGB)
```

Properties

Property	Value Type	What it is
length	number (long)	Read-only. The number of elements in the `documents` collection.
parent	object (Application) (page 75)	Read-only. The `documents` objects' container.
typename	string	Read-only. The class name of the referenced `documents` object.

Methods

Method	Parameter Type	Returns	What it does
index (itemKey)	number	Document (page 115)	Gets an element from the `documents` collection.
add ([width] [, height] [, resolution] [, name] [, mode] [, initialFill] [pixelAspectRatio])	UnitValue UnitValue number (double) string NewDocumentMode (page 337) DocumentFill (page 333) number (double)	Document (page 115)	Adds a `document` object (pixelAspectRatio: 0.100 0 10.00).
getByName (name)	string	Document (page 115)	Gets the first element in the `documents` collection with the provided name.

EPSOpenOptions

Options that can be specified when opening an EPS format document.

Properties

Property	Value Type	What it is
antiAlias	boolean	Read-write. Indication of whether to use antialias.
constrainProportions	boolean	Read-write. Indication of whether to constrain the proportions of the image.
height	UnitValue	Read-write. The height of the image (unit value).
mode	OpenDocumentMode (page 337)	Read-write. The color profile to use as the document mode.
resolution	number (double)	Read-write. The resolution of the document in pixels per inch.
typename	string	Read-only. The class name of the referenced EPSOpenOptions object.
width	UnitValue	Read-write. The width of the image (unit value).

EPSSaveOptions

Options that can be specified when saving a document in EPS format.

Properties

Property	Value Type	What it is
embedColorProfile	boolean	Read-write. Indication of whether to embed the color profile in this document.
encoding	SaveEncoding (page 342)	Read-write. The type of encoding to use (default: SaveEncoding.BINARY).
halftoneScreen	boolean	Read-write. Indication of whether to include the halftone screen (default: false).
interpolation	boolean	Read-write. Indication of whether to use image interpolation (default: false).
preview	Preview (page 340)	Read-write. The preview type.
psColorManagement	boolean	Read-write. Indication of whether to use PostScript color management (default: false).
transferFunction	boolean	Read-write. Indication of whether to include the Transfer functions to compensate for dot gain between the image and film (default: false).
transparentWhites	boolean	Read-write. Indication of whether to display white areas as transparent. **Note:** Valid only when *document*.mode – DocumentMode.BITMAP. See "mode" on page 116 (in the Properties table of the document object) or "changeMode" on page 118 (in the Methods table of the document object).
typename	string	Read-only. The class name of the referenced EPSSaveOptions object.
vectorData	boolean	Read-write. Indication of whether to include vector data. **Note:** Valid only if the document includes vector data (text).

ExportOptionsIllustrator

Options that can be specified when exporting a PathItem (page 167) object to an Adobe Illustrator® file.

Properties

Property	Value Type	What it is
path	IllustratorPathType (page 336)	Read-write. The type of path to export (default: IllustratorPathType.DOCUMENTBOUNDS).
pathName	string	Read-write. The name of the path to export. **Note:** Valid only when path = IllustratorPathType.NAMEDPATH. See "path" on page 132.
typename	string	Read-only. The class name of the referenced exportOptionsIllustrator object.

ExportOptionsSaveForWeb

Options that can be specified when optimizing a document for the web.

Properties

Property	Value type	What it is
blur	number (double)	Read-write. Applies blur to the image to reduce artifacts (default: 0.0).
colorReduction	ColorReductionTyp e (page 332)	Read-write. The color reduction algorithm (default: ColorReductionType.SELECTIVE).
colors	number (long)	Read-write. The number of colors in the palette (default: 256).
dither	Dither (page 333)	Read-write. The type of dither (default: Dither.DIFFUSION).
ditherAmount	number (long)	Read-write. The amount of dither (default: 100). **Note:** Valid only when dither = Dither.DIFFUSION. See "dither" on page 133.
format	SaveDocumentType (page 342)	Read-write. The file format to use (default: SaveDocumentType.COMPUSERVEGIF). **Note:** For this property, only COMPUSERVEGIF, JPEG, PNG-8, PNG-24, and BMP are supported.
includeProfile	boolean	Read-write. Indication of whether to include the document's embedded color profile (default: false).
interlaced	boolean	Read-write. Indication of whether to download in multiple passes; progressive (default: false).
lossy	number (long)	Read-write. The amount of lossiness allowed (default: 0).
matteColor	RGBColor (page 195)	Read-write. The colors to blend transparent pixels against.
optimized	boolean	Read-write. Indication of whether to create smaller but less compatible files (default: true). **Note:** Valid only when format = SaveDocumentType.JPEG. See "format" on page 133.

Property	Value type	What it is (Continued)
PNG8	boolean	Read-write. Indicates the number of bits; `true` = 8, `false` = 24 (default: `true`). **Note:** Valid only when `format = SaveDocumentType.PNG`. See "format" on page 133.
quality	number (long)	Read-write. The quality of the produced image (0 - 100 as percentage; default: `60`).
transparency	boolean	Read-write. Indication of transparent areas of the image should be included in the saved image(default: `true`).
transparencyAmount	number (long)	Read-write. The amount of transparency dither (default: 100). **Note:** Valid only if `transparency = true`. See "transparency" on page 134.
transparencyDither	Dither (page 333)	Read-write. The transparency dither algorithm (default: `transparencyDither = Dither.NONE`).
typename	string	Read-only. The class name of the referenced `ExportOptionsSaveForWeb` object.
webSnap	number (long)	Read-write. The tolerance amount within which to snap close colors to web palette colors (default: `0`).

GalleryBannerOptions

Options that define the `bannerOptions` property of the `galleryOptions` object. See "GalleryOptions" on page 139.

Tip: You can preserve default values for many `galleryBannerOptions` properties by setting the `galleryOptions` property `preserveAllMetadata` to `true` or by choosing **File > Automate > Web Photo Gallery**, and then choosing **Preserve all metadata on the Options area of the Web Photo Gallery dialog**.

Properties

Property	Value Type	What it is
contactInfo	string	Read-write. The web photo gallery contact info.
date	string	Read-write. The web photo gallery date (default: current date).
font	GalleryFontType (page 335)	Read-write. The font setting for the banner text (default: `GalleryFontType.ARIAL`).
fontSize	number (long)	Read-write. The font size for the banner text (1 - 7; default: 3).
photographer	string	Read-write. The web photo gallery photographer.
siteName	string	Read-write. The web photo gallery site name (default: `Adobe Web Photo Gallery`).
typename	string	Read-only. The class name of the referenced `galleryBannerOptions` object.

GalleryCustomColorOptions

Options that define the `customColorOptions` property of the `galleryOptions` object. See "GalleryOptions" on page 139.

Tip: You can preserve default values for many `galleryCustomColorOptions` properties by setting the `galleryOptions` property `preserveAllMetadata` to `true` or by choosing **File > Automate > Web Photo Gallery**, and then choosing **Preserve all metadata on the Options area of the Web Photo Gallery dialog**.

Properties

Property	Value Type	What it is
activeLinkColor	RGBColor (page 195)	Read-write. The color to use to indicate an active link.
backgroundColor	RGBColor (page 195)	Read-write. The background color.
bannerColor	RGBColor (page 195)	Read-write. The banner color.
linkColor	RGBColor (page 195)	Read-write. The color to use to indicate a link.
textColor	RGBColor (page 195)	Read-write. The text color.
typename	string	Read-only. The class name of the referenced `galleryCustomColorOptions` object.
visitedLinkColor	RGBColor (page 195)	Read-write. The color to use to indicate a visited link.

GalleryImagesOptions

Options that define the `imagesOptions` property of the `galleryOptions` object. See "GalleryOptions" on page 139.

Tip: You can preserve default values for many `galleryImagesOptions` properties by setting the `galleryOptions` property `preserveAllMetadata` to `true` or by choosing **File > Automate > Web Photo Gallery**, and then choosing **Preserve all metadata on the Options area of the Web Photo Gallery dialog**.

Properties

Property	Value Type	What it is
border	number (long)	Read-write. The size (in pixels) of the border that separates images (0 - 99; default: 0).
caption	boolean	Read-write. Indication of whether to generate image captions (default: `false`).
dimension	number (long)	Read-write. The resized image dimensions in pixels (default: 350). **Note:** Valid only when `resizeImages = true`. See "resizeImages" on page 138.
font	GalleryFontType (page 335)	Read-write. The font to use for image captions (default: `GalleryFontType.ARIAL`).
fontSize	number (long)	Read-write. The font size for image captions (1 - 7; default: 3). **Note:** Valid only when `caption = true`. See "caption" on page 137.
imageQuality	number (long)	Read-write. The quality setting for a JPEG image (0 - 12; default: 5).
includeCopyright	boolean	Read-write. Indication of whether to include copyright information in captions (default: `false`). **Note:** Valid only when `caption = true`. See "caption" on page 137.
includeCredits	boolean	Read-write. Indication of whether to include the credits in image captions (default: `false`). **Note:** Valid only when `caption = true`. See "caption" on page 137.
includeFilename	boolean	Read-write. Indication of whether to include the file name in image captions (default: `true`). **Note:** Valid only when `caption = true`. See "caption" on page 137.

Property	Value Type	What it is (Continued)
`includeTitle`	`boolean`	Read-write. Indication of whether to include the title in image captions (default: `false`). **Note:** Valid only when `caption = true`. See "caption" on page 137.
`numericLinks`	`boolean`	Read-write. Indication of whether to add numeric links (default: `true`).
`resizeConstraint`	`GalleryConstrainType` (page 335)	Read-write. The image dimensions to constrain in the gallery image (default: `GalleryConstrainType.CONSTRAINBOTH`). **Note:** Valid only when `resizeImages = true`. See "resizeImages" on page 138.
`resizeImages`	`boolean`	Read-write. Indication of whether to automatically resize images for placement on the gallery pages (default: `true`).
`typename`	`string`	Read-only. The class name of the referenced `galleryImagesOptions` object.

GalleryOptions

Options that can be specified for a Web photo gallery.

Tip: You can preserve default values for many `galleryOptions` properties by choosing **File > Automate > Web Photo Gallery**, and then choosing **Preserve all metadata on the Options area of the Web Photo Gallery dialog**.

Properties

Property	Value Type	What it is
addSizeAttributes	boolean	Read-write. Indicates whether width and height attributes for images will be added (default: `true`).
bannerOptions	GalleryBannerOptions (page 135)	Read-write. The options related to banner settings.
customColorOptions	GalleryCustomColorOptions (page 136)	Read-write. The options related to custom color settings.
emailAddress	string	Read-write. The email address to show on the web page.
imagesOptions	GalleryImagesOptions (page 137)	Read-write. The options related to images settings.
includeSubFolders	boolean	Read-write. Indication of whether to include all files found in sub folders of the input folder (default: `true`).
layoutStyle	string	Read-write. The style to use for laying out the web page (default: `Centered Frame 1 - Basic`).
preserveAllMetadata	boolean	Read-write. Indicates whether to save metadata (default: `false`).
securityOptions	GallerySecurityOptions (page 141)	Read-write. The options related to security settings.
thumbnailOptions	GalleryThumbnailOptions (page 142)	Read-write. The options related to thumbnail image settings.
typename	string	Read-only. The class name of the referenced `galleryOptions` object.

Property	Value Type	What it is (Continued)
`useShortExtension`	`boolean`	Read-write. Indicates whether the short web page extension `.htm` or number (long) web page extension `.html` will be used (default: `true`).
`useUTF8Encoding`	`boolean`	Read-write. Indicates whether the web page should use UTF-8 encoding (default: `false`).

GallerySecurityOptions

Options that define the `securityOptions` property of the `galleryOptions` object. See "GalleryOptions" on page 139.

Tip: You can preserve default values for many `gallerySecurityOptions` properties by setting the `galleryOptions` property `preserveAllMetadata` to `true` or by choosing **File > Automate > Web Photo Gallery**, and then choosing **Preserve all metadata on the Options area of the Web Photo Gallery dialog**.

Properties

Property	Value Type	What it is
content	GallerySecurityType (page 335)	Read-write. The web photo gallery security content (default: GallerySecurityType.NONE).
font	GalleryFontType (page 335)	Read-write. The web photo gallery security font (default: GalleryFontType.ARIAL).
fontSize	number (long)	Read-write. The web photo gallery security font size (1 - 72; default: 3).
opacity	number (long)	Read-write. The web page security opacity as a percent (default: 100).
text	string	Read-write. The web photo gallery security custom text.
textColor	RGBColor (page 195)	Read-write. The web page security text color.
textPosition	GallerySecurityTextPositionType (page 335)	Read-write. The web photo gallery security text position (default: GallerySecurityTextPositionType.CENTERED).
textRotate	GallerySecurityTextRotateType (page 335)	Read-write. The web photo gallery security text orientation to use (default: Gallery SecurityTextRotateType.ZERO).
typename	string	Read-only. The class name of the referenced gallerySecurityOptions object.

GalleryThumbnailOptions

Options that define the `thumbnailOptions` property of the `galleryOptions` object. See "GalleryOptions" on page 139.

Tip: You can preserve default values for many `galleryThumbnailOptions` properties by setting the `galleryOptions` property `preserveAllMetadata` to `true` or by choosing **File > Automate > Web Photo Gallery**, and then choosing **Preserve all metadata on the Options area of the Web Photo Gallery dialog**.

Properties

Property	Value Type	What it is
`border`	number (long)	Read-write. The amount of border pixels you want around your thumbnail images (0 - 99; default: `0`).
`caption`	boolean	Read-write. Indicates whether there is a caption (default: `false`).
`columnCount`	number (long)	Read-write. The number of columns on the page (default: `5`).
`dimension`	number (long)	Read-write. The web photo gallery thumbnail dimension in pixels (default: `75`).
`font`	GalleryFontType (page 335)	Read-write. The web photo gallery font (default: `GalleryFontType.ARIAL`).
`fontSize`	number (long)	Read-write. The font size for thumbnail images text (1 - 7; default: `3`).
`includeCopyright`	boolean	Read-write. Indication of whether to include copyright information for thumbnails (default: `false`).
`includeCredits`	boolean	Read-write. Indication of whether to include credits for thumbnails (default: `false`).
`includeFilename`	boolean	Read-write. Indication of whether to include file names for thumbnails (default: `false`).
`includeTitle`	boolean	Read-write. Indication of whether to include titles for thumbnails (default: `false`).
`rowCount`	number (long)	Read-write. The number of rows on the page (default: `3`).

Property	Value Type	What it is (Continued)
size	GalleryThumbSizeType (page 335)	Read-write. The thumbnail image size (default: GalleryThumbSizeType.MEDIUM).
typename	string	Read-only. The class name of the referenced GalleryThumbnailOptions object.

GIFSaveOptions

Options that can be specified when saving a document in GIF format.

Properties

Property	Value Type	What it is

`colors`	`number (long)`	Read-write. The number of palette colors.
		Note: Valid only when
		`palette = Palette.LOCALADAPTIVE;`
		`palette = Palette.LOCALPERCEPTUAL;`
		`palette = Palette.LOCALSELECTIVE;`
		`palette = Palette.MACOSPALETTE;`
		`palette = Palette.UNIFORM;`
		`palette = Palette.WEBPALETTE;` or
		`palette = Palette.WINDOWSPALETTE`.
		See "palette" on page 144.

`dither`	`Dither` (page 333)	Read-write. The dither type.
`ditherAmount`	`number (long)`	Read-write. The amount of dither. (1 - 100; default: `75`). **Note:** Valid only for when `dither = Dither.DIFFUSION`. See "dither" on page 150.
`forced`	`ForcedColors` (page 334)	Read-write. The type of colors to force into the color palette.
`interlaced`	`boolean`	Read-write. Indicates whether rows should be interlaced (default: `false`).
`matte`	`MatteType` (page 337)	Read-write. The color to use to fill anti-aliased edges adjacent to transparent areas of the image (default: `MatteType.WHITE`). **Note:** When `transparency = false`, the matte color is applied to transparent areas. See "transparency" on page 150.
`palette`	`Palette` (page 339)	Read-write. The type of palette to use (default: `Palette.LOCALSELECTIVE`).
`preserveExactColors`	`boolean`	Read-write. Indication of whether to protect colors in the image that contain entries in the color table from being dithered. **Note.** Valid only when `dither = Dither.DIFFUSION`. See "dither" on page 150.

Property	Value Type	What it is (Continued)
transparency	boolean	Read-write. Indication of whether to preserve transparent areas of the image during conversion to GIF format.
typename	string	Read-only. The class name of the referenced `GIFSaveOptions` object.

GrayColor

Options for defining a gray color.

Properties

Property	Value Type	What it is
gray	number (double)	Read-write. The gray value (0.0 - 100.0; default: 0.0).
typename	string	Read-only. The class name of the referenced grayColor object.

HistoryState

A version of the document stored automatically (and added to the `HistoryStates` collection), which preserves the document's state, each time the document is changed. See "HistoryStates" on page 148 for information about the `HistoryStates` collection.

Note: Because the `HistoryState` class is also a property of the Document (page 115) object, you use the object name, `historyState`, rather than the class name, `HistoryState`, in your code.

The following example uses correct syntax to refer to a `HistoryState` object named `AddLayerMask` and then assign its `snapshot` property value:

```
documents(0).historyState("AddLayerMask").snapshot =
true
```

The following example, which uses an uppercase *A* in the object name, is incorrect:

```
documents(0).HistoryState("AddLayerMask").snapshot =
true
```

Properties

Property	Value Type	What it is
name	string	Read-only. The `HistoryState` object's name.
parent	object (Document) (page 115)	Read-only. The `HistoryState` object's container.
snapshot	boolean	Read-only. Indicates whether the history state is a snapshot.
typename	string	Read-only. The class name of the referenced `HistoryState` object.

HistoryStates

The collection of `HistoryState` objects in the document. See "HistoryState" on page 147 for more information on `HistoryState` objects.

Note: Because the `HistoryStates` class is also a property of the Document (page 115) object, you use the object name, `historyStates`, rather than the class name, `HistoryStates`, in your code.

The following example uses correct syntax to fill a Selection object (referred to by the variable selRef) with an object in the `HistoryStates` collection:

```
selRef.fill(activeDocument.historyStates[7])
```

The following example, which uses an uppercase *H* in the object name, is incorrect:

```
selRef.fill(activeDocument.HistoryStates[7])
```

Properties

Property	Value Type	What it is
length	number (long)	Read-only. The number of elements in the `HistoryStates` collection.
parent	object (Document) (page 115)	Read-only. The `HistoryStates` object's container.
typename	string	Read-only. The class name of the referenced `HistoryStates` object.

Methods

Method	Parameter Type	Returns	What it does
index (itemKey)	number	HistoryState (page 147)	Gets an element from the `HistoryStates` collection.
getByName (name)	string	HistoryState (page 147)	Gets the first element in the `HistoryStates` collection with the provided name.

HSBColor

Options that can be specified for a color object using the HSB color model.

Properties

Property	Value Type	What it is
brightness	number (double)	Read-write. The brightness value (between 0.0 and 100.0).
hue	number (double)	Read-write. The hue value (between 0.0 and 360.0).
saturation	number (double)	Read-write. The saturation value (between 0.0 and 100.0).
typename	string	Read-only. The class name of the referenced HSBColor object.

IndexedConversionOptions

Options that can be specified when converting an RGB image to an indexed color model.

Properties

Property	Value Type	What it is

colors	number (long)	Read-write. The number of palette colors.
		Note: Valid only when
		`palette = Palette.LOCALADAPTIVE;`
		`palette = Palette.LOCALPERCEPTUAL;`
		`palette = Palette.LOCALSELECTIVE;`
		`palette = Palette.MACOSPALETTE;`
		`palette = Palette.UNIFORM;`
		`palette = Palette.WEBPALETTE;` or
		`palette = Palette.WINDOWSPALETTE` .
		See "palette" on page 150.

dither	Dither (page 333)	Read-write. The dither type.
ditherAmount	number (long)	Read-write. The amount of dither. (1 - 100). **Note:** Valid only when `dither = Dither.diffusion`.
forced	ForcedColors (page 334)	Read-write. The type of colors to force into the color palette.
matte	MatteType (page 337)	Read-write. Read-write. The color to use to fill anti-aliased edges adjacent to transparent areas of the image (default: `MatteType.WHITE`). **Note:** When `transparency = false`, the matte color is applied to transparent areas. See "transparency" on page 150.
palette	Palette (page 339)	Read-write. The palette type (default: `Palette.EXACT`).
preserveExactColors	boolean	Read-write.Indication of whether to protect colors in the image that contain entries in the color table from being dithered. **Note:** Valid only when `dither = Dither.DIFFUSION`. See "dither" on page 150.
transparency	boolean	Read-write. Indication of whether to preserve transparent areas of the image during conversion to GIF format.
typename	string	Read-only. The class name of the referenced `IndexedConversionOptions` object.

JPEGSaveOptions

Options that can be specified when saving a document in JPEG format.

Properties

Property	Value Type	What it is
embedColorProfile	boolean	Read-write. Indication of whether to embed the color profile in the document.
formatOptions	FormatOptions (page 335)	Read-write. The download format to use (default: FormatOptions.STANDARDBASELINE).
matte	MatteType (page 337)	Read-write. The color to use to fill anti-aliased edges adjacent to transparent areas of the image (default: MatteType.WHITE). **Note:** When transparency = false, the matte color is applied to transparent areas. See "transparency" on page 150.
quality	number (long)	Read-write. The image quality setting to use (affects file size and compression) (0 - 12; default: 3).
scans	number (long)	Read-write. The number of scans to make to incrementally display the image on the page (3 - 5; default: 3). **Note:** Valid only for when formatOptions = FormatOptions.PROGRESSIVE.
typename	string	Read-only. The class name of the referenced JPEGSaveOptions object.

LabColor

Options that can be specified when defining a color object using the LAB color model.

Properties

Property	Value Type	What it is
a	number (double)	Read-write. The a-value (-128.0 - 127.0).
b	number (double)	Read-write. The b-value (-128.0 - 127.0).
l	number (double)	Read-write. The L-value (0.0 - 100.0).
typename	string	Read-only. The class name of the referenced LabColor object.

LayerComp

A snapshot of a state of the layers in a document (can be used to view different page layouts or compositions).

Note: Because the `LayerComp` class is also a property of the Document (page 115) object, you use the object name, `layerComp`, rather than the class name, `LayerComp`, in your code.

The following example uses correct syntax to set the comment property value for a `LayerComp` object named `myLayerComp`:

```
activeDocument.layerComp("myLayerComp").comment =
"View from shoreline"
```

The following example, which uses an uppercase *L* in the object name, is incorrect:

```
activeDocument.LayerComp("myLayerComp").comment =
"View from shoreline"
```

Properties

Property	Value Type	What it is
appearance	boolean	Read-write. Indication of whether to use layer appearance (layer styles) settings.
comment	string	Read-write. A description of the layer comp.
name	string	Read-write. The name of the layer comp.
parent	object (Document) (page 115)	Read-write. The `layerComp` object's container.
position	boolean	Read-write. Indication of whether to use layer position.
selected	boolean	Read-only. Indication of whether the layer comp is currently selected.
typename	string	Read-only. The class name of the referenced `layerComp` object.
visibility	boolean	Read-write. Indication of whether to use layer visibility settings .

Methods

Method	Parameter Type	Returns	What it does
apply ( )			Applies the layer comp to the document.
recapture ( )			Recaptures the current layer state(s) for this layer comp.
remove ( )			Deletes the layerComp object.
resetfromComp ( )			Resets the layer comp state to the document state.

LayerComps

The collection of `layerComp` objects in the document. See "LayerComp" on page 153 for information on `layerComp` objects.

Note: Because the `LayerComps` class is also a property of the Document (page 115) object, you use the object name, `layerComps`, rather than the class name, `LayerComps`, in your code.

The following example uses correct syntax to add a `LayerComps`:

```
activeDocument.layerComps.add("myLayerComp",
    "View from Shoreline", true, true, true)
```

The following example, which uses an uppercase *L* in the object name, is incorrect:

```
activeDocument.LayerComps.add("myLayerComp",
    "View from Shoreline", true, true, true)
```

Properties

Property	Value Type	What it is
length	number (long)	Read-only. The number of elements in the `layerComps` collection.
parent	object (Document) (page 115)	Read-only. The `layerComps` object's container.
typename	string	Read-only. The class name of the referenced `layerComps` object.

Methods

Method	Parameter Type	Returns	What it does
index (itemKey)	number	LayerComp (page 153)	Gets an element from the `layerComps` collection.
add (name, comment, appearance, position, visibility)	string string boolean boolean boolean	LayerComp (page 153)	Adds a layer comp.
getByName (name)	string	LayerComp (page 153)	Gets the first element in the collection with the provided name.
removeAll ()			Removes all `layerComp` objects from the `layerComps` collection.

Layers

The collection of layer objects, including `artLayer` and `layerSet` objects, in the document. See ArtLayer (page 82) for information on `artLayer` objects. See LayerSet (page 157) for information on `layerSet` objects.

Note: Because the `Layers` object is a property of the Document (page 115) object (as well as several other objects), you use the object name, `layers`, rather than the class name, `Layers`, in your code. The following example uses the `length` property to count the number of `layer` objects in the active document, then displays the number on the screen:

```
var layerNum = app.activeDocument.layers.length
alert(layerNum)
```

The following example uses an uppercase *L*, which is incorrect:

```
var layerNum = app.activeDocument.Layers.length
alert(layerNum)
```

Properties

Property	Value Type	What it is
length	number (long)	Read-only. The number of elements in the `layers` collection.
parent	object (document or layerSet)	Read-only. The `layers` object's container.
typename	string	Read-only. The class name of the referenced `layers` object.

Methods

Method	Parameter Type	Returns	What it does
index (itemKey)	number	object(Layer)	Gets an element from the collection.
getByName (name)	string	Layer	Gets the first element in the `layers` collection with the provided name.
removeAll ()			Removes all layers from the collection.

LayerSet

A group of layer objects, which can include `artLayer` objects and other (nested) `layerSet` objects. A single command or set of commands manipulates all layers in a `layerSet` object.

Note: Most likely, you will use variables to refer to `layerSet` objects in your script. However, if you choose not to use a variable, be aware that, because the `LayerSet` class is also a property of the `Document` (page 115) object, you use the object name, `layerSet`, rather than the class name, `LayerSet`, in your code.

The following example uses correct syntax to refer to a `layerSet` object by name and then assign its `allLocked` property value:

```
documents(0).layerSet("myLayerSet").allLocked = true
```

The following example, which uses an uppercase *L* in the object name, is incorrect:

```
documents(0).LayerSet("myLayerSet").allLocked = true
```

Properties

Property	Value Type	What it is
allLocked	boolean	Read-write. Indicates whether the contents in the layers contained in the `layerSet` object are editable.
artLayers	ArtLayer (page 82)	Read-only. The `artLayer` objects in this layer set.
blendMode	BlendMode (page 330)	Read-write. The blend mode to use for the layer set.
bounds	Array(UnitValue)	Read-only. The bounding rectangle of the layer set.
enabledChannels	Array (Channel objects)	Read-write. The channels enabled for the layer set; must be a list of component channels. **Note:** See `kind` in the Properties table for the Channel object (`Channel`, page 102).
layers	LayerSets (page 159)	Read-only. The layers in this `layerSet` object.
layerSets	LayerSets (page 159)	Read-only. Layer Sets contained within a Layer Set.
linkedLayers	Array (layers)	Read-only. The layers linked to this `layerSet` object.
name	string	Read-write. The name of the `layerSet` object.
opacity	number (double)	Read-write. The master opacity of the `layerSet` object (0.0 - 100.0).
parent	object (document or layerSet)	Read-only. The `layerSet` object's container.

Property	Value Type	What it is (Continued)
typename	string	Read-only. The class name of the referenced `layerSet` object.
visible	boolean	Read-write. Indicates whether the `layerSet` object is visible.

Methods

Method	Parameter Type	Returns	What it does
duplicate ([relativeObject] [, insertionLocation])	object (ArtLayer, page 82,or LayerSet, page 157) ElementPlacement (page 334)	object (Layer)	Creates a duplicate of the `layerSet` object.
link (with)	object (Layer)		Links the layer set with another layer.
merge ()		ArtLayer	Merges the layerset; returns a reference to the art layer created by this method.
move (relativeObject, insertionLocation)	object (layer or layerSet) ElementPlacement (page 334)		Moves the `layerSet` object.
remove ()			Deletes the `layerSet` object.
resize ([horizontal] [, vertical] [, anchor])	number (double) number (double) AnchorPosition (page 329)		Resizes all layers in the layer set to the specified dimensions (as a percentage of its current size) and places the layer set in the specified position.
rotate (angle [, anchor])	number (double) AnchorPosition (page 329)		Rotates all layers in the layer set around the specified anchor point (default: `AnchorPosition.MIDDLECENTER`).
translate ([deltaX] [, deltaY])	UnitValue UnitValue		Moves the position relative to its current position.
unlink ()			Unlinks the layer set.

LayerSets

The collection of `layerSet` objects in the document. See LayerSet (page 157) for information on `layerSet` objects.

Note: Because the `LayerSets` class is a property of the Document (page 115) object, you use the object name, `layerSets`, rather than the class name, `LayerSets`, in your code. For example:

```
var laysetRef = docRef.layerSets.add()
```

The following sample uses the `layerSets` object incorrectly:

```
var laysetRef = docRef.LayerSets.add()
```

Properties

Property	Value Type	What it is
length	number (long)	Read-only. The number of elements in the `layerSets` collection.
parent	object (document or layerSet)	Read-only. The `layerSets` object's container.
typename	string	Read-only. The class name of the referenced `layerSets` object.

Methods

Method	Parameter Type	Returns	What it does
index (itemKey)	number	LayerSet	Gets an element from the `layerSets` collection.
add ()		LayerSet	Creates a new `layerSet` object.
getByName (name)	string	LayerSet	Gets the first element in the `layerSets` collection with the provided name.
removeAll ()			Removes the layer set, and any layers or layer sets it contains, from the document.

Sample Script

The following script creates three layer sets, then nests a second layer set in each layer set, and then creates a text layer in each nested set that displays the text "Layer in *n* Set Inside *n* Set", where *n* represents the ordinal number of the set (first, second, or third).

Note: The script uses the $ object, which is defined in "Dollar ($) Object" on page 362.

LayerSets.jsx

```
$.level = 1

//close all open documents
while (app.documents.length) {
   app.activeDocument.close()
}

// create a working document
var docRef = app.documents.add()

// create an array to hold the layer sets
var myLayerSets = new Array()

// Create an array to hold the text
var textArray = Array("First", "Second", "Third")

//Create an indexer variable
var i = 0

// Create three layer sets at the top level
for (i = 0; i < 3; i++) {
   myLayerSets[i] = new Array()
   myLayerSets[i][0] = docRef.layerSets.add()
}

// Rearrange the layer sets with the first one on top,
// second next, etc.
myLayerSets[1][0].moveAfter(myLayerSets[0][0])
myLayerSets[2][0].moveAfter(myLayerSets[1][0])

// Create a layer set inside each layer set
for (i = 0; i < 3; i++) {
   myLayerSets[i][0].name = textArray[i] + " Set"
   myLayerSets[i][1] = myLayerSets[i][0].layerSets.add()
   myLayerSets[i][1].name = "Inside " +
      textArray[i] + " Set"
}

// Create an array to hold the layers
var myLayers = new Array()

// Create a text layer with a description inside
// each layer set
for (i = 0; i < 3; i++) {
   myLayers[i] = myLayerSets[i][1].artLayers.add()
   myLayers[i].kind = LayerKind.TEXT
```

```
myLayers[i].textItem.contents = "Layer in " +
        textArray[i] + " Set Inside "
        + textArray[i] + " Set"
myLayers[i].textItem.position =
        Array(app.activeDocument.width * i * 0.33,
        app.activeDocument.height * (i + 1) * 0.25)
myLayers[i].textItem.size = 12
}
```

LensBlurOptions

Defines the optional parameter of the `artLayer` object's `applyLensBlur()` method.

Note: See "applyLensBlur" on page 86 (in the Methods table of the `artLayer` object).

Properties

Property	Value type	What it is
amount	number (long)	Read-write. The amount of noise (default: 0).
bladeCurvature	number (long)	Read-write. The blade curvature of the iris (default: 0).
brightness	number (long)	Read-write. The brightness for the specular highlights (default: 0).
distribution	NoiseDistribution (page 337)	Read-write. The distribution value for the noise (default: NoiseDistribution.UNIFORM).
focalDistance	number (long)	Read-write. The blur focal distance for the depth map (default: 0).
invertDepthMap	boolean	Read-write. Indicates whether the depth map is inverted (default: false).
monochromatic	boolean	Read-write. Indicates whether the noise is monochromatic (default: false).
radius	number (long)	Read-write. The radius of the iris (default: 15).
rotation	number (long)	Read-write. The rotation of the iris (default: 0).
shape	Geometry (page 335)	The shape of the iris (default: Geometry.HEXAGON).
source	DepthMapSource (page 332)	Read-write. The source for the depth map (default: DepthMapSource.NONE).
threshold	number (long)	Read-write. The threshold for the specular highlights (default: 0).
typename	string	Read-only. The class name of the referenced lensBlurOptions object.

NoColor

An object that represents a missing color.

Properties

Property	Value type	What it is
typename	string	Read-only. The class name of the referenced noColor object.

Notifier

An event-handler object that tells the script to execute specified code when a specified event occurs.

Note: Because the `Notifier` class is also a property of the Document (page 115) object, you use the object name, `notifier`, rather than the class name, `Notifier`, in your code.

Properties

Property	Value type	What it is
event	string	Read-only. The event ID in four characters or a unique string that the notifier is associated with.
eventClass	string	Read-only. The class ID of the event associated with the `Notifier` object, four characters or a unique string. **Note:** For a list of four-character codes, see "Appendix A: Event ID Codes" on page 389.
eventFile	file	Read-only. The path to the file to execute when the event occurs/activates the notifier.
parent	object (Application) (page 75)	Read-only. The `notifier` object's container.
typename	string	Read-only. The class name of the referenced `notifier` object.

Methods

Method	Parameter type	Returns	What it does
remove ()			Deletes the `notifier` object. **Note:** You can remove a `notifier` object from the Script Events Manager drop-down list by deleting the file named `Script Events Manager.xml` from in the Photoshop preferences folder. See Adobe Photoshop CS2 help for more information.

Notifiers

The collection of `notifier` objects in the document; the `notifiers` property of the `app` object. See "Notifier" on page 164 for information on `notifier` objects. See notifiers (page 76, in the Properties table of the `app` object).

Note: Because the `Notifiers` class is a property of the Document (page 115) object, you use the object name, `notifiers`, rather than the class name, `Notifiers`, in your code. For example:

```
var notRef =
activeDocument.notifiers.add("OnClickGoButton",
app.path + "/Presets/Scripts/Event Only
Scripts/4322.jsx"")
```

The following sample uses the `Notifiers` object incorrectly:

```
var notRef =
activeDocument.Notifiers.add("OnClickGoButton",
app.path + "/Presets/Scripts/Event Only
Scripts/4322.jsx"")
```

Properties

Property	Value type	What it is
length	number (long)	Read-only. The number of elements in the `notifiers` collection.
parent	object (Application) (page 75)	Read-only. The `notifiers` object's container
typename	string	Read-only. Read-only. The class name of the referenced `notifiers` object.

Methods

Method	Parameter type	Returns	What it does
index (itemKey)	number	Notifier (page 164)	Gets an element from the notifiers collection.
add (event, eventFile [, eventClass])	string string file	Notifier (page 164)	Creates a notifier object. **Note:** eventClass defines the class ID of the event: four characters or a unique string. For a list of four-character codes, see "Appendix A: Event ID Codes" on page 389. **Note:** Remember to omit the single quotes when including a four-character ID in your code. **Note:** An eventClass value corresponds to the value you would type in the Descriptive Label box when adding an event in the Script Events Manager in the Adobe Photoshop CS2 application. For more information on using the Script Events Manager, please refer to Adobe Photoshop CS2 help.
removeAll ()			Removes all notifier objects from the notifiers collection. **Note:** You can remove a notifier object from the Script Events Manager drop-down list by deleting the file named Script Events Manager.xml from in the Photoshop preferences folder. See Adobe Photoshop CS2 help for more information.

PathItem

A path or drawing object, such as the outline of a shape or a straight or curved line, which contains sub paths that comprise its geometry.

Note: Because the `PathItem` class is also a property of the Document (page 115) object, you use the object name, `pathItem`, rather than the class name, `PathItem`, in your code.

The following example uses correct syntax to select a `pathItem` object :

```
activeDocuments.pathItem("myPath").select()
```

The following example, which uses an uppercase *P* in the object name, is incorrect:

```
activeDocuments.PathItem("myPath").select()
```

Properties

Property	Value Type	What it is
kind	PathKind (page 339)	Read-write. The `pathItem` object's type.
name	string	Read-write. The `pathItem` object's name.
parent	object (document)	Read-only. The `pathItem` object's container.
SubPathItems	SubPathItems (page 206)	Read-only. The sub path objects for this `pathItem` object.
typename	string	Read-only. The class name of the referenced `pathItem` object.

Methods

Method	Parameter Type	Returns	What it does
deselect ()			Deselects this `pathItem` object.
duplicate (name)	string		Duplicates this `pathItem` object with the new name specified in the argument.

Method	Parameter Type	Returns	What it does (Continued)

fillPath
([fillColor]
[, mode]
[, opacity]
[,
preserveTransparency]
[, feather]
[, wholePath]
[, antiAlias])
	`Object (SolidColor,`
	page 203
	`ArtLayer,`page 82,
	`HistoryState,` page 147)
	`ColorBlendMode` (page 331)
	`number (double)`
	`boolean`
	`number (double)`
	`boolean`
	`boolean`
			Fills the area enclosed by the path (`opacity`: 0 - 100 as percent; `feather`: 0.0 - 250.0 in pixels).

makeClippingPath ([flatness])	`number (double)`		Makes this `pathItem` object the clipping path for this document; the optional parameter tells the PostScript printer how to approximate curves in the path (0.2 - 100).

makeSelection
([feather]
[, antiAlias]
[, operation])
	`number (double)`
	`boolean`
	`SelectionType` (page 342)
			Makes a `selection` object, whose border is the path, from this `pathItem` object (`feather`: 0.0 - 250.0 in pixels).
			Note: See "Selection" on page 196.

remove ()			Deletes this `pathItem` object.
select ()			Makes this `pathItem` object the active or selected `pathItem` object.
strokePath ([tool] [,simulatePressure])	`ToolType` (page 344) `boolean`		Strokes the path with the specified information.

Sample Script

The following creates a path in three segments: two diagonal lines that form a *V*, and a curved line above the *V* that makes it look like a 2D ice cream cone.

Paths.jsx

```
// Save the current preferences
var startRulerUnits = app.preferences.rulerUnits
var startTypeUnits = app.preferences.typeUnits
var startDisplayDialogs = app.displayDialogs
```

```
// Set Adobe Photoshop CS2 to use pixels and
// display no dialogs
app.preferences.rulerUnits = Units.PIXELS
app.preferences.typeUnits = TypeUnits.PIXELS
app.displayDialogs = DialogModes.NO

// first close all the open documents
while (app.documents.length) {
   app.activeDocument.close()
}

// create a document to work with
var docRef = app.documents.add(5000, 7000, 72, "Simple
Line")

//line #1--it's a straight line so the coordinates for
anchor, left, and //right
//for each point have the same coordinates
var lineArray = new Array()
   lineArray[0] = new PathPointInfo
   lineArray[0].kind = PointKind.CORNERPOINT
   lineArray[0].anchor = Array(100, 100)
   lineArray[0].leftDirection = lineArray[0].anchor
   lineArray[0].rightDirection = lineArray[0].anchor

   lineArray[1] = new PathPointInfo
   lineArray[1].kind = PointKind.CORNERPOINT
   lineArray[1].anchor = Array(150, 200)
   lineArray[1].leftDirection = lineArray[1].anchor
   lineArray[1].rightDirection = lineArray[1].anchor

var lineSubPathArray = new Array()
   lineSubPathArray[0] = new SubPathInfo()
   lineSubPathArray[0].operation =
ShapeOperation.SHAPEXOR
   lineSubPathArray[0].closed = false
   lineSubPathArray[0].entireSubPath = lineArray

//line#2
var lineArray2[0] = new Array()
   lineArray2[0].kind = PointKind.CORNERPOINT
   lineArray2[0].anchor = Array(150, 200)
   lineArray2[0].leftDirection = lineArray2[0].anchor
   lineArray2[0].rightDirection = lineArray2[0].anchor

   lineArray2[1] = new PathPointInfo
   lineArray2[1].kind = PointKind.CORNERPOINT
   lineArray2[1].anchor = Array(200, 100)
   lineArray2[1].leftDirection = lineArray2[1].anchor
```

```
   lineArray2[1].rightDirection = lineArray2[1].anchor

   lineSubPathArray[1] = new SubPathInfo()
   lineSubPathArray[1].operation =
ShapeOperation.SHAPEXOR
   lineSubPathArray[1].closed = false
   lineSubPathArray[1].entireSubPath = lineArray2

//ice cream curve
//it's a curved line, so there are 3 points, not 2
//coordinates for the middle point (lineArray3[1])
//are different.
//The left direction is positioned "above" the anchor
// on the screen.
//The right direction is positioned "below" the anchor
//You can change the coordinates for these points to see
//how the curve works...
var lineArray3[0] = new Array()
   lineArray3[0].kind = PointKind.CORNERPOINT
   lineArray3[0].anchor = Array(200, 100)
   lineArray3[0].leftDirection = lineArray3[0].anchor
   lineArray3[0].rightDirection = lineArray3[0].anchor

   lineArray3[1] = new PathPointInfo
   lineArray3[1].kind = PointKind.CORNERPOINT
   lineArray3[1].anchor = Array(150, 50)
   lineArray31].leftDirection = Array(100, 50)
   lineArray3[1].rightDirection = Array(200, 50)

   lineArray3[2] = new PathPointInfo
   lineArray3[2].kind = PointKind.CORNERPOINT
   lineArray3[2].anchor = Array(100, 100)
   lineArray3[2].leftDirection = lineArray3[2].anchor
   lineArray3[2].rightDirection = lineArray3[2].anchor

   lineSubPathArray[1] = new SubPathInfo()
   lineSubPathArray[1].operation =
      ShapeOperation.SHAPEXOR
   lineSubPathArray[1].closed = false
   lineSubPathArray[1].entireSubPath = lineArray3

//create the path item
var myPathItem = docRef.pathItems.add("A Line",
lineSubPathArray);

// stroke it so we can see something
myPathItem.strokePath(ToolType.BRUSH)
```

```
// Reset the application preferences
preferences.rulerUnits = startRulerUnits;
preferences.typeUnits = startTypeUnits;
displayDialogs = startDisplayDialogs
```

PathItems

The collection of `pathItem` objects in the document. See PathItem (page 167) for information on `pathItem` objects.

Note: Because the `PathItems` class is a property of the Document (page 115) object, you use the object name, `pathItems`, rather than the class name, `PathItems`, in your code. For example:

```
var myPathItem = docRef.pathItems.add("A Line",
lineSubPathArray)
```

The following sample uses the `PathItems` object incorrectly:

```
var myPathItem = docRef.PathItems.add("A Line",
lineSubPathArray)
```

Properties

Property	Value Type	What it is
length	number (long)	Read-only. The number of `pathItem` objects in the `pathItems` collection.
parent	object (document)	Read-only. The `pathItems` object's container.
typename	string	Read-only. The class name of the referenced `pathItems` object.

Methods

Method	Parameter Type	Returns	What it does
index (itemKey)	number	PathItem (page 167)	Gets a `pathItem` object from the `pathItems` collection.
add (name, entirePath)	string Array (SubPathItem objects) (page 205)	PathItem (page 167)	Creates a new `pathItem` object.
getByName (name)	string	PathItem (page 167)	Gets the first element in the `pathItems` collection with the provided name.
removeAll ()			Removes all `pathItem` objects from the `pathItems` collection.

PathPoint

Information about an array of `PathPointInfo` objects.

Note: You do not use the `PathPoint` object to create points that make up a path. Rather, you use the `PathPoint` object to retrieve information about the points that describe path segments. To create path points, use the `PathPointInfo` objects. See "PathPointInfo" on page 174.

Properties

Property	Value Type	What it is
anchor	`Array(UnitValue)`	Read-write. The point on the curve (`leftDirection`/`rightDirection` are points representing the control handle end points).
kind	`PointKind` (page 340)	Read-write. The `PathPoint` object's type.
leftDirection	`Array(UnitValue)`	Read-write. The x and y coordinates that define the left handle.
parent	`object` `(SubPathItem)` (page 205)	Read-only. The `PathPoint` object's container.
rightDirection	`Array(UnitValue)`	Read-write. The x and y coordinates that define the right handle.
typename	`string`	Read-only. The class name of the referenced `PathPoint` object.

PathPointInfo

A point on a path, expressed as an array of three coordinate arrays: the anchor point, left direction point, and right direction point. For paths that are straight segments (not curved), the coordinates of all three points are the same. For curved segments, the coordinates are different. The difference between the anchor point and the left or right direction points determines the arc of the curve. You use the left direction point to bend the curve "outward" or make it convex; you use the right direction point to bend the curve "inward" or make it concave.

Properties

Property	Value Type	What it is
anchor	Array	Read-write. The x and y coordinates of one end point of the path segment.
kind	PointKind (page 340)	Read-write. The `PathPointInfo` object's kind.
leftDirection	Array (UnitValue)	Read-write. The location of the left direction point ("in" position).
rightDirection	Array (UnitValue)	Read-write. The location of the right handle ("out" position).
typename	string	Read-only. The class name of the referenced `PathPointInfo` object.

PathPoints

A collection of `PathPoint` objects that comprises the `PathPoints` property of the `SubPathItem` object. See "SubPathItem" on page 205 for more information.

Properties

Property	Value Type	What it is
length	number (long)	Read-only. The number of elements in the `PathPoints` collection.
parent	object (SubPathItem) (page 205)	Read-only. The `PathPoints` object's container.
typename	string	Read-only. The class name of the referenced `PathPoints` object.

Method	Parameter type	Returns	What it does
index (itemKey)	number	PathPoint (page 173)	Gets an element from the `PathPoints` collection.

PDFOpenOptions

Options that can be specified when opening a document in generic Adobe PDF format.

Properties

Property	Value Type	What it is
`antiAlias`	`boolean`	Read-write. Indication of whether to use antialias.
`bitsPerChannel`	`BitsPerChannelType` (page 330)	Read-write. The number of bits per channel.
`constrainProportions`	`boolean`	Deprecated for Adobe Photoshop CS2.
`cropPage`	`CropToType` (page 332)	Read-write. The method of cropping to use.
`height`	`UnitValue`	Deprecated for Adobe Photoshop CS2.
`mode`	`OpenDocumentMode` (page 337)	Read-write. The color model to use.
`name`	`string`	Read-write. The name of the document.
`page`	`number (long)`	Read-write. The page to which to open the document.
`resolution`	`number (double)`	Read-write. The resolution of the document (in pixels per inch).
`suppressWarnings`	`boolean`	Read-write. Indication of whether to suppress warnings when opening the document.
`typename`	`string`	Read-only. The class name of the referenced `PDFOpenOptions` object.
`usePageNumber`	`boolean`	Read-write. Indication of whether the value specified in the `page` property will refer to an image number when `usePageNumber = false`. See "page" on page 176.
`width`	`UnitValue`	Deprecated for Adobe Photoshop CS2.

PDFSaveOptions

Options that can be specified when saving a document in Adobe PDF format.

Properties

Property	Value Type	What it is
alphaChannels	boolean	Read-write. Indication of whether to save the alpha channels with the file.
annotations	boolean	Read-write. Indication of whether to save comments with the file.
colorConversion	boolean	Read-write. Indication of whether to convert the color profile to a destination profile.
convertToEightBit	boolean	Read-write. Indication of whether to convert a 16-bit image to 8-bit for better compatibility with other applications.
description	string	Read-write. Description of the save options to use.
destinationProfile	string	Read-write. Description of the final RGB or CMYK output device, such as a monitor or a press standard.
downgradeColorProfile	boolean	Deprecated for Adobe Photoshop CS2.
downSample	PDFResample (page 339)	Read-write. The down sample method to use.
downSampleSize	number (double)	Read-write. The size to downsample images if they exceed the limit in pixels per inch.
downSampleSizeLimit	number (double)	Read-write. Limits downsampling or subsampling to images that exceed this value in pixels per inch.
embedColorProfile	boolean	Read-write. Indication of whether to embed the color profile in the document.
embedFonts	boolean	Deprecated for Adobe Photoshop CS2.
embedThumbnail	boolean	Read-write. Indication of whether to include a small preview image in Adobe PDF files.
encoding	PDFStandard (page 339)	Read-write. The encoding method to use (default: PDFEncoding.PDFZIP).
interpolation	boolean	Deprecated for Adobe Photoshop CS2.

Property	Value Type	What it is (Continued)
`jpegQuality`	number (long)	Read-write. The quality of the produced image (0 - 12), which is inversely proportionate to the compression amount. **Note:** Valid only when `encoding = PDFEncoding.JPEG.`
`layers`	boolean	Read-write. Indication of whether to save the document's layers.
`optimizeForWeb`	boolean	Read-write. Indication of whether to improve performance of PDF files on Web servers.
`outputCondition`	string	Read-write. An optional comment field for inserting descriptions of the output condition. The text is stored in the PDF/X file.
`outputConditionID`	string	Read-write. Identifier for the output condition.
`PDFCompatibility`	PDFCompatibility (page 339)	Read-write. The PDF version to make the document compatible with.
`PDFStandard`	PDFStandard (page 339)	Read-write. The PDF standard to make the document compatible with.
`preserveEditing`	boolean	Read-write. Indication of whether to reopen the PDF in Adobe Photoshop CS2 with native Photoshop data intact.
`presetFile`	string	Read-write. The preset file to use for settings. **Note:** This option overrides other settings.
`profileInclusionPolicy`	boolean	Read-write. Indication of whether to show which profiles to include.
`registryName`	string	Read-write. URL where the output condition is registered.
`spotColors`	boolean	Read-write. Indication of whether to save spot colors.
`tileSize`	number (long)	Read-write. Compression option. **Note:** Valid only when `encoding =` `PDFEncoding.JPEG2000.`
`transparency`	boolean	Deprecated for Adobe Photoshop CS2.
`typename`	string	Read-only. The class name of the referenced `PDFSaveOptions` object.
`useOutlines`	boolean	Deprecated for Adobe Photoshop CS2.

Property	Value Type	What it is (Continued)
vectorData	boolean	Deprecated for Adobe Photoshop CS2.
view	boolean	Read-write. Indication of whether to open the saved PDF in Adobe Acrobat.

PhotoCDOpenOptions

Options to be specified when opening a Kodak Photo CD (PCD) files, including high-resolution files from Pro Photo CD discs.

Properties

Property	Value Type	What it is
colorProfileName	string	Read-write. The profile to use when reading the image.
colorSpace	PhotoCDColorSpace (page 339)	Read-write. The colorspace for the image.
orientation	Orientation (page 338)	Read-write. The image orientation.
pixelSize	PhotoCDSize (page 340)	Read-write. The image dimensions.
resolution	number (double)	Read-write. The image resolution (in pixels per inch).
typename	string	Read-only. The class name of the referenced photoCDOpenOptions object.

PhotoshopSaveOptions

Options that can be specified when saving a document in PSD format.

Properties

Property	Value Type	What it is
alphaChannels	boolean	Read-write. Indication of whether to save the alpha channels.
annotations	boolean	Read-write. Indication of whether to save the annotations.
embedColorProfile	boolean	Read-write. Indication of whether to embed the color profile in the document.
layers	boolean	Read-write. Indication of whether to preserve the layers.
spotColors	boolean	Read-write. Indication of whether to save the spot colors.
typename	string	Read-only. The class name of the referenced photoshopSaveOptions object.

PICTFileSaveOptions

Options that can be specified when saving a document in PICT format.

Properties

Property	Value Type	What it is
alphaChannels	boolean	Read-write. Indication of whether to save the alpha channels.
compression	PICTCompression (page 340)	Read-write. (default: PICTCompression.NONE)
embedColorProfile	boolean	Read-write. Indication of whether to embed the color profile in the document.
resolution	PICTBitsPerPixels (page 340)	Read-write. The number of bits per pixel.
typename	string	Read-only. The class name of the referenced PICTFileSaveOptions object.

PICTResourceSaveOptions

Options that can be specified when saving a document as a PICT Resource file.

Properties

Property	Value Type	What it is
alphaChannels	boolean	Read-write. Indication of whether to save the alpha channels.
compression	PICTCompression (page 340)	Read-write. The type of compression to use (default: `PICTCompression.NONE`).
embedColorProfile	boolean	Read-write. Indication of whether to embed the color profile in the document.
name	string	Read-write. The name of the PICT resource.
resolution	PICTBitsPerPixels (page 340)	Read-write. The number of bits per pixel.
resourceID	number (long)	Read-write. The ID of the PICT resource (default: `128`).
typename	string	Read-only. The class name of the referenced `PICTResourceSaveOptions` object.

PicturePackageOptions

Options that can be specified for a Picture Package.

Properties

Property	Value type	What it is
content	PicturePackageTextType (page 340)	Read-write. The content information (default: PicturePackageTextType.NONE).
flatten	boolean	Read-write. Indicates whether all layers in the final document are flattened (default: true).
font	GalleryFontType (page 335)	Read-write. The font used for security text (default: GalleryFontType.ARIAL).
fontSize	number (long)	Read-write. The font size used for security text (default: 12).
layout	string	Read-write. The layout to use to generate the picture package (default: " (2) 5x7").
mode	NewDocumentMode (page 337)	Read-write. Read-write. The color profile to use as the document mode (default: NewDocumentMode.RGB).
opacity	number (long)	Read-write. The web page security opacity as a percent (default: 100).
resolution	number (double)	Read-write. The resolution of the document in pixels per inch (default: 72.0).
text	string	Read-write. The picture package custom text. **Note:** Valid only when content = PicturePackageType.USER. See "content" on page 184.
textColor	RGBColor (page 195)	Read-write. The color to use for security text.
textPosition	GallerySecurityTextPositionType (page 335)	Read-write. The security text position (default: GallerySecurityTextPositionType. CENTERED).
textRotate	GallerySecurityTextRotateType (page 335)	Read-write. The orientation to use for security text (default: GallerySecurityTextRotateType.ZERO).
typename	string	Read-only. The class name of the referenced PicturePackageOptions object.

PixarSaveOptions

Options that can be specified when saving a document in Pixar format.

Properties

Property	Value Type	What it is
alphaChannels	boolean	Read-write. Indication of whether to save the alpha channels.
typename	string	Read-only. The class name of the referenced PixarSaveOptions object.

PNGSaveOptions

Options that can be specified when saving a document in PNG format.

Properties

Property	Value Type	What it is
`interlaced`	`boolean`	Read-write. Indicates whether the should rows be interlaced (default: `false`).
`typename`	`string`	Read-only. The class name of the referenced `PNGSaveOptions` object.

Preferences

Options to define for the `preferences` property of the `app` object. See "preferencesFolder" on page 76 (in the Properties table for the `app` object).

Note: Because the `Preferences` class is a property of the Document (page 115) object, you use the object name, `preferences`, rather than the class name, `Preferences`, in your code. For example:

```
app.preferences.rulerUnits = Units.PIXELS
app.preferences.typeUnits = TypeUnits.PIXELS
```

The following code incorrectly uses an uppercase *P*:

```
app.Preferences.rulerUnits = Units.PIXELS
app.Preferences.typeUnits = TypeUnits.PIXELS
```

Note: Defining the `preferences` properties is basically equivalent to selecting **Edit > Preferences** (Windows) or **Photoshop > Preferences** in the Adobe Photoshop CS2 application. For explanations of individual settings, please refer to Adobe Photoshop CS2 Help.

Properties

Property	Value Type	What it is
additionalPluginFolder	file	Read-write. The path to an additional plug-in folder. **Note:** Valid only when `useAdditionalPluginFolder = true`. See "useAdditionalPluginFolder" on page 190.
appendExtension	SaveBehavior (page 341)	Read-write. Save files with extensions on Windows.
askBeforeSavingLayeredTIFF	boolean	Read-write. Indication of whether to ask the user to verify layer preservation options when saving a file in TIFF format.
autoUpdateOpenDocuments	boolean	Read-write. Indication of whether to automatically update open documents.
beepWhenDone	boolean	Read-write. Indication of whether to beep when a process finishes.
colorChannelsInColor	boolean	Read-write. Indication of whether to display component channels in the Channels palette in color.

Property	Value Type	What it is (Continued)
`colorPicker`	`ColorPicker` (page 332)	Read-write.
`columnGutter`	`number (double)`	Read-write. The width of the column gutters (in points). (0.1 - 600.0).
`columnWidth`	`number (double)`	Read-write. Column width (in points) (0.1 - 600.0).
`createFirstSnapshot`	`boolean`	Read-write. Indication of whether to automatically make the first snapshot when a new document is created.
`dynamicColorSliders`	`boolean`	Read-write. Indication of whether dynamic color sliders appear in the Color palette.
`editLogItems`	`EditLogItemsType` (page 333)	Read-write. The options for editing history log items. **Note:** Valid only when `useHistoryLog = true`. See "useHistoryLog" on page 190.
`exportClipboard`	`boolean`	Read-write. Indication of whether to retain Adobe Photoshop CS2 contents on the clipboard after you exit the application.
`fontPreviewSize`	`FontPreviewType` (page 334)	Read-write. Indication of whether to show font previews in the type tool font menus.
`fullSizePreview`	`boolean`	Read-write. (Mac only.) Indication of whether to show image preview as a full size image or thumbnail.
`gamutWarningOpacity`	`number (double)`	Read-write. (0 - 100 as percent).
`gridSize`	`GridSize` (page 336)	Read-write. The size to use for squares in the grid.
`gridStyle`	`GridLineStyle` (page 336)	Read-write. The formatting style for non-printing grid lines.
`gridSubDivisions`	`number (long)`	Read-write. (1 - 100)
`guideStyle`	`GuideLineStyle` (page 336)	Read-write. The formatting style for non-printing guide lines.
`iconPreview`	`boolean`	Read-write. (Mac only.)
`imageCacheForHistograms`	`boolean`	Read-write. Indication of whether to use the sampled data cache for histograms in the Level dialog (faster but not as accurate).

Property	Value Type	What it is (Continued)
`imageCacheLevels`	number (long)	Read-write. The number of images to hold in the cache (1 - 8).
`imagePreviews`	SaveBehavior (page 341)	Read-write. The behavior mode to use when saving files.
`interpolation`	ResampleMethod (page 341)	Read-write. The method to use to assign color values to any new pixels created when an image is resampled or resized.
`keyboardZoomResizesWindows`	boolean	Read-write. Indication of whether to automatically resize the window when zooming in or out using keyboard shortcuts.
`macOSThumbnail`	boolean	Read-write. (Mac only.) Indication of whether to create a thumbnail when saving the image.
`maximizeCompatibility`	QueryStateType (page 341)	Read-write. The behavior to use to check whether to maximize compatibility when opening Adobe Photoshop CS2 (PSD) files .
`maxRAMuse`	number (long)	Read-write. The maximum percentage of available RAM used by Adobe Photoshop CS2 (5 - 100).
`nonLinearHistory`	boolean	Read-write. Indication of whether to allow non-linear history.
`numberofHistoryStates`	number (long)	Read-write. The number of history states to preserve (1 - 100).
`otherCursors`	OtherPaintingCursors (page 338)	Read-write. The type of pointer to use.
`paintingCursors`	PaintingCursors (page 338)	Read-write. The type of pointer to use.
`parent`	object (Application) (page 75)	Read-write. The `preferences` object's container.
`pixelDoubling`	boolean	Read-write. Indication of whether to halve the resolution or (double the size of pixels) to make previews display more quickly.
`pointSize`	PointType (page 340)	Read-write. The point/pica size.
`recentFileListLength`	number (long)	Read-write. The number of items in the recent file list (0 - 30).

Property	Value Type	What it is (Continued)
`rulerUnits`	Units (page 345)	Read-write. The unit the scripting system will use when receiving and returning values.
`saveLogItems`	SaveLogItemsType (page 342)	Read-write. The options for saving the history items.
`saveLogItemsFile`	file	Read-write. The path to the history log file.
`savePaletteLocations`	boolean	Read-write. Indication of whether to make new palette locations the default location.
`showAsianTextOptions`	boolean	Read-write. Indication of whether to display Asian text options in the Paragraph palette.
`showEnglishFontNames`	boolean	Read-write. Indication of whether to list Asian font names in English.
`showSliceNumber`	boolean	Read-write. Indication of whether to display slice numbers in the document window when using the Slice tool.
`showToolTips`	boolean	Read-write. Indication of whether to show pop up definitions on mouse over.
`smartQuotes`	boolean	Read-write. Indication of whether to use curly or straight quote marks.
`typename`	string	Read-only. The class name of the referenced preferences object.
`typeUnits`	TypeUnits (page 344)	Read-write. The unit type-size that the numeric inputs are assumed to represent.
`useAdditionalPluginFolder`	boolean	Read-write. Indication of whether to use an additional folder for compatible plug-ins stored with a different application.
`useDiffusionDither`	boolean	Read-write. Indication of whether to use diffusion dithering to minimize distinctive patterning caused by pattern dithering.
`useHistoryLog`	boolean	Read-write. Indication of whether to create a log file for history states.
`useLowerCaseExtension`	boolean	Read-write. Indicates whether the file extension should be lowercase.
`useShiftKeyForToolSwitch`	boolean	Read-write. Indication of whether to enable cycling through a set of hidden tools.

Property	Value Type	What it is (Continued)
`useVideoAlpha`	`boolean`	Read-write. Indication of whether to enable Adobe Photoshop CS2 to send transparency information to your computer's video board. (Requires hardware support.)
`windowsThumbnail`	`boolean`	Read-write. (Requires hardware support.) Indication of whether to create a thumbnail when saving the image on Windows.

PresentationOptions

Options that can be specified for Adobe PDF presentations.

Properties

Property	Value Type	What it is
`autoAdvance`	`boolean`	Read-write. Indication of whether to auto advance images when viewing the presentation (default: `true`). **Note:** Valid only when `presentation = true`. See "presentation" on page 192.
`includeFilename`	`boolean`	Read-write. Indication of whether to include the file name for the image (default: `false`).
`interpolation`	`boolean`	Read-write. Indication of whether to use image interpolation (default: `false`).
`loop`	`boolean`	Read-write. Indication of whether to begin the presentation again after the last page (default: `false`). **Note:** Valid only when `autoAdvance = true`. See "autoAdvance" on page 192.
`magnification`	`MagnificationType` (page 337)	Read-write. The magnification type to use when viewing the image.
`pDFFileOptions`	`PDFSaveOptions` (page 177)	Read-write. Options to use when creating the PDF file.
`presentation`	`boolean`	Read-write. Indication of whether the output will be a presentation (default: `false`); when `false`, the output is a Multi-Page document.
`transition`	`TransitionType` (page 344)	Read-write. The transition from one image to the next (default: `TransitionType.NONE`). **Note:** Valid only when `autoAdvance = true`. See "autoAdvance" on page 192.
`typename`	`string`	Read-only. The class name of the referenced `PresentationOptions` object.

RawFormatOpenOptions

Options that can be specified when opening a document in RAW format.

Properties

Property	Value Type	What it is
bitsPerChannel	number (long)	Read-write. The number of bits for each channel. **Note:** The only valid values are bitsPerChannel = BitsPerChannelType.EIGHT or bitsPerChannel = BitsPerChannelType.SIXTEEN.
byteOrder	ByteOrder (page 330)	Read-write. The order in which bytes will be read. **Note:** Valid only when bitsPerChannel = BitsPerChannelType.SIXTEEN. See "bitsPerChannel" on page 193.
channelNumber	number (long)	Read-write. The number of channels in the image (1 - 56). **Note:** The value of channelNumber cannot exceed the number of channels in the image. When bitsPerChannel = BitsPerChannelType.SIXTEEN, only the following values are valid: 1, 3, or 4. See "bitsPerChannel" on page 193.
headerSize	number (long)	Read-write. The number of bytes of information that will appear in the file before actual image information begins; that is, the number of zeroes inserted at the beginning of the file as placeholders (0 - 1919999).
height	number (long)	Read-write. The height of the image (in pixels).
interleaveChannels	boolean	Read-write. Indication of whether to store color values sequentially.
retainHeader	boolean	Read-write. Indication of whether to retain the header when saving. **Note:** Valid only when headerSize (page 193) is 1 or greater.
typename	string	Read-only. The class name of the referenced RawFormatOpenOptions object.
width	number (long)	Read-write. The image width in pixels.

RawSaveOptions

Options that can be specified when saving a document in RAW format.

Properties

Property	Value Type	What it is
alphaChannels	boolean	Read-write. Indicates whether alpha channels should be saved.
spotColors	boolean	Read-write. Indicates whether the spot colors should be saved.
typename	string	Read-only. The class name of the referenced RawSaveOptions object.

RGBColor

The definition of a color in RGB color mode.

Properties

Property	Value Type	What it is
blue	number (double)	Read-write. The blue color value (0.0 - 255.0; default: 255.0).
green	number (double)	Read-write. The green color value (0.0 - 255.0; default: 255.0).
hexValue	string	Read-write. The hex representation of the color.
red	number (double)	Read-write. The red color value (0.0 - 255.0; default: 255.0).
typename	string	Read-only. The class name of the referenced RGBColor object.

Selection

The selected area of a document or layer.

Note: Because the `Selection` class is a property of the Document (page 115) object, you use the object name, `selection`, rather than the class name, `Selection`, in your code, as in the following example:

```
checkersDoc.selection.fill(app.foregroundColor)
```

Properties

Property	Value Type	What it is
bounds	`array of UnitValues`	Read-only. The bounding rectangle of the entire selection.
parent	`object (Document)` (page 115)	Read-only. The object's container.
typename	`string`	Read-only. The class name of the referenced `selection` object.

Methods

Method	Parameter Type	Returns	What it does
clear ()			Clears the selection and does not copy it to the clipboard.
contract (by)	`UnitValue`		Contracts the selection by the specified amount.
copy ([merge])	`boolean`		Copies the selection to the clipboard. When the optional argument is used and set to `true`, a merged copy is performed (all visible layers in the selection are copied).
cut ()			Clears the current selection and copies it to the clipboard.
deselect ()			Deselects the current selection.
expand (by)	`UnitValue`		Expands the selection by the specified amount.
feather (by)	`UnitValue`		Feathers the edges of the selection by the specified amount.

Adobe® Photoshop® CS2 Official JavaScript Reference

Method	Parameter Type	Returns	What it does (Continued)
fill (filltype [, mode] [, opacity] [, preserveTransparency])	Object (SolidColor, page 203, ArtLayer, page 82, HistoryState, page 147); or String ColorBlendMode (page 331) number (long) boolean		Fills the selection (opacity: 1 - 100 as percent).
grow (tolerance, antiAlias)	number (long) boolean		Grows the selection to include all adjacent pixels falling within the specified tolerance range.
invert ()			Inverts the selection (deselects the selection and selects the rest of the layer or document). **Note:** To flip the selection shape, see "rotate" on page 197.
load (from [, combination] [, inverting])	Channel (page 102) SelectionType (page 342) boolean		Loads the selection from the specified channel.
makeWorkPath ([tolerance])	number (double)		Makes this selection item the work path for this document.
resize ([horizontal] [, vertical] [, anchor])	number (double) number (double) AnchorPosition (page 329)		Resizes the selected area to the specified dimensions and anchor position.
resizeBoundary ([horizontal] [, vertical] [, anchor])	number (double) number (double) AnchorPosition (page 329)		Changes the size of the selection to the specified dimensions around the specified anchor.
rotate (angle [, anchor])	number (double) AnchorPosition (page 329)		Rotates the selection by the specified amount around the specified anchor point.
rotateBoundary (angle [, anchor])	number (double) AnchorPosition (page 329)		Rotates the boundary of the selection around the specified anchor.
select (region [, type] [, feather] [, antiAlias])	Array (points: Array (Array (x,y),...) SelectionType (page 342) number (double) boolean		Selects the specified region.

Method	Parameter Type	Returns	What it does (Continued)
selectAll ()			Selects the entire layer.
selectBorder (width)	UnitValue		Selects the selection border only (in the specified width); subsequent actions do not affect the selected area within the borders.
similar (tolerance, antiAlias)	number (long) boolean		Grows the selection to include pixels throughout the image falling within the tolerance range.
smooth (radius)	number (long)		Cleans up stray pixels left inside or outside a color-based selection (within the radius specified in pixels).
store (into [, combination])	Channel (page 102) SelectionType (page 342)		Saves the selection as a channel.
stroke (strokeColor, width [, location] [, mode] [, opacity] [, preserveTransparency])	Object (color) number (long) StrokeLocation (page 343) ColorBlendMode (page 331) number (long) boolean		Strokes the selection border (opacity: 1 - 100 as percent).
translate ([deltaX] [, deltaY])	UnitValue UnitValue		Moves the entire selection relative to its current position.
translateBoundary ([deltaX] [, deltaY])	UnitValue UnitValue		Moves the selection relative to its current position.

Sample Script

The following script creates a checkerboard using the following steps:

- Create an 800 x 800 pixel document.
- Divide the entire document into 100 x 100 pixel squares.
- Select every other square in the first row, then shift the selection criteria to select the alternate squares in the following row. Repeat until every other square in the document is selected.
- Fill the selected squares with the foreground color from the palette.

- Invert the selection and fill the newly selected squares with the background color from the palette.
- Deselect the squares to remove the selection outlines (the "marching ants").

Selection.jsx

```
// Save the current preferences
var startRulerUnits = app.preferences.rulerUnits
var startTypeUnits = app.preferences.typeUnits
var startDisplayDialogs = app.displayDialogs

// Set Adobe Photoshop CS2 to use pixels and
// display no dialogs
app.preferences.rulerUnits = Units.PIXELS
app.preferences.typeUnits = TypeUnits.PIXELS
app.displayDialogs = DialogModes.NO

//Close all the open documents
while (app.documents.length) {
   app.activeDocument.close()
}

//Create variables for the 800 pixel board divided
//in even 100 x 100 squares
var docSize = 800
var cells = 8
var cellSize = docSize / cells

// create a new document
var checkersDoc = app.documents.add(docSize, docSize, 72,
"Checkers")

// Create a variable to use for selecting
// the checker board
// That allows me to shift the selection
// one square to the right
// on every other row, and then shift back
// for the rows in between.
var shiftIt = true

// loop through vertically to create the first row
for (var v = 0; v < docSize; v += cellSize) {

   // Switch the shift for a new row
   shiftIt = !shiftIt

   // loop through horizontally
```

```
       for (var h = 0; h < docSize; h += (cellSize * 2)) {

              // push over the cellSize to start with only
              if (shiftIt && h == 0) {
                 h += cellSize
          }

              // Select a square
              selRegion = Array(Array(h, v),
                         Array(h + cellSize, v),
                         Array(h + cellSize, v + cellSize),
                         Array(h, v + cellSize),
                         Array(h, v))

              // In the first iteration of the loop,
              // start the selection
              // In subsequent iterations, use the
              // EXTEND constant value
              //of the select() method to add to the selection
              // (in the loop's else clause)
              if (h == 0 && v == 0) {
                 checkersDoc.selection.select(selRegion)
              } else {
                 checkersDoc.selection.select(selRegion,
                     SelectionType.EXTEND)
          }

              // turn this off for faster execution
              // turn this on for debugging
              WaitForRedraw()
       }
}

// Fill the current selection with the foreground color
checkersDoc.selection.fill(app.foregroundColor)

//Invert the selection
checkersDoc.selection.invert()

// Fill the new selection with the background color
checkersDoc.selection.fill(app.backgroundColor)

// Clear the selection to get rid of the
// non-printing borders
checkersDoc.selection.deselect()

// Reset the application preferences
app.preferences.rulerUnits = startRulerUnits
app.preferences.typeUnits = startTypeUnits
```

```
app.displayDialogs = startDisplayDialogs

// A helper function for debugging
// It also helps the user see what is going on
// if you turn it off for this example you
// get a flashing cursor for a number (long) time
function WaitForRedraw()
{
   var eventWait = charIDToTypeID('Wait')
   var enumRedrawComplete = charIDToTypeID('RdCm')
   var typeState = charIDToTypeID('Stte')
   var keyState = charIDToTypeID('Stte')

   var desc = new ActionDescriptor()

   desc.putEnumerated(keyState, typeState,
enumRedrawComplete)

   executeAction(eventWait, desc, DialogModes.NO)
}
```

SGIRGBSaveOptions

Options that can be specified when saving a document in SGIRGB format.

Note: The SGIRGB format is not installed automatically with Adobe Photoshop CS2.

Properties

Property	Value Type	What it is
alphaChannels	boolean	Read-write. Indication of whether to save the alpha channels.
spotColors	boolean	Read-write. Indication of whether to save the spot colors.
typename	string	Read-only. The class name of the referenced SGIRGBSaveOptions object.

SolidColor

A color definition used in the document.

Properties

Property	Value Type	What it is
cmyk	CMYKColor (page 110)	Read-write. The CMYK color mode.
gray	GrayColor (page 146)	Read-write. The Grayscale color mode.
hsb	HSBColor (page 149)	Read-write. The HSB color mode.
lab	LabColor (page 152)	Read-write. The LAB color mode.
model	ColorModel (page 332)	Read-write. The color model.
nearestWebColor	RGBColor (page 195)	Read-only. The nearest web color to the current color.
rgb	RGBColor (page 195)	Read-write. The RGB color mode.
typename	string	Read-only. The class name of the referenced SolidColor object.

Methods

Method	Parameter Type	Returns	What it does
isEqual (color)	SolidColor (page 203)	boolean	Indication of whether the SolidColor object is visually equal to the specified color.

SubPathInfo

An array of `PathPointInfo` objects that describes a straight or curved segment of a path.

Properties

Property	Value Type	What it is
closed	boolean	Read-write. Indication of whether the path describes an enclosed area.
entireSubPath	Array (PathPoint objects) (page 173)	Read-write.
operation	ShapeOperation (page 342)	Read-write. The sub path's operation on other sub paths.
typename	string	Read-only. The class name of the referenced SubPathInfo object.

SubPathItem

Information about a path.

Note: You do not use the `SubPathItem` object to create a path. Rather, you use the `SubPathInfo` object to retrieve information about a path. (Note that all of the `SubPathItem` object's properties are *Read-only*.) To create path segments, see "SubPathInfo" on page 204.

Properties

Property	Value Type	What it is
`closed`	`boolean`	Read-only. Indicates whether the path is closed.
`operation`	`ShapeOperation` (page 342)	Read-only. The sub path operation on other sub paths.
`parent`	`object (PathItem)` (page 167)	Read-only. The object's container.
`pathPoints`	`PathPoints` (page 175)	Read-only. The `PathPoints` collection.
`typename`	`string`	Read-only. The class name of the referenced `SubPathItem` object.

SubPathItems

A collection of `SubPathItem` objects. See "SubPathItem" on page 205.

Properties

Property	Value Type	What it is
length	number (long)	Read-only. The number of elements in the `SubPathItems` collection.
parent	object (PathItem) (page 167)	Read-only. The `SubPathItems` object's container.
typename	string	Read-only. The class name of the referenced `SubPathItems` object.

Methods

Method	Parameter type	Returns	What it does
index (itemKey)	number	SubPathItem (page 205)	Gets an element from the `SubPathItems` collection.

TargaSaveOptions

Options that can be set when saving a document in TGA (Targa) format.

Properties

Property	Value Type	What it is
`alphaChannels`	`boolean`	Read-write. Indication of whether to save the alpha channels.
`resolution`	`TargaBitsPerPixels` (page 343)	Read-write. The number of bits per pixel (default: `TargaBitsPerPixels.TWENTYFOUR`).
`rleCompression`	`boolean`	Read-write. Indicates whether RLE compression should be used (default: `true`).
`typename`	`string`	Read-only. The class name of the referenced `TargaSaveOptions` object.

TextFont

Details about a font in the `TextFonts` collection. See "TextFonts" on page 209 for more information on the `TextFonts` collection.

Properties

Property	Value Type	What it is
family	string	Read-only. The font family.
name	string	Read-only. The name of the font.
parent	object (Application) (page 75)	Read-only. The object's container.
postScriptName	string	Read-only. The PostScript name of the font.
style	string	Read-only. The font style.
typename	string	Read-only. The class name of the referenced textFont object.

TextFonts

The collection of fonts available on your computer.

Note: The `TextFonts` class corresponds to the `fonts` property of the `TextFonts` object. In a script, you use the object name `fonts`, rather than the class name `TextFonts`, to refer to a `TextFonts` object. The following example uses the length property to determine, and then display, the number of `TextFonts` installed on the machine.

- Correct:

  ```
  alert(app.fonts.length)
  ```

- Incorrect:

  ```
  alert(app.TextFonts.length)
  ```

See `Application` (page 75), specifically the `fonts` property, for more information.

Properties

Property	Value Type	What it is
length	number (long)	Read-only. The number of elements in the TextFonts collection.
parent	object (Application) (page 75)	Read-only. The object's container.
typename	string	Read-only. The class name of the referenced TextFonts object.

Methods

Method	Parameter Type	Returns	What it does
index (itemKey)	number	TextFont (page 208)	Gets an element from the TextFonts collection.
getByName (name)	string	TextFont (page 208)	Gets the first element in the TextFonts collection with the provided name.

TextItem

The text in an `artLayer` object whose `kind` property is `LayerKind.TEXT`. See "ArtLayer" on page 82, specifically the `kind` property, for more information.

Note: Because the `TextItem` class is a property of the `ArtLayer` class, you use the object name, `textItem`, rather than the class name, `TextItem`, in your code. For example:

```
myLayers[i].textItem.contents = "Layer in " +
textArray[i] + " Set Inside "
```

Properties

Property	Value Type	What it is
alternateLigatures	boolean	Read-write. Indication of whether to use alternate ligatures. **Note:** Alternate ligatures are the same as Discretionary Ligatures. Please refer to Adobe Photoshop CS2 Help for more information.
antiAliasMethod	AntiAlias (page 329)	Read-write. The method of anti aliasing to use.
autoKerning	AutoKernType (page 329)	Read-write. The auto kerning option to use.
autoLeadingAmount	number (double)	Read-write. The percentage to use for auto (default) leading (0.01 - 5000.00 in points). **Note:** Valid only when `useAutoLeading = true`. See "useAutoLeading" on page 217.
baselineShift	UnitValue	Read-write. The unit value to use in the baseline offset of text.
capitalization	TextCase (page 343)	Read-write. The text case.
color	SolidColor (page 203)	Read-write. The text color.
contents	string	Read-write. The actual text in the layer.

Property	Value Type	What it is (Continued)
`desiredGlyphScaling`	`number (double)`	Read-write. The desired amount (percentage) to scale the horizontal size of the text letters (50 - 200; at 100, the width of characters is not scaled). **Note:** Valid only when `justification = Justification.CENTERJUSTIFIED;` `justification = Justification.FULLYJUSTIFIED;` `justification = Justification.LEFTJUSTIFIED;` or `justification = Justification.RIGHTJUSTIFIED`. See "justification" on page 213. The following values are also required: minimumGlyphScaling (page 215) and maximumGlyphScaling (page 214).
`desiredLetterScaling` **Note:** "Letter Scaling" is basically equivalent to "Letter Spacing" in the Adobe Photoshop CS2 application Justification dialog (Select Justification on the Paragraphs palette menu).	`number (double)`	Read-write. The amount of space between letters (100 - 500; at 0, no space is added between letters). **Note:** Valid only when `justification = Justification.CENTERJUSTIFIED;` `justification = Justification.FULLYJUSTIFIED;` `justification = Justification.LEFTJUSTIFIED;` or `justification = Justification.RIGHTJUSTIFIED`. See "justification" on page 213. The following values are also required: minimumLetterScaling (page 216) and maximumLetterScaling (page 214).

Property	Value Type	What it is (Continued)
desiredWordScaling **Note:** "Word Scaling" is basically equivalent to "Word Spacing" in the Adobe Photoshop CS2 application Justification dialog (Select Justification on the Paragraphs palette menu).	number (double)	Read-write. The amount (percentage) of space between words (0 -1000; at 100, no additional space is added between words). **Note:** Valid only when `justification = Justification.CENTERJUSTIFIED;` `justification = Justification.FULLYJUSTIFIED;` `justification = Justification.LEFTJUSTIFIED;` or `justification = Justification.RIGHTJUSTIFIED.` See "justification" on page 213. The following values are also required: minimumWordScaling (page 216) and maximumWordScaling (page 215).
direction	Direction (page 333)	Read-write. The text orientation.
fauxBold	boolean	Read-write. Indication of whether to use faux bold (default: `false`). **Note:** Using `fauxBold.true` is equivalent to selecting text and clicking the Faux Bold button in the Character palette.
fauxItalic	boolean	Read-write. Indication of whether to use faux italic (default: `false`). **Note:** Using `fauxItalic.true` is equivalent to selecting text and clicking the Faux Italic button in the Character palette.
firstLineIndent	UnitValue	Read-write. The amount (unit value) to indent the first line of paragraphs (-1296 - 1296).
font	string	Read-write. The text face of the character.
hangingPunctuation	boolean	Read-write. Indication of whether to use roman Hanging Punctuation.
height	UnitValue	Read-write. The height of the bounding box (unit value) for paragraph text. **Note:** Valid only when `kind = TextType.PARAGRAPHTEXT.` See "kind" on page 213.
horizontalScale	number (long)	Read-write. Character scaling (horizontal) in proportion to vertical scale (0 - 1000 in percent). See "verticalScale" on page 217.

Property	Value Type	What it is (Continued)
hyphenateAfterFirst	number (long)	Read-write. The number of letters after which hyphenation in word wrap is allowed (1 - 15).
hyphenateBeforeLast	number (long)	Read-write. The number of letters before which hyphenation in word wrap is allowed (1 - 15).
hyphenateCapitalWords	boolean	Read-write. Indication of whether to allow hyphenation in word wrap of capitalized words.
hyphenateWordsLongerThan	number (long)	Read-write. The minimum number of letters a word must have in order for hyphenation in word wrap to be allowed (2 - 25).
hyphenation	boolean	Read-write. Indication of whether to use hyphenation in word wrap.
hyphenationZone	UnitValue	Read-write. The distance at the end of a line that will cause a word to break in unjustified type (0 - 720 pica).
hyphenLimit	number (long)	Read-write. The maximum number of consecutive lines that can end with a hyphenated word.
justification	Justification (page 336)	Read-write. The paragraph justification.
kind	TextType (page 343)	Read-write. The text-wrap type.
language	Language (page 336)	Read-write. The language to use.
leading	UnitValue	Read-write. The leading amount (unit value).
leftIndent	UnitValue	Read-write. The amount (unit value) of space to indent text from the left (-1296 - 1296).
ligatures	boolean	Read-write. Indication of whether to use ligatures.

Property	Value Type	What it is (Continued)
`maximumGlyphScaling`	`number (double)`	Read-write. The maximum amount (percentage) to scale the horizontal size of the text letters (50 - 200; at 100, the width of characters is not scaled). **Note:** Valid only when `justification = Justification.CENTERJUSTIFIED;` `justification = Justification.FULLYJUSTIFIED;` `justification = Justification.LEFTJUSTIFIED;` or `justification = Justification.RIGHTJUSTIFIED.` See "justification" on page 213. The following values are also required: minimumGlyphScaling (page 215) and desiredGlyphScaling (page 211).
`maximumLetterScaling` **Note:** "Letter Scaling" is basically equivalent to "Letter Spacing" in the Adobe Photoshop CS2 application Justification dialog (Select Justification on the Paragraphs palette menu).	`number (double)`	Read-write. The maximum amount of space to allow between letters (100 - 500; at 0, no space is added between letters). **Note:** Valid only when `justification = Justification.CENTERJUSTIFIED;` `justification = Justification.FULLYJUSTIFIED;` `justification = Justification.LEFTJUSTIFIED;` or `justification = Justification.RIGHTJUSTIFIED.` See "justification" on page 213. The following values are also required: minimumLetterScaling (page 216) and desiredLetterScaling (page 211).

Property	Value Type	What it is (Continued)
`maximumWordScaling` **Note:** "Word Scaling" is basically equivalent to "Word Spacing" in the Adobe Photoshop CS2 application Justification dialog (Select Justification on the Paragraphs palette menu).	`number (double)`	Read-write. The maximum amount (percentage) of space to allow between words (0 -1000; at 100, no additional space is added between words). **Note:** Valid only when `justification = Justification.CENTERJUSTIFIED`; `justification = Justification.FULLYJUSTIFIED`; `justification = Justification.LEFTJUSTIFIED`; or `justification = Justification.RIGHTJUSTIFIED`. See "justification" on page 213. The following values are also required: minimumWordScaling (page 216) and desiredWordScaling (page 212).
`minimumGlyphScaling`	`number (double)`	Read-write. The minimum amount (percentage) to scale the horizontal size of the text letters (50 - 200; at 100, the width of characters is not scaled). **Note:** Valid only when `justification = Justification.CENTERJUSTIFIED`; `justification = Justification.FULLYJUSTIFIED`; `justification = Justification.LEFTJUSTIFIED`; or `justification = Justification.RIGHTJUSTIFIED`. See "justification" on page 213. The following values are also required: minimumGlyphScaling (page 215) and desiredGlyphScaling (page 211).

Property	Value Type	What it is (Continued)
`minimumLetterScaling` **Note:** "Letter Scaling" is basically equivalent to "Letter Spacing" in the Adobe Photoshop CS2 application Justification dialog (Select Justification on the Paragraphs palette menu).	`number (double)`	Read-write. The minimum amount (percentage) of space between letters (100 - 500; at 0, no space is removed between letters). **Note:** Valid only when `justification = Justification.CENTERJUSTIFIED`; `justification = Justification.FULLYJUSTIFIED`; `justification = Justification.LEFTJUSTIFIED`; or `justification = Justification.RIGHTJUSTIFIED`. See "justification" on page 213. The following values are also required: maximumLetterScaling (page 214) and desiredLetterScaling (page 211).
`minimumWordScaling` **Note:** "Word Scaling" is basically equivalent to "Word Spacing" in the Adobe Photoshop CS2 application Justification dialog (Select Justification on the Paragraphs palette menu).	`number (double)`	Read-write. The minimum amount (percentage) of space between words (0 -1000; at 100, no space is removed between words). **Note:** Valid only when `justification = Justification.CENTERJUSTIFIED`; `justification = Justification.FULLYJUSTIFIED`; `justification = Justification.LEFTJUSTIFIED`; or `justification = Justification.RIGHTJUSTIFIED`. See "justification" on page 213. The following values are also required: maximumWordScaling (page 215) and desiredWordScaling (page 212).
`noBreak`	`boolean`	Read-write. Indication of whether to allow words to break at the end of a line. **Note:** When enacted on large amounts of consecutive characters, `noBreak = true` can prevent word wrap and thus may prevent some text from appearing on the screen.
`oldStyle`	`boolean`	Read-write. Indication of whether to use old style type.

`parent`	`object`
	`(ArtLayer)`
	`(page 82)`
		Read-write. The `textItem` object's container.

Property	Value Type	What it is (Continued)
position	Array (UnitValue)	Read-write. The position of origin for the text. The array must contain two values (unit value). **Note:** Setting the position property is basically equivalent to clicking the text tool at a point in the document to create the point of origin for text.
rightIndent	UnitValue	Read-write. The amount of space (unit value) to indent text from the right (-1296 - 1296).
size	number (double)	Read-write. The font size in points.
spaceAfter	UnitValue	Read-write. The amount of space (unit value) to use after each paragraph (-1296 - 1296).
spaceBefore	UnitValue	Read-write. The amount of space (unit value) to use before each paragraph (-1296 - 1296).
strikeThru	StrikeThruType (page 343)	Read-write. The text strike through option to use.
textComposer	TextComposer (page 343)	Read-write. The composition method to use to evaluate line breaks and optimize the specified hyphenation and justification options. **Note:** Valid only when `kind = TextType.PARAGRAPHTEXT.` See "kind" on page 213.
tracking	number (double)	Read-write. The amount of uniform spacing between multiple characters (-1000 - 10000). **Note:** Tracking units are 1/1000 of an em space. The width of an em space is relative to the current type size. In a 1-point font, 1 em equals 1 point; in a 10-point font, 1 em equals 10 points. So, for example, 100 units in a 10-point font are equivalent to 1 point.
typename	string	Read-only. The class name of the referenced textItem object.
underline	UnderlineType (page 345)	Read-write. The text underlining options.
useAutoLeading	boolean	Read-write. Indication of whether to use a font's built-in leading information.
verticalScale	number (long)	Read-write. Character scaling (vertical) in proportion to horizontal scale (0 - 1000 in percent). See "horizontalScale" on page 212.
warpBend	number (double)	Read-write. The warp bend percentage (-100 - 100).

Property	Value Type	What it is (Continued)
`warpDirection`	`Direction` (page 333)	Read-write. The warp direction.
`warpHorizontalDistortion`	`number (double)`	Read-write. The horizontal distortion (as percentage) of the warp (-100 - 100).
`warpStyle`	`WarpStyle` (page 345)	Read-write. The style of warp to use.
`warpVerticalDistortion`	`number (double)`	Read-write. The vertical distortion (as percentage) of the warp (-100 - 100).
`width`	`UnitValue`	Read-write. The width of the bounding box (unit value) for paragraph text. **Note:** Valid only when `kind = TextType.PARAGRAPHTEXT`. See "kind" on page 213.

Methods

Method	Parameter Type	Returns	What it does
`convertToShape ()`			Converts the text item and its containing layer to a fill layer with the text changed to a clipping path.
`createPath ()`			Creates a clipping path from the outlines of the actual text items (such as letters or words).

TiffSaveOptions

Options that can be specified when saving a document in TIFF format.

Properties

Property	Value Type	What it is
`alphaChannels`	`boolean`	Read-write. Indication of whether to save the alpha channels.
`annotations`	`boolean`	Read-write. Indication of whether to save the annotations.
`byteOrder`	`ByteOrder` (page 330)	Read-write. The order in which the document's bytes will be read. (The default is `ByteOrder.MACOS` when running on MacOS and `ByteOrder.IBM` when running on a PC.)
`embedColorProfile`	`boolean`	Read-write. Indication of whether to embed the color profile in the document.
`imageCompression`	`TIFFEncoding` (page 343)	Read-write. The compression type (default: `TIFFEncoding.NONE`).
`interleaveChannels`	`boolean`	Read-write. Indication of whether the channels in the image will be interleaved.
`jpegQuality`	`number (long)`	Read-write. The quality of the produced image (0 - 12), which is inversely proportionate to the amount of JPEG compression. **Note:** Valid only when `imageCompression = TIFFEncoding.JPEG`.
`layerCompression`	`LayerCompression` (page 336)	Read-write. The method of compression to use when saving layers (as opposed to saving composite data). **Note:** Valid only when `layers = true`. See "layers" on page 219
`layers`	`boolean`	Read-write. Indication of whether to save the layers.
`saveImagePyramid`	`boolean`	Read-write. Indication of whether to preserve multi-resolution information (default: `false`).
`spotColors`	`boolean`	Read-write. Indication of whether to save the spot colors.
`transparency`	`boolean`	Read-write. Indication of whether to save the transparency as an additional alpha channel when the file is opened in another application.
`typename`	`string`	Read-only. The class name of the referenced `tiffSaveOptions` object.

xmpMetadata

Camera raw image file settings stored in an XMP file in the same folder as the raw file with the same base name and an XMP extension.

Properties

Property	Value Type	What it is
parent	object (Document) (page 115)	Read-only. The object's container.
rawData	string	Read-only. The raw XML form of file information.
typename	string	Read-only. The class name of the referenced xmpMetadata object.

6 | Action Manager

Adobe Photoshop CS2 actions allow you to save time by automating repetitive tasks. You create and run actions in the application interface using the Actions palette.

You can also manage actions in scripts using a utility called the *Action Manager*. The Action Manager allows you to write scripts that target Adobe Photoshop CS2 functionality that is not otherwise accessible in the scripting interface, such as third party plug-ins and filters. The only requirement for using the Action Manager is that the task that you want to access from the Action Manager is recordable.

This chapter describes how to use the Action Manager and the scripting interface objects it includes.

The ScriptListener plug-in

Before you use the Action Manager, you must install the ScriptListener plug-in. ScriptListener records a file with scripting code corresponding to the actions you perform in the UI.

Tip: Because ScriptListener records most of your actions, install ScriptListener only when you are creating Action Manager. Leaving ScriptListener installed continuously will not only create large files that occupy memory on your hard drive, it can slow Adobe Photoshop CS2 performance.

When you perform a task or series of tasks in Adobe Photoshop CS2, ScriptListener creates a file, `ScriptingListenerJS.log`, which contains JavaScript code that represents your actions.

- On Windows, ScriptListener places file the file on your C:\ drive.
- On Mac OS, ScriptListener creates the file on the desktop.

Note: There is no AppleScript interface to the Action Manager. However, you can access the Action Manager from an AppleScript by executing a JavaScript via the AppleScript.

Installing ScriptListener

The ScriptListener plug-in is located in the `..\Adobe Photoshop CS2\Scripting Guide\Utilities` folder.

➤ **To install the ScriptListener:**

1. Select the file `ScriptListener.8li` and then choose **Edit > Copy**.

2. Paste the file copy to the following location:

   `..\Adobe Photoshop CS\Plug-Ins\Adobe Photoshop Only\Automate`

3. Open Adobe Photoshop CS2.

   Note: If Adobe Photoshop CS2 is already open, close it and then start it again.

➤ **To uninstall the ScriptListener:**

1. Close Adobe Photoshop CS2.

2. Verify that a copy of the file `ScriptListener.8li` still exists in the `..\Adobe Photoshop CS2\Scripting Guide\Utilities` folder.

3. Delete the file `ScriptListener.8li` from the following location:

   `..\Adobe Photoshop CS\Plug-Ins\Adobe Photoshop Only\Automate`

4. Delete the log file `ScriptingListenerJS.log` from your C:\ drive (Windows) or desktop (Mac OS).

   Note: In Windows, even though you remove the ScriptListener from the Automate folder, it may continue to record actions. To prevent the `ScriptingListenerJS.log` file from becoming too large, delete it each time you finish playing a Adobe Photoshop CS2 action.

Action Manager scripting objects

The objects ActionDescriptor (page 67), ActionList (page 70), and ActionReference (page 73) are part of the Action Manager functionality.

Using the Action Manager from JavaScript

The section demonstrates how to create the `ScriptingListenerJS.log` log file and use its contents to create your script.

The procedures in this section uses the Action Manager to make the Emboss filter available to the scripting interface. (By default, the Emboss filter is available only via the Adobe Photoshop CS2 interface.)

Note: ScriptListener must be installed in the `Automate` folder before you begin the following procedure. See "Installing ScriptListener" on page 221.

➤ **To make the Emboss filter scriptable:**

1. Open Adobe Photoshop CS2, then open a document.

2. Choose **Window > Actions**, then choose **New Action** from the Actions palette menu.

3. Name the action, then click **Record**.

4. Choose **Filter > Stylize > Emboss**.

5. Using the following settings:
   - Angle: 135
   - Height: 3
   - Amount: 100

6. Do one of the following:
   - In Windows, open `C:\ScriptingListenerJS.log`.
   - On Mac OS, open `ScriptingListenerJS.log` on the desktop.

   At the end of the file you will see code similar to the following (although your numbers may be different):

   ```
   var id19 = charIDToTypeID( "Embs" );
   var desc4 = new ActionDescriptor();
   var id20 = charIDToTypeID( "Angl" );
   desc4.putInteger( id20, 135 );
   var id21 = charIDToTypeID( "Hght" );
   desc4.putInteger( id21, 3 );
   var id22 = charIDToTypeID( "Amnt" );
   desc4.putInteger( id22, 100 );
   executeAction( id19, desc4 );
   ```

Note: ScriptListener separates logged commands with horizontal lines composed of hyphens (-----...). If this is not the first action recorded in the log, you can easily locate the most recent action; it follows the final hyphen-line.

7. In the script, identify the values that you used with the filter (135, 3 and 100), then copy the JavaScript code from `ScriptListenerJS.log` to another file and substitute the filter specification values with variable names.

   In the following example, `135` has been replaced with `angle`; `3` has been replaced with `height`; `100` has been replaced with `amount`.

   ```
   var id19 = charIDToTypeID( "Embs" );
   ```

```
var desc4 = new ActionDescriptor();
var id20 = charIDToTypeID( "Angl" );
desc4.putInteger( id20, angle );
var id21 = charIDToTypeID( "Hght" );
desc4.putInteger( id21, height );
var id22 = charIDToTypeID( "Amnt" );
desc7.putInteger( id22, amount );
executeAction( id19, desc4 );
```

8. Wrap the code in a JavaScript function. In the following example, the function name is emboss.

```
function emboss( angle, height, amount )
{
    var id19 = charIDToTypeID( "Embs" );
    var desc4 = new ActionDescriptor();
    var id20 = charIDToTypeID( "Angl" );
    desc4.putInteger( id20, angle );
    var id21 = charIDToTypeID( "Hght" );
    desc4.putInteger( id21, height );
    var id22 = charIDToTypeID( "Amnt" );
    desc7.putInteger( id22, amount );
    executeAction( id19, desc4 );
}
```

9. To use a JavaScript to apply the Emboss filter to a document, include the emboss function in the JavaScript and call the function with the desired parameters. For example, the following example applies the Emboss filter with angle 75, height 2, and amount 89.

```
// Open the document in the script
//Call emboss with desired parameters
emboss( 75, 2, 89 );
//finish the script

//include the function in the script file
function emboss(angle, height, amount )
{
    var id32 = charIDToTypeID( "Embs" );
    var desc7 = new ActionDescriptor();
    var id33 = charIDToTypeID( "Angl" );
    desc7.putInteger( id33, angle );
    var id34 = charIDToTypeID( "Hght" );
    desc7.putInteger( id34, height );
    var id35 = charIDToTypeID( "Amnt" );
    desc7.putInteger( id35, amount );
    executeAction( id32, desc7 );
}
```

7 | Using ScriptUI

Overview

ScriptUI is a component that works with the ExtendScript JavaScript interpreter to provide JavaScript programs with the ability to create and interact with user interface elements. It provides an object model for windows and UI control elements within an Adobe Creative Suite 2 application. ScriptUI objects are available to JavaScript scripts for the following applications:

- Adobe Photoshop CS2
- Adobe Bridge CS2

Note: Adobe GoLive CS SDK includes another version of these objects, which have diverged somewhat in usage and functionality. See the *Adobe GoLive CS SDK Programmer's Guide* and *Adobe GoLive CS SDK Programmer's Reference* for details.

This chapter describe how to work with these objects, and Chapter 8, "ScriptUI Object Reference," provides the details of the objects with their properties, methods, and creation parameters.

ScriptUI Programming Model

ScriptUI defines `Window` objects that represent platform-specific windows, and various control elements such as `Button` and `StaticText`, that represent user-interface controls. These objects share a common set of properties and methods that allow you to query the type, move the element around, set the title, caption or content, and so on. Many element types also have properties unique to that class of elements.

Creating a window

ScriptUI defines the following types of windows:

- Modal dialog boxes: not resizable, holds focus when shown.
- Floating palettes: also called modeless dialogs, not resizable. (Photoshop CS2 does not support script creation of palette windows.)
- Main windows: resizable, suitable for use as an application's main window. (Main windows are not normally created by script developers for Adobe Creative Suite 2 applications. Photoshop CS2 does not support script creation of main windows.)

To create a new window, use the `Window` constructor function. The constructor takes the desired type of the window. The type is `"dialog"` for a modal dialog, or `"palette"` for a modeless dialog or floating palette. You can supply optional arguments to specify an initial window title and bounds.

The following example creates an empty dialog with the variable name `dlg`, which is used in subsequent examples:

```
// Create an empty dialog window near
// the upper left of the screen
var dlg = new Window('dialog', 'Alert Box Builder',
[100,100,480,490]);
```

Newly created windows are initially hidden; the `show` method makes them visible and responsive to user interaction. For example:

```
dlg.show();
```

Container elements

All `Windows` are containers—that is, they contain other elements within their bounds. Within a `Window`, you can create other types of container elements: `Panels` and `Groups`. These can contain control elements, and can also contain other `Panel` and `Group` containers. However, a `Window` cannot be added to any container.

- A `Group` is the simplest container used to visually organize related controls. You would typically define a group and populate it with related elements, for instance an `edittext` box and its descriptive `statictext` label.

- A `Panel` is a frame object, also typically used to visually organize related controls. It has a text property to specify a title, and can have a border to visually separate the collection of elements from other elements of a dialog.

You might create a `Panel` and populate it with several `Groups`, each with their own elements. You can create nested containers, with different layout properties for different containers, in order to define a relatively complex layout without any explicit placement.

You can add elements to any container using the `add` method (see "Adding elements to containers" on page 228). An element added to a container is considered a child of that container. Certain operations on a container apply to its children; for example, when you hide a container, its children are also hidden.

Window layout

When a script creates a `Window` and adds various UI elements to it, the locations and sizes of elements and spacing between elements is known as the *layout* of the window. Each UI element has properties which define its location and dimensions: `location`, `size`, and `bounds`. These properties are initially undefined, and a script that employs Automatic layout (page 243) should leave them undefined for the main window as well as its contained elements, allowing the automatic layout mechanism to set their values.

Your script can access these values , and (if not using auto-layout) set them as follows:

- The `location` of a window is defined by a Point (page 290) object containing a pair of coordinates (`x` and `y`) for the top left corner (the *origin*), specified in the screen coordinate system. The `location` of an element within a window or other container is defined as the origin point specified in the container's coordinate system. That is, the `x` and `y` values are relative to the origin of the container.

  The following examples show equivalent ways of placing the content region of an existing window at screen coordinates [10, 50]:

  ```
  win.location = [10, 50];
  win.location = {x:10, y:50};
  win.location = "x:10, y:50";
  ```

- The `size` of an element's region is defined by a Dimension (page 290) object containing a `width` and `height` in pixels.

  The following examples show equivalent ways of changing an existing window's width and height to 200 and 100:

  ```
  win.size = [200, 100];
  win.size = {width:200, height:100};
  win.size = "width:200, height:100";
  ```

  This example shows how to change a window's height to 100, leaving its location and width unchanged:

  ```
  win.size.height = 100;
  ```

- The `bounds` of an element are defined by a Bounds (page 290) object containing both the origin point (`x`, `y`) and size (`width`, `height`) To define the size and location of windows and controls in one step, use the `bounds` property.

  The value of the `bounds` property can be a string with appropriate contents, an inline JavaScript `Bounds` object, or a four-element array. The following examples show equivalent ways of placing a 380 by 390 pixel window near the upper left corner of the screen:

```
var dlg = new Window('dialog', 'Alert Box Builder',
[100,100,480,490]); dlg.bounds = [100,100,480,490];
dlg.bounds = {x:100, y:100, width:380, height:390};
dlg.bounds = {left:100, top:100, right:480,
bottom:490};
dlg.bounds = "left:100, top:100, right:480,
bottom:490";
```

The `window` dimensions define the size of the *content region* of the window, or that portion of the window that a script can directly control. The actual window size is typically larger, because the host platform's window system typically adds title bars and borders. The `bounds` property for a `Window` refers only to its content region. To determine the bounds of the frame surrounding the content region of a window, use the Window object's frameBounds (page 270) property.

Adding elements to containers

To add elements to a `window`, `panel`, or `group`, use the container's add (page 275) method. This method accepts the `type` of the element to be created and some optional parameters, depending on the element type. It creates and returns an object of the specified type.

In additions to windows, ScriptUI defines the following user-interface elements and controls:

- Panels (frames) and groups, to collect and organize other control types
- Push buttons with text or icons, radio buttons, checkbox buttons
- Static text or images, edit text
- Progressbars, scrollbars, sliders
- Lists, which include list boxes and drop-down (also called popup) lists. Each item in a list is a control of type `item`, and the parent list's `items` property contains an array of child items. You can add list items with the parent list's add (page 275) method.

You can specify the initial size and position of any new element relative to the working area of the parent container, in an optional `bounds` parameter. Different types of elements have different additional parameters. For elements which display text, for example, you can specify the initial text. See the "ScriptUI Object Reference" on page 267 for details.

The order of optional parameters must be maintained. Use the value `undefined` for a parameter you do not wish to set. For example, if you want to use automatic layout to determine the bounds, but still set the title and text in a panel and button, the following creates `Panel` and `Button` elements with an initial `text` value, but no `bounds` value:

```
dlg.btnPnl = dlg.add('panel', undefined, 'Build it');
dlg.btnPnl.testBtn = dlg.btnPnl.add('button', undefined,
'Test');
```

Tip: This example creates a dynamic property, `btnPnl`, on the parent window object, which contains the returned reference to the child control object. This is not required, but provides a useful way to access your controls.

A new element is initially set to be visible, but it not shown unless its parent object is shown.

Creation properties

Some element types have attributes that can only be specified when the element is created. These are not normal properties of the element, in that they cannot be changed during the element's lifetime, and they are only needed once. For these element types, you can supply an optional *creation-properties* argument to the `add` method. This argument is an object with one or more properties that control aspects of the element's appearance, or special functions such as whether an edit text element is editable or read-only. See "Control object constructors" on page 275 for details.

All UI elements have an optional creation property called `name`, which assigns a name for identifying that element. For example, the following creates a new `Button` element with the name 'ok':

```
dlg.btnPnl.buildBtn =
    dlg.btnPnl.add('button', undefined, 'Build',
{name:'ok'});
```

Accessing child elements

A reference to each element added to a container is appended to the container's `children` property. You can access the child elements through this array, using a 0-based index. For controls that are not containers, the `children` collection is empty.

In this example, the `msgPnl` panel was the first element created in `dlg`, so the script can access the panel object at index 0 of the parent's `children` property to set the text for the title:

```
var dlg = new Window('dialog', 'Alert Box Builder');
dlg.msgPnl = dlg.add('panel');
dlg.children[0].text = 'Messages';
```

If you use a creation property to assign a name to a newly created element, you can access that child by its name, either in the `children` array of its parent, or directly as a property of its parent. For example, the `Button` in a previous example was named "`ok`", so it can be referenced as follows:

```
dlg.btnPnl.children['ok'].text = "Build";
dlg.btnPnl.ok.text = "Build";
```

For list controls (type `list` and `dropdown`), you can access the child list-item objects through the `items` array.

Removing elements

To add elements to a `window`, `panel`, or `group`, use the container's remove (page 287) method. This method accepts an object representing the element to be removed, or the name of the element, or the index of the element in the container's `children` collection (see "Accessing child elements" on page 229).

The specified element is removed from view if it was currently visible, and it is no longer accessible from the container or window. The results of any further references by a script to the object representing the element are undefined.

To remove list items from a list, use the parent list control's remove (page 287) method in the same way. It removes the item from the parent's `items` list, hides it from view, and deletes the item object.

Types of controls

The following sections introduce the types of controls you can add to a `Window` or other container element (`panel` or `group`). For details of the properties and functions, and of how to create each type of element, see "ScriptUI Object Reference" on page 267.

Containers

These are types of Control objects (page 275) which are contained in windows, and which contain and group other controls.

Panel	Typically used to visually organize related controls.
	● Set the `text` property to define a title which appears at the top of the `Panel`.
	● An optional `borderStyle` creation property controls the appearance of the border drawn around the panel.
	You can use `Panels` as separators: those with `width` = 0 appear as vertical lines and those with `height` = 0 appear as horizontal lines.
	
	``
	var dlg = new Window('dialog', 'Alert Box Builder',[100,100,480,245]);
	dlg.msgPnl = dlg.add('panel', [25,15,355,130], 'Messages');
	``

Group	Used to visually organize related controls. Unlike `Panels`, `Groups` have no title or visible border. You can use them to create hierarchies of controls, and for fine control over layout attributes of certain groups of controls within a larger panel. For examples, see "Creating more complex arrangements" on page 249.

User interface controls

These are types of Control objects (page 275) which are contained in windows, panels, and groups, and which provide specific kinds of display and user interaction.

StaticText	Typically used to display text strings that are not intended for direct manipulation by a user, such as informative messages or labels.
	
	This example creates a `Panel` and adds several `StaticText` elements:
	
	``
	var dlg = new Window('dialog', 'Alert Box
	Builder',[100,100,480,245]);
	  dlg.msgPnl = dlg.add('panel', [25,15,355,130], 'Messages');
	  dlg.msgPnl.titleSt = dlg.msgPnl.add('statictext', [15,15,105,35],
	    'Alert box title:');
	  dlg.msgPnl.msgSt = dlg.msgPnl.add('statictext', [15,65,105,85],
	    'Alert message:');
	  dlg.show();
	``

EditText	Allows users to enter text, which is returned to the script when the dialog is dismissed. Text in `EditText` elements can be selected, copied, and pasted.
	
	● Set the `text` property to assign the initial displayed text in the element, and read it to obtain the current text value, as entered or modified by the user.
	
	● Set the `textselection` property to replace the current selection with new text, or to insert text at the cursor (insertion point). Read this property to obtain the current selection, if any.
	
	This example adds some `EditText` elements, with initial values that a user can accept or replace:
	
	``
	var dlg = new Window('dialog', 'Alert Box
	Builder',[100,100,480,245]);
	  dlg.msgPnl = dlg.add('panel', [25,15,355,130], 'Messages');
	  dlg.msgPnl.titleSt = dlg.msgPnl.add('statictext', [15,15,105,35],
	    'Alert box title:');
	  dlg.msgPnl.titleEt = dlg.msgPnl.add('edittext', [115,15,315,35],
	    'Sample Alert');
	  dlg.msgPnl.msgSt = dlg.msgPnl.add('statictext', [15,65,105,85],
	    'Alert message:');
	  dlg.msgPnl.msgEt = dlg.msgPnl.add('edittext', [115,45,315,105],
	    '<your message here>', {multiline:true});
	  dlg.show();
	``
	Note the creation property on the second `EditText` field, where `multiline:true` indicates a field in which a long text string can be entered. The text wraps to appear as multiple lines.

Button	Typically used to initiate some action from a window when a user clicks the button; for example, accepting a dialog's current settings, canceling a dialog, bringing up a new dialog, and so on.
	• Set the `text` property to assign a label to identify a `Button`'s function.
	• The `onClick` callback method provides behavior.

	<pre>var dlg = new Window('dialog', 'Alert Box
	Builder',[100,100,480,245]);
	    dlg.btnPnl = dlg.add('panel', [15,50,365,95], 'Build it');
	    dlg.btnPnl.testBtn = dlg.btnPnl.add('button', [15,15,115,35],
	    'Test');
	    dlg.btnPnl.buildBtn = dlg.btnPnl.add('button', [125,15,225,35],
	        'Build', {name:'ok'});
	    dlg.btnPnl.cancelBtn = dlg.btnPnl.add('button', [235,15,335,35],
	        'Cancel', {name:'cancel'});
	    dlg.show();</pre>

IconButton	A button that displays an icon instead of text. Like a text button, typically initiates an action in response to a click.
	• The `icon` property identifies the icon image; see "Displaying icons" on page 235.
	• The `onClick` callback method provides behavior.
Image	Displays an iconic image.
	• The `icon` property identifies the icon image; see "Displaying icons" on page 235.
Checkbox	Allows the user to set a boolean state.
	• Set the `text` property to assign an identifying text string that appears next to the clickable box.
	• The user can click to select or deselect the box, which shows a checkmark when selected. The `value=true` when it is selected (checked) and `false` when it is not.
	When you create a `Checkbox`, you can set its `value` property to specify its initial state and appearance.

	<pre>// Add a checkbox to control the buttons that dismiss an alert box
	dlg.hasBtnsCb = dlg.add('checkbox', [125,145,255,165],
	    'Should there be alert buttons?');
	dlg.hasBtnsCb.value = true;</pre>

RadioButton	Allows the user to select one choice among several.
	
	● Set the `text` property to assign an identifying text string that appears next to the clickable button.
	
	● The `value=true` when the button is selected. The button shows the state in a platform-specific manner, with a filled or empty dot, for example.
	
	You group a related set of radio buttons by creating all the related elements one after another. When any button's value becomes `true`, the value of all other buttons in the group becomes `false`. When you create a group of radio buttons, you should set the state of one of them `true`:
	
	``
	var dlg = new Window('dialog', 'Alert Box
	Builder',[100,100,480,245]);
	dlg.alertBtnsPnl = dlg.add('panel', [45,50,335,95], 'Button
	alignment');
	dlg.alertBtnsPnl.alignLeftRb = dlg.alertBtnsPnl.add('radiobutton',
	    [15,15,95,35], 'Left');
	dlg.alertBtnsPnl.alignCenterRb = dlg.alertBtnsPnl.add('radiobutton',
	    [105,15,185,35], 'Center');
	dlg.alertBtnsPnl.alignRightRb = dlg.alertBtnsPnl.add('radiobutton',
	    [195,15,275,35], 'Right');
	dlg.alertBtnsPnl.alignCenterRb.value = true;
	dlg.show();
	``

Progressbar	Typically used to display the progress of a time-consuming operation. A colored bar covers a percentage of the area of the control, representing the percentage completion of the operation. The `value` property reflects and controls how much of the visible area is colored, relative to the maximum value (`maxvalue`). By default the range is 0 to 100, so the `value=50` when the operation is half done.
Slider	Typically used to select within a range of values. The slider is a horizontal bar with a draggable indicator, and you can click a point on the slider bar to jump the indicator to that location. The `value` property reflects and controls the position of the indicator, within the range determined by `minvalue` and `maxvalue`. By default the range is 0 to 100, so setting `value=50` moves the indicator to the middle of the bar.

Scrollbar	Like a slider, the scrollbar is a bar with a draggable indicator. It also has "stepper" buttons at each end, that you can click to jump the indicator by the amount in the `stepdelta` property. If you click a point on the bar outside the indicator, the indicator jumps by the amount in the `jumpdelta` property.
	
	You can create scrollbars with horizontal or vertical orientation; if `width` is greater than `height`, it is horizontal, otherwise it is vertical.
	
	Scrollbars are often created with an associated `EditText` field to display the current value of the scrollbar, and to allow setting the scrollbar's position to a specific value. This example creates a scrollbar with associated `StaticText` and `EditText` elements within a panel:
	
	``
	dlg.sizePnl = dlg.add('panel', [60,240,320,315], 'Dimensions');
	dlg.sizePnl.widthSt = dlg.sizePnl.add('statictext', [15,15,65,35],
	   'Width:');
	dlg.sizePnl.widthScrl = dlg.sizePnl.add('scrollbar', [75,15,195,35],
	   300, 300, 800);
	dlg.sizePnl.widthEt = dlg.sizePnl.add('edittext', [205,15,245,35]);
	``
	The last three arguments to the `add` method that creates the scrollbar define the values for the `value`, `minvalue` and `maxvalue` properties.

ListBox **DropDownList**	These controls display lists of items, which are represented by `ListItem` objects in the `items` property. You can access the items in this array using a 0-based index. ● A `ListBox` control displays a list of choices. When you create the object, you specify whether it allows the user to select only one or multiple items. If a list contains more items than can be displayed in the available area, a scrollbar may appear that allows the user to scroll through all the list items. ● A `DropDownList` control displays a single visible item. When you click the control, a list drops down and allows you to select one of the other items in the list. Drop-down lists can have nonselectable separator items for visually separating groups of related items, as in a menu. You can specify the choice items on creation of the list object, or afterward using the list object's add (page 287) method. You can remove items programmatically with the list object's remove (page 287) and removeAll (page 287) method.
ListItem	Items added to or inserted into any type of list control are `ListItem` objects, with properties that can be manipulated from a script. `ListItem` elements can be of the following types: ● `item`: the typical item in any type of list. It displays text or an icon, and can be selected. To display an icon, set the item object's `icon` property; see "Displaying icons" on page 235. ● `separator`: a separator is a nonselectable visual element in a drop-down list. Although it has a `text` property, the value is ignored, and the item is displayed as a horizontal line.

Displaying icons

You can display icon images in Image or IconButton controls, or in place of strings as the selectable items in a Listbox or DropdownList control. In each case, the image is defined by setting the element's `icon` property, either to a named icon resource, a File object (page 311), or the pathname of a file containing the iconic image (see "Specifying paths" on page 305).

The image data for an icon must be in Portable Network Graphics (PNG) format. See http://www.libpng.org for detailed information on the PNG format.

You can set or reset the `icon` property at any time to change the image displayed in the element.

The scripting environment can define icon *resources*, which are available to scripts by name. To specify an icon resource, set a control's `icon` property to the resource's JavaScript name, or refer to the resource by name when creating the control. For example, to create a button with an application-defined icon resource:

```
myWin.upBtn = myWin.add ("iconbutton", undefined,
"SourceFolderIcon");
```

If a script does not explicitly set the `preferredSize` or `size` property of an element that displays a icon image, the value of `preferredSize` is determined by the dimensions of the iconic image. If the size values are explicitly set to dimensions smaller than those of the actual image graphic, the displayed image is clipped. If they are set to dimensions larger than those of the image graphic, the displayed image is centered in the larger space. An image is never scaled to fit the available space.

Prompts and alerts

Static functions on the Window Class (page 268) are globally available to display short messages in standard dialogs. The host application controls the appearance of these simple dialogs, so they are consistent with other alert and message boxes displayed by the application. You can often use these standard dialogs for simple interactions with your users, rather than designing special-purpose dialogs of your own.

Use the static functions alert (page 268), confirm (page 268), and prompt (page 269) on the `Window` class to invoke these dialogs with your own messages. You do not need to create a `window` object to call these functions.

Modal dialogs

A modal dialog is initially invisible. Your script invokes it using the show (page 273) method, which does not return until the dialog has been dismissed. The user can dismiss it by using a platform-specific window gesture, or by using one of the dialog controls that you supply, typically an **OK** or **Cancel** button. The onClick (page 288) method of such a button must call the close (page 273) or hide (page 273) method to close the dialog. The `close` method allows you to pass a value to be returned by the `show` method.

For an example of how to define such buttons and their behavior, see "Defining behavior for controls with event callbacks" on page 241.

Creating and using modal dialogs

A dialog typically contains some controls that the user must interact with, to make selections or enter values that your script will use. In some cases, the result of the user action is stored in the object, and you can retrieve it after the dialog has been dismissed. For example, if the user changes the state of a `Checkbox` or `RadioButton`, the new state is found in the control's `value` property.

However, if you need to respond to a user action while the dialog is still active, you must assign the control a callback function for the interaction event, either onClick (page 288) or onChange (page 288). The callback function is the value of the `onClick` or `onChange` property of the control.

For example, if you need to validate a value that the user enters in a `edittext` control, you can do so in an `onChange` callback handler function for that control. The callback can perform the validation, and perhaps display an alert to inform the user of errors.

Sometimes, a modal dialog presents choices to the user that must be correct before your script allows the dialog to be dismissed. If your script needs to validate the state of a dialog after the user clicks **OK**, you can define an onClose (page 274) event handler for the dialog. This callback function is invoked whenever a window is closed. If the function returns `true`, the window is closed, but if it returns `false`, the close operation is cancelled and the window remains open.

Your `onClose` handler can examine the states of any controls in the dialog to determine their correctness, and can show alert (page 268) messages or use other modal dialogs to alert the user to any errors that must be corrected. It can then return `true` to allow the dialog to be dismissed, or `false` to allow the user to correct any errors.

Dismissing a modal dialog

Every modal dialog should have at least one button that the user can click to dismiss the dialog. Typically modal dialogs have an **OK** and a **Cancel** button to close the dialog with or without accepting changes that were made in it.

You can define onClick (page 288) callbacks for the buttons that close the parent dialog by calling its close (page 273) method. You have the option of sending a value to the `close` method, which is in turn passed on to and returned from the show (page 273) method that invoked the dialog. This return value allows your script to distinguish different closing events; for example, clicking **OK** can return 1, clicking **Cancel** can return 2. However, for this typical behavior, you do not need to define these callbacks explicitly; see "Default and cancel elements" on page 238.

For some dialogs, such as a simple alert with only an **OK** button, you do not need to return any value. For more complex dialogs with several possible user actions, you might need to distinguish more outcomes. If you need to distinguish more than two closing states, you must define your own closing callbacks rather than relying on the default behavior.

If, by mistake, you create a modal dialog with no buttons to dismiss it, or if your dialog does have buttons, but their onClick handlers do not function properly, a user can still dismiss the dialog by typing Esc. In this case, the system will execute a call to the dialog's close method, passing a value of 2. This is not, of course, a recommended way to design your dialogs, but is provided as an escape hatch to prevent the application from hanging in case of an error in the operations of your dialog.

Default and cancel elements

The user can typically dismiss a modal dialog by clicking an **OK** or **Cancel** button, or by typing certain keyboard shortcuts. By convention, typing ENTER is the same as clicking **OK** or the default button, and typing Esc is the same as clicking **Cancel**. The keyboard shortcut has the same effect as calling notify (page 287) for the associated button control.

To determine which control is notified by which keyboard shortcut, set the dialog object's defaultElement (page 270) and cancelElement (page 270) properties. The value is the control object that should be notified when the user types the associated keyboard shortcut.

- For buttons assigned as the defaultElement, if there is no onClick handler associated with the button, clicking the button or typing ENTER calls the parent dialog's close (page 273) method, passing a value of 1 to be returned by the show (page 273) call that opened the dialog.

- For buttons assigned as the cancelElement, if there is no onClick handler associated with the button, clicking the button or typing Esc calls the parent dialog's close (page 273) method, passing a value of 2 to be returned by the show (page 273) call that opened the dialog.

If you do not set the defaultElement and cancelElement properties explicitly, ScriptUI tries to choose reasonable defaults when the dialog is about to be shown for the first time. For the default element, it looks for a button whose name or text value is "ok" (disregarding case). For the cancel element, it looks for a button whose name or text value is "cancel" (disregarding case). Because it looks at the `name` value first, this works even if the `text` value is localized. If there is no suitable button in the dialog, the property value remains `null`, which means that the keyboard shortcut has no effect in that dialog.

To make this feature most useful, it is recommended that you always provide the `name` creation property for buttons meant to be used in this way.

Resource specifications

You can create one or more UI elements at a time using a *resource specification*. This specially formatted string provides a simple and compact means of creating an element, including any container element and its component elements. The resource-specification string is passed as the `type` parameter to the `Window()` or `add()` constructor function.

The general structure of a resource specification is an element type specification (such as `dialog`), followed by a set of braces enclosing one or more property definitions.

```
var myResource = "dialog{ control_specs }";
var myDialog = new Window ( myResource );
```

Controls are defined as properties within windows and other containers. For each control, give the class name of the control, followed by the properties of the control enclosed in braces. For example, the following specifies a `Button`:

```
testBtn: Button { text: 'Test' }
```

The following resource string specifies a panel that contains several `StaticText` and `EditText` controls:

```
"msgPnl: Panel { text: 'Messages',\
    bounds:[25,15,355,130], \
    titleSt: StaticText { text:'Alert box title:', \
        bounds:[15,15,105,35] }, \
    titleEt: EditText { text:'Sample Alert',\
        bounds:[115,15,315,35] }, \
    msgSt: StaticText { text:'Alert message:', \
        bounds:[15,65,105,85] }, \
    msgEt: EditText { text:'<your message here>', \
        bounds:[115,45,315,105],
properties:{multiline:true} } \
    }"
```

The property with name `properties` specifies creation properties; see "Creation properties" on page 229.

A property value can be specified as null, true, false, a string, a number, an inline array, or an object.

- An inline array contains one or more values in the form:

   ```
   [value, value,...]
   ```

- An object can be an inline object, or a named object, in the form :

   ```
   {classname inlineObject}
   ```

- An inline object contains one or more properties, in the form:

   ```
   {propertyName:propertyValue,propertyName:propertyValue,... }
   ```

The Resource specification example (page 262) shows how to build a complete window and all its contents with a resource specification. The resource specification format can also be used to create a single element or container and its child elements. For example, if the alertBuilderResource in Resource specification example did not contain the panel btnPnlResource, you could define that resource separately, then add it to the dialog as follows:

```
var btnPnlResource =
    "panel { text: 'Build it', bounds:[15,330,365,375], \
        testBtn: Button { text:'Test', \
            bounds:[15,15,115,35] }, \
        buildBtn: Button { text:'Build',\
            bounds:[125,15,225,35], \
        properties:{name:'ok'} }, \
        cancelBtn: Button { text:'Cancel',\
            bounds:[235,15,335,35], \
        properties:{name:'cancel'} } \
    }";
dlg = new Window(alertBuilderResource);
dlg.btnPnl = dlg.add(btnPnlResource);
dlg.show();
```

Defining behavior for controls with event callbacks

You must define the behavior of your controls in order for them to respond to user interaction. You do this by defining event-handling callback functions as part of the definition of the control or window. To respond to a specific event, define a handler function for it, and assign a reference to that function in the corresponding property of the window or control object. Different types of windows and controls respond to different actions, or events:

- Windows generate events when the user moves or resizes the window. To handle these events, define callback functions for onMove (page 274), onMoving (page 274), onResize (page 274), and onResizing (page 274). To respond to the user opening or closing the window, define callback functions for onShow (page 274) and onClose (page 274).

- Button, radiobutton, and checkbox controls generate events when the user clicks within the control bounds. To handle the event, define a callback function for onClick (page 288).

- Edittext, scrollbar, and slider controls generate events when the content or value changes—that is, when the user types into an edit field, or moves the scroll or slider indicator. To handle these events, define callback functions for onChange (page 288) and onChanging (page 288).

Defining event handler functions

Your script can define an event handler as a named function referenced by the callback property, or as an unnamed function defined inline in the callback property.

- If you define a named function, assign its name as the value of the corresponding callback property. For example:

```
function hasBtnsCbOnClick { /* do something
interesting */ }
hasBtnsCb.onClick = hasBtnsCbOnClick;
```

- For a simple, unnamed function, set the property value directly to the function definition:

```
UI_element.callback_name = function () {
handler_definition};
```

Event-handler functions take no arguments.

For example, the following sets the onClick property of the checkbox hasBtnsCb, to a function that enables another control in the same dialog:

```
hasBtnsCb.onClick = function ()
    { this.parent.alertBtnsPnl.enabled = this.value; };
```

The following statements set the `onClick` event handlers for buttons that close the containing dialog, returning different values to the `show` method that invoked the dialog, so that the calling script can tell which button was clicked:

```
buildBtn.onClick = function () {
this.parent.parent.close(1); };
cancelBtn.onClick = function () {
this.parent.parent.close(2); };
```

Simulating user events

You can simulate user actions by sending an event notification directly to a window or control with the `notify` method. A script can use this method to generate events in the controls of a window, as if a user was clicking buttons, entering text, or moving the window. If you have defined an event-handler callback for the element, the `notify` method invokes it.

The `notify` method takes an optional argument that specifies which event it should simulate. If a control can generate only one kind of event, notification generates that event by default.

The following controls generate the `onClick` event:

```
button
checkbox
iconbutton
radiobutton
```

The following controls generate the `onChange` event:

```
dropdownlist
edittext
listbox
scrollbar
slider
```

The following controls generate the `onChanging` event:

```
edittext
scrollbar
slider
```

In `radiobutton` and `checkbox` controls, the boolean `value` property automatically changes when the user clicks the control. If you use `notify()` to simulate a click, the `value` changes just as if the user had clicked. For example, if the `value` of a checkbox `hasBtnsCb` is `true`, this code changes the value to `false`:

```
if (dlg.hasBtnsCb.value == true) dlg.hasBtnsCb.notify();
// dlg.hasBtnsCb.value is now false
```

Automatic layout

When a script creates a window and its associated UI elements, it can explicitly control the size and location of each element and of the container elements, or it can take advantage of the automatic layout capability provided by ScriptUI. The automatic layout mechanism uses certain available information about UI elements, along with a set of layout rules, to establish a visually pleasing layout of the controls in a dialog, automatically determining the proper sizes for elements and containers.

Automatic layout is easier to program than explicit layout. It makes a script easier to modify and maintain, and it also makes the script easier to localize for different languages.

The script programmer has considerable control over the automatic layout process. Each container has an associated layout manager object, specified in the `layout` property. The layout manager controls the sizes and positions of the contained elements, and also sizes the container itself.

There is a default layout manager object, or you can create a new one:

```
myWin.layout = new AutoLayoutManager(myWin);
```

Default layout behavior

By default, the `autoLayoutManager` object implements the default layout behavior. A script can modify the properties of the default layout manager object, or create a new, custom layout manager if it needs more specialized layout behavior. See "Custom layout manager example" on page 253.

Child elements of a container can be organized in a single row or column, or in a stack, where the elements overlap one other in the same region of the container, and only the top element is fully visible. This is controlled by the container's `orientation` property, which can have the value `row`, `column`, or `stack`.

You can nest `Panel` and `Group` containers to create more complex organizations. For example, to display two columns of controls, you can create a panel with a row orientation that in turn contains two groups, each with a column orientation.

Containers have properties to control inter-element spacing and margins within their edges. The layout manager provides defaults if these are not set.

The alignment of child elements within a container is controlled by the `alignChildren` property of the container, and the `alignment` property of the individual controls. The `alignChildren` property determines an overall

---

strategy for the container, which can be overridden by a particular child element's `alignment` value.

A layout manager can determine the best size for a child element through the element's `preferredSize` property. The value defaults to dimensions determined by the UI framework based on characteristics of the control type and variable characteristics such as a displayed text string.

For details of how you can set these property values to affect the automatic layout, see "Automatic layout properties" on page 244.

Note: ScriptUI does not offer direct control of fonts, and fonts are chosen differently on different platforms, so windows that are created the same way can appear different on different platforms.

Automatic layout properties

Your script establishes rules for the layout manager by setting the values of certain properties, both in the container object and in the child elements. The following examples show the effects of various combinations of values for these properties. The examples are based on a simple window containing a `StaticText`, `Button` and `EditText` element, created (using Resource specifications, page 239) as follows:

```
var w = new Window(
    "window { \
        orientation: 'row', \
        st: StaticText { }, \
        pb: Button { text: 'OK' }, \
        et: EditText { size:[20, 30] } \
    }");
w.show();
```

Each example shows the effects of setting particular layout properties in various ways. In each window, `w. text` is set so that the window title shows which property is being varied, and `w.st.text` is set to display the particular property value being demonstrated.

Container orientation

The `orientation` property of a container specifies the organization of child elements within it. It can have these values:

- `row`: Child elements are arranged next to each other, in a single row from left to right across the container. The height of the container is based on the height of the tallest child element in the row, and the width of the container is based on the combined widths of all the child elements.

- `column`: Child elements are arranged above and below each other, in a single column from top to bottom across the container. The height of the container is based on the combined heights of all the child elements, and the width of the container is based on the widest child element in the column.

- `stack`: Child elements are arranged overlapping one another, as in a stack of papers. The elements overlie one another in the same region of the container. Only the top element is fully visible. The height of the container is based on the height of the tallest child element in the stack, and the width of the container is based on the widest child element in the stack.

The following figure shows the results of laying out the sample window with each of these orientations:

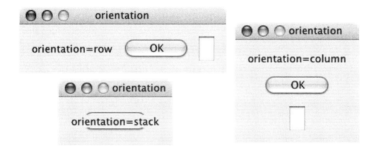

Aligning children

The alignment of child elements within a container is controlled by two properties: `alignChildren` in the parent container, and `alignment` in each child. The `alignChildren` value in the parent container controls the alignment of all children within that container, unless it is overridden by the `alignment` value set on an individual child element.

These properties use the same values, which specify alignment along one axis, depending on the orientation of the container. The property values are not case-sensitive; for example, the strings `FILL`, `Fill`, and `fill` are all valid.

Elements in a row can be aligned along the vertical axis, in these ways:

- `top`: The element's top edge is located at the top margin of its container.
- `bottom`: The element's bottom edge is located at the bottom margin of its container.
- `center`: The element is centered within the top and bottom margins of its container.
- `fill`: The element's height is adjusted to fill the height of the container between the top and bottom margins.

Elements in a column can be aligned along the horizontal axis, in these ways:

- `left`: The element's left edge is located at the left margin of its container.
- `right`: The element's right edge is located at the right margin of its container.
- `center`: The element is centered within the right and left margins of its container.
- `fill`: The element's width is adjusted to fill the width of the container between the right and left margins.

Elements in a stack can be aligned along either the vertical or the horizontal axis, in these ways:

- `top`: The element's top edge is located at the top margin of its container, and the element is centered within the right and left margins of its container.
- `bottom`: The element's bottom edge is located at the bottom margin of its container, and the element is centered within the right and left margins of its container.
- `left`: The element's left edge is located at the left margin of its container, and the element is centered within the top and bottom margins of its container.
- `right`: The element's right edge is located at the right margin of its container, and the element is centered within the top and bottom margins of its container.
- `center`: The element is centered within the top, bottom, right, and left margins of its container.
- `fill`: The element's height is adjusted to fill the height of the container between the top and bottom margins, and the element's width is adjusted to fill the width of the container between the right and left margins.

The following figure shows the results of creating the sample window with row orientation and the `bottom` and `top` alignment settings in the parent's `alignChildren` property:

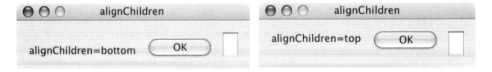

The following figure shows the results of creating the sample window with column orientation and the `right`, `left`, and `fill` alignment settings in the parent's `alignChildren` property. Notice how in the `fill` case, each element is made as wide as the widest element in the container:

You can override the container's child alignment, as specified by `alignChildren`, by setting the `alignment` property of a particular child element. The following diagram shows the result of setting `alignment` to `right` for the `EditText` element, when the parent's `alignChildren` value is left:

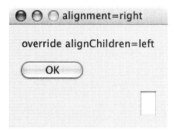

Setting margins

The `margins` property of a container specifies the number of pixels between the edges of a container and the outermost edges of the child elements. You can set this property to a simple number to specify equal margins, or using a Margins (page 290) object, which allows you to specify different margins for each edge of the container.

The following figure shows the results of creating the sample window with row orientation and margins of 5 and 15 pixels:

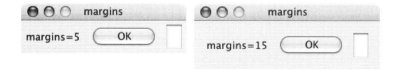

This figure shows the results of creating the sample window with column orientation, a top margin of 0 pixels, a bottom margin of 20 pixels, and left and right margins of 15 pixels:

Spacing between children

The `spacing` property of a container specifies the number of pixels separating one child element from its adjacent sibling element.

This figure shows the results of creating the sample window with row orientation, and spacing of 15 and 5 pixels, respectively:

This figure shows the results of creating the sample window with column orientation, and spacing of 20 pixels:

Determining a preferred size

Each element has a `preferredSize` property, which is initially defined with reasonable default dimensions for the element. The default value is calculated by ScriptUI, and is based on constant characteristics of each type of element, and variable characteristics such as the text string to be displayed in a button or text element.

If an element's `size` property is not defined, the layout manager uses the value of `preferredSize` to determine the dimensions of each element during the layout process. Generally, you should avoid setting the `preferredSize` property explicitly, and let ScriptUI determine the best value based on the state of an element at layout time. This allows you to set the `text` properties of your UI elements using localizable strings (see "Localization in ScriptUI objects" on page 264). The width and height of each element are calculated at layout time based on the chosen language-specific text string, rather than relying on the script to specify a fixed size for each element.

However, a script can explicitly set the `preferredSize` property to give hints to the layout manager about the intended sizes of elements for which a reasonable default size is not easily determined, such as an `EditText` element that has no initial text content to measure.

Creating more complex arrangements

You can easily create more complex arrangements by nesting `Group` containers within `Panel` containers and other `Group` containers.

Many dialogs consist of rows of information to be filled in, where each row has columns of related types of controls. For instance, an edit field is typically in a row next to a static text label that identifies it, and a series of such rows are arranged in a column. This example (created using Resource specifications, page 239) shows a simple dialog in which a user can enter information into two `EditText` fields, each arranged in a row with its `StaticText` label. To create the layout, a `Panel` with a column orientation contains two `Group` elements with row orientation. These groups contain the control rows. A third `Group`, outside the panel, contains the row of buttons.

```
res =
"dialog { \
   info: Panel { orientation: 'column', \
      text: 'Personal Info', \
      name: Group { orientation: 'row', \
         s: StaticText { text:'Name:' }, \
         e: EditText { preferredSize: [200, 20] } \
      }, \
      addr: Group { orientation: 'row', \
         s: StaticText { text:'Street / City:' }, \
         e: EditText { preferredSize: [200, 20] } \
      } \
   }, \
   buttons: Group { orientation: 'row', \
      okBtn: Button { text:'OK', properties:{name:'ok'} }, \
      cancelBtn: Button { text:'Cancel', \
properties:{name:'cancel'} } \
```

```
       } \
     }";
     win = new Window (res);
     win.center();
     win.show();
```

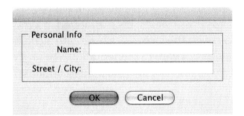

In this simplest example, the columns are not vertically aligned. When you are using fixed-width controls in your rows, a simple way to get an attractive alignment of the `StaticText` labels for your `EditText` fields is to align the child rows in the `Panel` to the right of the panel. In the example, add the following to the `Panel` specification:

```
     info: Panel { orientation: 'column',
     alignChildren:'right', \
```

This creates the following result:

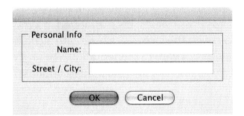

Suppose now that you need two panels, and want each panel to have the same width in the dialog. You can specify this at the level of the dialog window object, the parent of both panels. Specify `alignChildren='fill'`, which makes each child of the dialog match its width to the widest child.

```
     res =
         "dialog { alignChildren: 'fill', \
             info: Panel { orientation: 'column',
     alignChildren:'right', \
                 text: 'Personal Info', \
                 name: Group { orientation: 'row', \
                     s: StaticText { text:'Name:' }, \
                     e: EditText { preferredSize: [200, 20] } \
                 } \
             }, \
             workInfo: Panel { orientation: 'column', \
                 text: 'Work Info', \
```

Adobe® Photoshop® CS2 Official JavaScript Reference

```
            name: Group { orientation: 'row', \
                s: StaticText { text:'Company name:' }, \
                e: EditText { preferredSize: [200, 20] } \
            } \
        }, \
        buttons: Group { orientation: 'row', \
            alignment: 'right', \
            okBtn: Button { text:'OK', \
    properties:{name:'ok'} }, \
            cancelBtn: Button { text:'Cancel', \
    properties:{name:'cancel'} } \
        } \
    }";
win = new Window (res); win.center(); win.show();
```

To make the buttons to appear at the right of the dialog, the `buttons` group overrides the `fill` alignment of its parent (the dialog), and specifies `alignment='right'`.

Creating dynamic content

Many dialogs need to present different sets of information based on the user selecting some option within the dialog. You can use the `stack` orientation to present different views in the same region of a dialog.

A `stack` orientation of a container places child elements so they are centered in a space which is wide enough to hold the widest child element, and tall enough to contain the tallest child element. If you arrange groups or panels in such a stack, you can show and hide them in different combinations to display a different set of controls in the same space, depending on other choices in the dialog.

For example, this dialog changes dynamically according to the user's choice in the `DropDownList`.

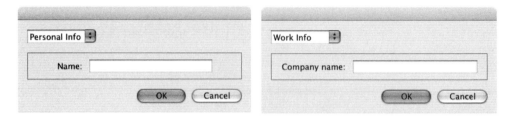

The following script creates this dialog. It compresses the "Personal Info" and "Work Info" panels from the previous example into a single `Panel` that has two `Groups` arranged in a stack. A `DropDownList` allows the user to choose which set of information to view. When the user makes a choice in the list, its onChange (page 288) function shows one group, and hides the other.

```
res =
    "dialog { \
        whichInfo: DropDownList { alignment:'left' }, \
        allGroups: Panel { orientation:'stack', \
            info: Group { orientation: 'column', \
                name: Group { orientation: 'row', \
                    s: StaticText { text:'Name:' }, \
                    e: EditText { preferredSize: [200, 20] } \
                } \
            }, \
            workInfo: Group { orientation: 'column', \
                name: Group { orientation: 'row', \
                    s: StaticText { text:'Company name:' }, \
                    e: EditText { preferredSize: [200, 20] } \
                } \
                }, \
            }, \
        buttons: Group { orientation: 'row', alignment:
'right', \
            okBtn: Button { text:'OK',
properties:{name:'ok'} }, \
            cancelBtn: Button { text:'Cancel',
properties:{name:'cancel'} } \
        } \
    }";
win = new Window (res);
win.whichInfo.onChange = function () {
    if (this.selection != null) {
        for (var g = 0; g < this.items.length; g++)
            this.items[g].group.visible = false;
                //hide all other groups
```

```
                  this.selection.group.visible = true;//show this
group
        }
    }
}
var item = win.whichInfo.add ('item', 'Personal Info');
item.group = win.allGroups.info;
item = win.whichInfo.add ('item', 'Work Info');
item.group = win.allGroups.workInfo;
win.whichInfo.selection = win.whichInfo.items[0];
win.center();
win.show();
```

Custom layout manager example

This script creates a dialog almost identical to the one in the previous example, except that it defines a layout-manager subclass, and assigns an instance of this class as the `layout` property for the last `Group` in the dialog. (The example also demonstrates the technique for defining a reusable class in JavaScript.)

This script-defined layout manager positions elements in its container in a stair-step fashion, so that the buttons are staggered rather than in a straight line.

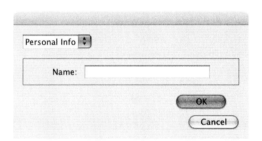

```
/* Define a custom layout manager that arranges the children
** of 'container' in a stair-step fashion.*/

function StairStepButtonLayout (container) {
this.initSelf(container); }

// Define its 'method' functions
function SSBL_initSelf (container) { this.container =
container; }

function SSBL_layout() {
    var top = 0, left = 0;
    var width;
    var vspacing = 10, hspacing = 20;
```

```
      for (i = 0; i < this.container.children.length; i++) {
         var child = this.container.children[i];
         if (typeof child.layout != "undefined")
            // If child is a container, call its layout method
            child.layout.layout();
         child.size = child.preferredSize;
         child.location = [left, top];
         width = left + child.size.width;
         top += child.size.height + vspacing;
         left += hspacing;
      }
      this.container.preferredSize = [width, top - vspacing];
}

// Attach methods to Object's prototype
StairStepButtonLayout.prototype.initSelf = SSBL_initSelf;
StairStepButtonLayout.prototype.layout = SSBL_layout;

// Define a string containing the resource specification for
the controls
res =
 "dialog { \
   whichInfo: DropDownList { alignment:'left' }, \
   allGroups: Panel { orientation:'stack', \
      info: Group { orientation: 'column', \
         name: Group { orientation: 'row', \
            s: StaticText { text:'Name:' }, \
            e: EditText { preferredSize: [200, 20] } \
         } \
      }, \
      workInfo: Group { orientation: 'column', \
         name: Group { orientation: 'row', \
            s: StaticText { text:'Company name:' }, \
            e: EditText { preferredSize: [200, 20] } \
         } \
      }, \
   }, \
   buttons: Group { orientation: 'row', alignment: 'right', \
      okBtn: Button { text:'OK', properties:{name:'ok'} }, \
      cancelBtn: Button { text:'Cancel',
properties:{name:'cancel'} } \
   } \
 }",
// Create window using resource spec
win = new Window (res);
// Create list items, select first one
win.whichInfo.onChange = function () {
   if (this.selection != null) {
```

```
                for (var g = 0; g < this.items.length; g++)
                    this.items[g].group.visible = false;
                this.selection.group.visible = true;
            }
        }
    }
    var item = win.whichInfo.add ('item', 'Personal Info');
    item.group = win.allGroups.info;
    item = win.whichInfo.add ('item', 'Work Info');
    item.group = win.allGroups.workInfo;
    win.whichInfo.selection = win.whichInfo.items[0];

    // Override the default layout manager for the 'buttons'
    group
    // with custom layout manager
    win.buttons.layout = new
    StairStepButtonLayout(win.buttons);

    win.center();
    win.show();
```

The AutoLayoutManager algorithm

When a script creates a `window` object and its elements and shows it the first time, the visible UI-platform window and controls are created. At this point, if no explicit placement of controls was specified by the script, all the controls are located at [0, 0] within their containers, and have default dimensions. Before the window is made visible, the layout manager's `layout` method is called to assign locations and sizes for all the elements and their containers.

The default `AutoLayoutManager`'s `layout` method performs these steps when invoked during the initial call to a `window` object's `show` method.

➤ **For example:**

1. Read the `bounds` property for the managed container; if undefined, proceed with auto layout. If defined, assume that the script has explicitly placed the elements in this container, and cancel the layout operation (if both the `location` and `size` property have been set, this is equivalent to setting the `bounds` property, and layout does not proceed).

2. Determine the container's margins and inter-element spacing from its `margins` and `spacing` properties, and the orientation and alignment of its child elements from the container's `orientation` and `alignChildren` properties. If any of these properties are undefined, use default settings obtained from platform and UI framework-specific default values.

---

3. Enumerate the child elements, and for each child:
   - If the child is a container, call its layout manager (that is, execute this entire algorithm again for the container).
   - Read its `alignment` property; if defined, override the default alignment established by the parent container with its `alignChildren` property.
   - Read its `size` property: if defined, use it to determine the child's dimensions. If undefined, read its `preferredSize` property to get the child's dimensions. Ignore the child's `location` property.

   All the per-child information is collected for later use.

4. Based on the orientation, calculate the trial location of each child in the row or column, using inter-element spacing and the container's margins.

5. Determine the column, row, or stack dimensions, based on the dimensions of the children.

6. Using the desired alignment for each child element, adjust its trial location relative to the edges of its container. For stack orientation, center each child horizontally and vertically in its container.

7. Set the `bounds` property for each child element.

8. Set the container's `preferredSize` property, based on the margins and dimensions of the row or column of child elements.

Automatic layout restrictions

The following restrictions apply to the automatic layout mechanism:

- The default layout manager does not attempt to lay out a container that has a defined `bounds` property. The script programmer can override this behavior by defining a custom layout manager for the container.

- The layout mechanism does not track changes to element sizes after the initial layout has occurred. The script can initiate another layout by calling the layout manager's `layout` method, and can force the manager to recalculate the sizes of all child containers by passing the optional argument as `true`.

- The layout mechanism does not support re-layout if a dialog window is resized.

Example scripts

These examples demonstrate two ways of building and populating a ScriptUI dialog. The first creates each control with a separate `add` method, while the second defines a resource string that creates the control hierarchy.

The two examples create the same dialog, which collects values from the user. When the Alert Box Builder dialog is dismissed, the script builds a resource string from the collected values, and saves it to a file. That resource string can later be used to create and display the user-configured alert box.

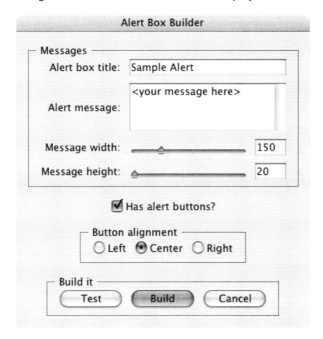

Alert box builder

This variation builds the dialog using the window and panel `add` methods to create each control.

```
//------------- Functions -------------//
/* This function creates the builder dialog
** using the add method
** An alternative that uses a resource specification
** is shown in the following section */

function createBuilderDialog() {
   // Create an empty dialog window near
   // the upper left of the screen
```

```
var dlg = new Window('dialog', 'Alert Box Builder');
dlg.frameLocation = [100, 100];
// Add a panel to hold title and 'message text' strings
dlg.msgPnl = dlg.add('panel', undefined, 'Messages');
dlg.msgPnl.alignChildren = "right";
dlg.msgPnl.title = dlg.msgPnl.add('group');
dlg.msgPnl.msg = dlg.msgPnl.add('group');
dlg.msgPnl.msgWidth = dlg.msgPnl.add('group');
dlg.msgPnl.msgHeight = dlg.msgPnl.add('group');
with (dlg.msgPnl) {
    title.st = title.add('statictext', undefined,
       'Alert box title:');
    title.et = title.add('edittext', undefined,
       'Sample Alert');
    title.et.preferredSize = [200,20];
    msg.st = msg.add('statictext', undefined,
       'Alert message:');
    msg.et = msg.add('edittext', undefined,
       '<your message here>',
       {multiline:true});
    msg.et.preferredSize = [200,60];
    msgWidth.st = msgWidth.add('statictext', undefined,
       'Message width:');
    msgWidth.sl = msgWidth.add('slider', undefined,
       150, 100, 300);
    msgWidth.sl.preferredSize = [150, 20];
    msgWidth.et = msgWidth.add('edittext');
    msgWidth.et.preferredSize = [40, 20];
    msgHeight.st = msgHeight.add('statictext', undefined,
       'Message height:');
    msgHeight.sl = msgHeight.add('slider', undefined,
       20, 20, 300);
    msgHeight.sl.preferredSize = [150, 20];
    msgHeight.et = msgHeight.add('edittext');
    msgHeight.et.preferredSize = [40, 20];
}
// Add a checkbox to control the presence of buttons
// to dismiss the alert box
dlg.hasBtnsCb = dlg.add('checkbox', undefined,
    'Has alert buttons?');
// Add panel to determine alignment of buttons
// on the alert box
dlg.alertBtnsPnl = dlg.add('panel', undefined,
    'Button alignment');
dlg.alertBtnsPnl.orientation = "row";
dlg.alertBtnsPnl.alignLeftRb =
    dlg.alertBtnsPnl.add('radiobutton', undefined,
       'Left');
```

```
   dlg.alertBtnsPnl.alignCenterRb =
      dlg.alertBtnsPnl.add('radiobutton', undefined,
'Center');
   dlg.alertBtnsPnl.alignRightRb =
      dlg.alertBtnsPnl.add('radiobutton', undefined,
'Right');
   // Add a panel with buttons to test parameters and
   // create the alert box specification
   dlg.btnPnl = dlg.add('panel', undefined, 'Build it');
   dlg.btnPnl.orientation = "row";
   dlg.btnPnl.testBtn = dlg.btnPnl.add('button', undefined,
'Test');
   dlg.btnPnl.buildBtn = dlg.btnPnl.add('button',
undefined, 'Build',
      {name:'ok'});
   dlg.btnPnl.cancelBtn =
      dlg.btnPnl.add('button', undefined, 'Cancel',
{name:'cancel'});

   return dlg;
} // createBuilderDialog

/* This function initializes the values in the controls
** of the builder dialog */

function initializeBuilder(builder) {
   // Set up initial control states
   with (builder) {
      hasBtnsCb.value = true;
      alertBtnsPnl.alignCenterRb.value = true;
      with (msgPnl) {
         msgWidth.et.text = msgWidth.sl.value;
         msgHeight.et.text = msgHeight.sl.value;
      }
   }
   // Attach event callback functions to controls
   /* The 'has buttons' checkbox enables or disables
      the panel that determines the
      justification of the 'alert' button group */
   builder.hasBtnsCb.onClick =
      function () { this.parent.alertBtnsPnl.enabled =
this.value; };
   /* The edittext fields and scrollbars in
      msgPnl are connected */
   with (builder.msgPnl) {
      msgWidth.et.onChange =
         function () {
            this.parent.parent.msgWidth.sl.value =
               this.text; };
```

```
        msgWidth.sl.onChanging =
            function () { this.parent.parent.msgWidth.et.text =
    this.value; };
        msgHeight.et.onChange =
            function () { this.parent.parent.msgHeight.sl.value
    = this.text; };
        msgHeight.sl.onChanging =
            function () { this.parent.parent.msgHeight.et.text
    = this.value; };
        }
    with (builder.btnPnl) {
        // The Test button creates a trial Alert box from
        // the current specifications
        testBtn.onClick =
            function () {
                Window.alert('Type Enter or Esc to dismiss the
    test Alert box');

    createTestDialog(createResource(this.parent.parent));
            };
        // The Build and Cancel buttons close this dialog
        buildBtn.onClick =
            function () { this.parent.parent.close(1); };
        cancelBtn.onClick =
            function () { this.parent.parent.close(2); };
        };
} // initializeBuilder

/* This function invokes the dialog an returns its result */
function runBuilder(builder) {
    return builder.show();
}
/* This function creates and returns a string
** containing a dialog
** resource specification that will create
** an Alert dialog using
** the parameters the user entered in the builder dialog. */
function createResource(builder) {
    // Define the initial part of the resource spec with
dialog parameters
    var res = "dialog { " +
        stringProperty("text", builder.msgPnl.title.et.text)

        "\n";
    // Define the alert message statictext element,
    // sizing it as user specified
    var textWidth = Number(builder.msgPnl.msgWidth.et.text);
    var textHeight =
        Number(builder.msgPnl.msgHeight.et.text);
```

```
            res += "  msg: StaticText { " +
               stringProperty("text", builder.msgPnl.msg.et.text) +
               " preferredSize: [" + textWidth + ", " +
                           textHeight + "],\n" +
               "    justify:'center', properties:{multiline:true} }";
            // Define buttons if desired
            var hasButtons = builder.hasBtnsCb.value;
            if (hasButtons) {
               var groupAlign = "center";
               // Align buttons as specified
               if (builder.alertBtnsPnl.alignLeftRb.value)
                  groupAlign = "left";
               else if (builder.alertBtnsPnl.alignRightRb.value)
                  groupAlign = "right";
               res += ",\n" +
                  " btnGroup: Group {\n" +
                  stringProperty("    alignment", groupAlign) +
                  "\n" +
                  "    okBtn: Button { " +
                  stringProperty("text", "OK") +"},\n";
               res += "    cancelBtn: Button { " +
                  stringProperty("text", "Cancel") +"}" +
                  "  }";
            }
            // done
            res += "\n}";
            return res;
         }
         function stringProperty(pname, pval) {
            return pname + ":'" + pval + "', ";
         }
         function createTestDialog(resource) {
            var target = new Window (resource);
            target.center();
            return target.show();
         }
         //------------ Main script ------------//
         var builder = createBuilderDialog();
         //for an alternative, see below
         initializeBuilder(builder);
         if (runBuilder(builder) == 1) {
            // Create the Alert dialog resource specification string
            var resSpec = createResource(builder);
            // Write the resource spec string to
            // a file w/platform file-open dialog
            var fname =
               File.openDialog('Save resource specification');
            var f = File(fname);
            if (f.open('w')) {
```

```
      var ok = f.write(resSpec);
      if (ok)
          ok = f.close();
      if (! ok)
          Window.alert("Error creating " + fname + ": " +
f.error);
    }
}
```

Resource specification example

This example provides an alternative method of building the same initial
Alert box builder (page 257) dialog, using a resource specification instead of
explicit calls to the add method of a container element. To use this alternate
version, add this code to the beginning of the previous example in place of
the createBuilderDialog function. In the main script, replace the line:

```
var builder = createBuilderDialog();
```

with this line:

```
var builder = createBuilderDialogFromResource();
```

The new code follows:

```
var alertBuilderResource =
    "dialog { \
      text: 'Alert Box Builder', frameLocation:[100,100], \
      msgPnl: Panel { orientation:'column', \
        alignChildren:'right', \
        text: 'Messages', \
        title: Group { \
          st: StaticText { text:'Alert box title:' }, \
          et: EditText { text:'Sample Alert', \
              preferredSize:[200, 20] } \
        }, \
        msg: Group { \
          st: StaticText { text:'Alert message:' }, \
          et: EditText { text:'<your message here>', \
              preferredSize:[200, 60],\
              properties:{multiline:true} } \
        }, \
        msgWidth: Group { alignChildren:'center', \
          st: StaticText { text:'Message width:' }, \
          sl: Slider { minvalue:100, maxvalue:300,\
              value:150, \
              preferredSize:[150, 20] }, \
          et: EditText { preferredSize:[40, 20] } \
        }, \
        msgHeight: Group { alignChildren:'center', \
          st: StaticText { text:'Message height:' }, \
          sl: Slider { minvalue:20, maxvalue:300, \
```

```
                    preferredSize:[150, 20] }, \
            et: EditText { preferredSize:[40, 20] } \
         } \
      }, \
      hasBtnsCb: Checkbox { text:'Has alert buttons?', \
                alignment:'center' }, \
      alertBtnsPnl: Panel { orientation:'row', \
         text: 'Button alignment', \
         alignLeftRb: RadioButton { text:'Left' }, \
         alignCenterRb: RadioButton { text:'Center' }, \
         alignRightRb: RadioButton { text:'Right' } \
      }, \
      btnPnl: Panel { orientation:'row', \
         text: 'Build it', \
         testBtn: Button { text:'Test' }, \
         buildBtn: Button { text:'Build', \
            properties:{name:'ok'} }, \
         cancelBtn: Button { text:'Cancel', \
            properties:{name:'cancel'} } \
      } \
   }";

// This function creates the builder dialog
// from the resource string
function createBuilderDialogFromResource() {
   var builder = new Window(alertBuilderResource);
   return builder;
} // createBuilderDialogFromResource
```

Localization in ScriptUI objects

For portions of your user interface that are displayed on the screen, you may want to localize the displayed text. You can localize the display strings in any ScriptUI object (including MenuElement Objects, page 292) simply and efficiently, using the Global localize function (page 372). This function takes as its argument a *localization object* containing the localized versions of a string.

For complete details of this ExtendScript feature, see "Localizing ExtendScript Strings" on page 369.

A localization object is a JavaScript object literal whose property names are locale names, and whose property values are the localized text strings. The locale name is an identifier as specified in the ISO 3166 standard. In this example, a btnText object contains localized text strings for several locales. This object supplies the text for a Button to be added to a window w:

```
btnText = { en: "Yes", de: "Ja", fr: "Oui" };
b1 = w.add ("button", undefined, localize (btnText));
```

The localize function extracts the proper string for the current locale. It matches the current locale and platform to one of the object's properties and returns the associated string. On a German system, for example, the property de provides the string "Ja".

When your script uses localization to provide language-appropriate strings for UI elements, it should also take advantage of the Automatic layout (page 243) feature. The layout manager can determine the best size for each UI element based on its localized text value, automatically adjusting the layout of your script-defined dialogs to allow for the varying widths of strings for different languages.

Variable values in localized strings

The localize function allows you to include variables in the string values. Each variable is replaced with the result of evaluating an additional argument. For example:

```
today = {
   en: "Today is %1/%2.",
   de: "Heute ist der %2.%1."
   };
d = new Date();
Window.alert (localize (today, d.getMonth()+1,
d.getDate()));
```

Enabling automatic localization

If you do not need variable replacement, you can use automatic localization. To turn on automatic localization, set the global value:

```
$.localization=true
```

When it is enabled, you can specify a localization object directly as the value of any property that takes a localizable string, without using the `localize` function. For example:

```
btnText = { en: "Yes", de: "Ja", fr: "Oui" };
b1 = w.add ("button", undefined, btnText);
```

The `localize` function always performs its translation, regardless of the setting of the `$.localize` variable. For example:

```
//Only works if the $.localize=true
b1 = w.add ("button", undefined, btnText);
//Always works, regardless of $.localize value
b1 = w.add ("button", undefined, localize (btnText));
```

If you need to include variables in the localized strings, use the `localize` function.

8 | ScriptUI Object Reference

Overview

ScriptUI is a component that works with the ExtendScript JavaScript interpreter to provide JavaScript programs with the ability to create and interact with user interface elements. It provides an object model for windows and UI control elements within an Adobe Creative Suite 2 application.

For an overview of the ScriptUI object model and a description of usage, see Chapter 7, "Using ScriptUI."

This chapter provides the details of the ScriptUI classes and objects with their properties, methods, and creation parameters.

- Window Class
- Window object
- Control objects
- Size and Location Objects
- LayoutManager object
- MenuElement Object

Window Class

The `Window` class defines these static properties and functions which are available globally through reference to the class. Window instances created with `new Window()` do not have these properties and functions.

Window class properties

`coreVersion`	String	The internal core version number of the ScriptUI components. Read only.
`version`	String	The main version number of the ScriptUI components. Read only.

Window class functions

`alert`
`Window.alert`
  `(message[, title, errorIcon])`
	Displays the localizable *message* string in a user alert box that provides an **OK** button. For details, see the ExtendScript alert (page 373) function.
	
	The alert dialog is not intended for lengthy messages. When the string argument is too long, the alert dialog truncates it.

`confirm`
`Window.confirm`
  `(message[,noAsDflt ,title ])`
	Displays the localizable *message* string in a self-sizing modal dialog box with **Yes** and **No** buttons. Returns `true` if the user clicks **Yes**, `false` if the user clicks **No**.
	
	For details, see the ExtendScript confirm (page 374) function.
	
	The confirmation dialog can show longer messages than the alert and prompt dialogs, but if this string is too long, the dialog truncates it.

`find`
`Window.find (resourceName)`
`Window.find (type, title)`
	Finds and returns an existing window object, which can be a window already created by a script, or a windows created by the application (if the application supports this case).
	    resourceName: A named resource that identifies a window that the application exposes to JavaScript. (Not supported in all ScriptUI implementations.)
	    type: The window creation type, `dialog`, `palette`, or `window`. Used to distinguish between windows with the same title. If the type is unimportant, pass `null` or an empty string.
	    title: The title of the window to find.
	If it finds an existing window, the method returns the corresponding JavaScript `window` object. If not, it returns `null`.

getResourceText Window.getResourceText (*textResource*)	Finds and returns a text string representation of the *textResource* from the host application's resource data. If no string resource matches the *textResource* name, the name is treated as literal text.
prompt Window.prompt (*message, preset*[, *title*])	Displays a modal dialog that returns the user's text input. • When the user clicks **OK** to dismiss the dialog, the method returns the text the user entered. • When the user clicks the **Cancel** button, the method returns null. For details, see the ExtendScript prompt (page 375) function.

Window object

Window object constructor

Creates and returns a new window object, or null if window creation failed. To create a new Window object:

```
new Window (type [, title, bounds,
    {creation_properties}]);
```

type	The window type. The value is: dialog: Creates a modal dialog. palette: Creates a modeless dialog, also called a floating palette. window: Creates a simple window that can be used as a main window for an application
title	Optional. The window title. A localizable string.

bounds	Optional. The window's position and size.
`creation_properties`	Optional. An object that can contain any of these properties: `resizeable`: When `true`, the window can be resized by the user. Default is `false`. `closeButton`: When `true`, the title bar includes a button to close the window, if the platform and window type allow it. When `false`, it does not. Default is `true`. Not used for dialogs. `maximizeButton`: When `true`, the title bar includes a button to expand the window to its maximum size (typically, the entire screen), if the platform and window type allow it. When `false`, it does not. Default is `false` for type `palette`, `true` for type `window`. Not used for dialogs. `minimizeButton`: When `true`, the title bar includes a button to minimize or iconify the window, if the platform and window type allow it. When `false`, it does not. Default is `false` for type `palette`, `true` for type `window`. Main windows cannot have a minimize button in Mac OS. Not used for dialogs. `independent`: When `true`, a window of type `window` is independent of other application windows, and can be hidden behind them in Windows. In Mac OS, has no effect. Default is `false`.

Window object properties

Window elements contain the following properties, in addition to those common to all ScriptUI elements:

`defaultElement`	Object	For a window of type `dialog`, the control to notify when a user types the ENTER key. By default, looks for a `button` whose name or text is `"ok"` (case disregarded).
`cancelElement`	Object	For a window of type `dialog`, the control to notify when a user types the ESC key in Windows®, or the CMD. combination in Mac OS®. By default, looks for a `button` whose name or text is `"cancel"` (case disregarded).
`frameBounds`	Bounds	A Bounds (page 290) object for the boundaries of the Window's frame in screen coordinates. The frame consists of the title bar and borders that enclose the content region of a window, depending on the windowing system. Read only.
`frameLocation`	Point	A Point (page 290) object for the location of the top left corner of the Window's frame. The same as `[frameBounds.x, frameBounds.y]`. Set this value to move the window frame to the specified location on the screen. The `frameBounds` value changes accordingly.
`frameSize`	Dimension	A Dimension (page 290) object for the size and location of the Window's frame in screen coordinates. Read only.

Container properties

The following table shows properties that are available on `window` objects and container objects (controls of type `panel` and `group`).

`alignChildren`	String	Tells the layout manager how unlike-sized children of a container should be aligned within a column or row. Order of creation determines which children are at the top of a column or the left of a row; the earlier a child is created, the closer it is to the top or left of its column or row.
		If defined, `alignment` for a child element overrides the `alignChildren` setting for the parent container.
		Allowed values depend on the `orientation` value. For `orientation=row`:

		<pre> top
		  bottom
		  center (default)
		  fill</pre>

		For `orientation=column`:

		<pre> left
		  right
		  center (default)
		  fill</pre>

		For `orientation=stack`:

		<pre> top
		  bottom
		  left
		  right
		  center (default)
		  fill</pre>

		Values are not case sensitive.
`children`	Array of Object	The collection of UI elements that have been added to this container (`window`, `panel`, `group`). An array indexed by number or by a string containing an element's `name`. The `length` property of this array is the number of child elements for container elements, and is zero for controls. Read only.
`layout`	LayoutManager	A LayoutManager object (page 291) for a container (`window`, `panel`, `group`). The first time a container object is made visible, ScriptUI invokes this layout manager by calling its `layout` function. Default is an instance of the `LayoutManager` class that is automatically created when the container element is created.
`margins`	Margins	A Margins (page 290) object describing the number of pixels between the edges of this container and the outermost child elements. You can specify different margins for each edge of the container. The default value is based on the type of container, and is chosen to match the standard Adobe UI guidelines.

orientation	String	How elements are organized within this container. Interpreted by the layout manager for the container. The default LayoutManager object (page 291) accepts the (case-insensitive) values:
		`row`
		`column`
		`stack`
		The default orientation depends on the type of container. For `Window` and `Panel`, the default is `column`, and for `Group` the default is `row`.
		The allowed values for the container's `alignChildren` and its children's `alignment` properties depend on the orientation.

spacing	Number	The number of pixels separating one child element from its adjacent sibling element. Because each container holds only a single row or column of children, only a single spacing value is needed for a container. The default value is based on the type of container, and is chosen to match standard Adobe UI guidelines.

Window object functions

These functions are defined for `window` objects.

add
`(type [, bounds, text,`
`{ creation_props> } ]);`
	Creates and returns a new control or container object and adds it to the children of this window. Returns `null` if unable to create the object.

type	The control type. See "Control types and creation parameters" on page 275.
bounds	Optional. A bounds specification that describes the size and position of the new control or container, relative to its parent. See Bounds (page 290) object for specification formats. If supplied, this value creates a new Bounds object which is assigned to the new object's `bounds` property.
text	Optional. String. Initial text to be displayed in the control as the title, label, or contents, depending on the control type. If supplied, this value is assigned to the new object's `text` property.
creation_props	Optional. Object. The properties of this object specify creation parameters, which are specific to each object type. See "Control types and creation parameters" on page 275.

center
`windowObj.center`
`([window])`
	Centers this window on the screen, or with respect to another specified window.

window	Optional. A Window object (page 269).

close
`windowObj.close`
`([result])`
	Closes this window. If an onClose (page 274) callback is defined for the window, calls that function before closing the window.

`result`	Optional. A number to be returned from the `show` method that invoked this window as a modal dialog.
hide `windowObj.hide()`	Hides this window. When a window is hidden, its children are also hidden, but when it is shown again, the children retain their own visibility states. For a modal dialog, closes the dialog and sets its result to 0.
notify `windowObj.notify([event])`	Sends a notification message, simulating the specified user interaction event. For example, to simulate a dialog being moved by a user: `    myDlg.notify("onMove")`

`event`	Optional. The name of the window event handler to call. One of:
	`        onClose`
	`        onMove`
	`        onMoving`
	`        onResize`
	`        onResizing`
	`        onShow`

remove
`windowObj.remove(index)`
`windowObj.remove(text)`
`windowObj.remove(child)`
	Removes the specified child control from this window's `children` array. No error results if the child does not exist. Returns `undefined`.

`index`
`text`
`child`
	The child control to remove, specified by 0-based index, `text` value, or as a `control` object.

show `windowObj.show()`	Shows this window, container, or control. If an onShow (page 274) callback is defined for a window, calls that function before showing the window. When a window or container is hidden, its children are also hidden, but when it is shown again, the children retain their own visibility states. For a modal dialog, opens the dialog and does not return until the dialog is dismissed. If it is dismissed via the close (page 273) method, this method returns any `result` value passed to that method. Otherwise, returns 0.

Window event-handling callbacks

The following callback functions can be defined to respond to events in windows. To respond to an event, define a function with the corresponding name in the `window` object.

Callback	Description
onClose	Called when a request is made to close the window, either by an explicit call to the close (page 273) function or by a user action (clicking the OS-specific close icon in the title bar). The function is called before the window actually closes; it can return `false` to cancel the close operation.
onMove	Called when the window has been moved.
onMoving	Called while a window in being moved, each time the position changes. A handler can monitor the move operation.
onResize	Called when the window has been resized.
onResizing	Called while a window is being resized, each time the height or width changes. A handler can monitor the resize operation.
onShow	Called when a request is made to open the window using the show (page 273) method, before the window is made visible, but after automatic layout is complete. A handler can modify the results of the automatic layout.

Control objects

Control object constructors

Use the `add` method to create new containers and controls. The `add` method is available on `window` and container (`panel` and `group`) objects. (See also "add" on page 287 for dropdownlist and listbox controls.)

add
 	
  `(type [, bounds, text,`
    `{ creation_props> }`
`]);`
	Creates and returns a new control or container object and adds it to the children of this window or container. Returns `null` if unable to create the object.

`type`	The control type. See "Control types and creation parameters" on page 275.
`bounds`	Optional. A bounds specification that describes the size and position of the new control or container, relative to its parent. See Bounds (page 290) object for specification formats. If supplied, this value creates a new Bounds object which is assigned to the new object's `bounds` property.
`text`	Optional. String. Initial text to be displayed in the control as the title, label, or contents, depending on the control type. If supplied, this value is assigned to the new object's `text` property.
`creation_props`	Optional. Object. The properties of this object specify creation parameters, which are specific to each object type. See "Control types and creation parameters" on page 275.

Control types and creation parameters

The following type names can be used in string literals as the `type` specifier for the `add` method, available on `window` and container (`panel` and `group`) objects. The class names can used in resource specifications to define controls within a window or panel.

Type name	Class name	Description

button	Button	A pushbutton containing a text string. Calls the onClick (page 288) callback if the control is clicked or if its notify (page 287) method is called.
		
		To add to a window w:
		
		`w.add ("button" [, bounds, text ]);`
		    bounds: Optional. The control's position and size.
		    text: Optional. The text displayed in the control.

checkbox	Checkbox	A dual-state control showing a box with a checkmark when `value=true`, empty when `value=false`. Calls the onClick (page 288) callback if the control is clicked or if its notify (page 287) method is called.
		
		To add to a window w:
		
		`w.add ("checkbox" [, bounds, text ]);`
		    bounds: Optional. The control's position and size.
		    text: Optional. The text displayed in the control.

dropdownlist	DropDownList	A drop-down list with zero or more items. Calls the onChange (page 288) callback if the item selection is changed or if its notify (page 287) method is called.
		
		To add to a window w:
		
		`w.add ("dropdown list", bounds [, items]`
		`       [, {creation_properties}]);`
		    bounds: The control's position and size.
		    items: Optional. Supply this argument or the
		        creation_properties argument, not both. An array of
		        strings for the text of each list item. An `item` object is
		        created for each item. An item with the text string "-"
		        creates a separator item.
		    creation_properties: Optional. Supply this argument or
		        the *items* argument, not both. This form is most useful for
		        elements defined using Resource specifications
		        (page 239). An object that contains the following property:
		    items: An array of strings for the text of each list item. An
		        `item` object is created for each item. An item with the text
		        string "-" creates a separator item.

Type name	Class name	Description

edittext	EditText	An edit text field that the user can change. Calls the onChange (page 288) callback if the text is changed and the user types ENTER or the control loses focus, or if its notify (page 287) method is called. Calls the onChanging (page 288) callback when any change is made to the text. The `textselection` property contains currently selected text.
		
		To add to a window `w`:
		
		`w.add ("edittext" [, bounds, text, {creation_properties}]);`
		    bounds: Optional. The control's position and size.
		    text: Optional. The text displayed in the control.
		    creation_properties: Optional. An object that contains any of the following properties:
		        multiline: When `false` (the default), the control accepts a single line of text. When `true`, the control accepts multiple lines, in which case the text wraps within the width of the control.
		        readonly: When `false` (the default), the control accepts text input. When `true`, the control does not accept input but only displays the contents of the `text` property.
		        noecho: When `false` (the default), the control displays input text. When `true`, the control does not display input text (used for password input fields).
		        enterKeySignalsOnChange: When `false` (the default), the control signals an onChange (page 288) event when the editable text is changed and the control loses the keyboard focus (that is, the user tabs to another control, clicks outside the control, or types ENTER). When `true`, the control only signals an `onChange` event when the editable text is changed and the user types ENTER; other changes to the keyboard focus do not signal the event.

group	Group	A container for other controls. Containers have additional properties that control the children; see "Container properties" on page 271. Hiding a group hides all its children. Making it visible makes visible those children that are not individually hidden. To add to a window `w`: `w.add ("group" [, bounds]);` *bounds*: Optional. The element's position and size.

Type name	Class name	Description

iconbutton	IconButton	A pushbutton containing an icon. Calls the onClick (page 288) callback if the control is clicked or if its notify (page 287) method is called.
		
		To add to a window w:
		
		`w.add ("iconbutton" [, bounds, icon,`
		`        {creation_properties}]);`
		   bounds: Optional. The control's position and size.
		   icon: Optional. The named resource for the icon or family of icons displayed in the button control, or a pathname or File object (page 311) for an image file. Images must be in PNG format.
		   creation_properties: Optional. An object that contains the following property:
		     style: A string for the visual style, one of:
		   button: Has a visible border with a raised or 3D appearance.
		   toolbutton: Has a flat appearance, appropriate for inclusion in a toolbar

image	Image	Displays an icon or image.
		To add to a window w:
		
		`w.add ("image" [, bounds, icon]);`
		   bounds: Optional. The control's position and size.
		   icon: Optional. The named resource for the icon or family of icons displayed in the image control, or a pathname or File object (page 311) for an image file. Images must be in PNG format.

item	ListItem	A choice item in a list box or drop-down list. The objects are created when items are specified on creation of the parent list object, or afterward using the list control's add (page 287) method.
		
		• Items in a drop-down list can be of type separator, in which case they cannot be selected, and are shown as a horizontal line.
		
		Item objects have these properties which are not found in other controls:
		   index (page 284)
		   selected (page 285)

Type name	Class name	Description
listbox	ListBox	A list box with zero or more items. Calls the onChange (page 288) callback if the item selection is changed or if its notify (page 287) method is called. To add to a window w: `w.add ("listbox", bounds [, items, {creation_properties}]);` *bounds*: Optional. The control's position and size. *items*: Optional. An array of strings for the text of each list item. An `item` object is created for each item. Supply this argument, or the `items` property in *creation_properties*, not both. *creation_properties*: Optional. An object that contains any of the following properties: **multiselect**: When `false` (the default), only one item can be selected. When `true`, multiple items can be selected. **items**: An array of strings for the text of each list item. An `item` object is created for each item. An item with the text string "–" creates a separator item. Supply this property, or the `items` argument, not both. This form is most useful for elements defined using Resource specifications (page 239).
panel	Panel	A container for other types of controls, with an optional frame. Containers have additional properties that control the children; see "Container properties" on page 271. Hiding a panel hides all its children. Making it visible makes visible those children that are not individually hidden. To add to a window w: `w.add ("panel" [, bounds, text, {creation_properties} ]);` *bounds*: Optional. The element's position and size. A panel whose width is 0 appears as a vertical line. A panel whose height is 0 appears as a horizontal line. *text*: Optional. The text displayed in the border of the panel. *creation_properties*: Optional. An object that contains the following property: **borderStyle**: A string that specifies the appearance of the border drawn around the panel. One of `black`, `etched`, `gray`, `raised`, `sunken`. Default is `etched`.

Type name	Class name	Description

progressbar	Progressbar	A horizontal rectangle that shows progress of an operation. All progressbar controls have a horizontal orientation. The value property contains the current position of the progress indicator; the default is 0. There is a minvalue property, but it is always 0; attempts to set it to a different value are silently ignored.
		
		To add to a window w:
		
		w.add ("progressbar" [, *bounds*, *value*, *maxvalue*]);
		    bounds: Optional. The control's position and size.
		    value: Optional. The initial position of the progress indicator. Default is 0.
		    maxvalue: Optional. The maximum value that the value property can be set to. Default is 100.

radiobutton	RadioButton	A dual-state control, grouped with other radiobuttons, of which only one can be in the selected state. Shows the selected state when value=true, empty when value=false. Calls the onClick (page 288) callback if the control is clicked or if its notify (page 287) method is called.
		
		All radiobuttons in a group must be created sequentially, with no intervening creation of other element types. Only one radiobutton in a group can be set at a time; setting a different radiobutton unsets the original one.
		
		To add to a window w:
		
		w.add ("radiobutton" [, *bounds*, *text*]);
		    bounds: Optional. The control's position and size.
		    text: Optional. The text displayed in the control.

Type name	Class name	Description

scrollbar	Scrollbar	A scrollbar with a draggable scroll indicator and stepper buttons to move the indicator. The `scrollbar` control has a horizontal orientation if the `width` is greater than the `height` at creation time, or vertical if its `height` is greater than its `width`.
		
		Calls the onChange (page 288) callback after the position of the indicator is changed or if its notify (page 287) method is called. Calls the onChanging (page 288) callback repeatedly while the user is moving the indicator.
		
		The `value` property contains the current position of the scrollbar's indicator within the scrolling area, within the range of `minvalue` and `maxvalue`.
		
		The `stepdelta` property determines the scrolling unit for the up or down arrow; default is 1.
		
		The `jumpdelta` property determines the scrolling unit for a jump (as when the bar is clicked outside the indicator or arrows); default is 20% of the range between `minvalue` and `maxvalue`.
		
		To add to a window `w`:
		<pre>w.add ("scrollbar" [, bounds, value, minvalue, maxvalue]);</pre> *bounds*: Optional. The control's position and size.
		    value: Optional. The initial position of the scroll indicator. Default is 0.
		    minvalue: Optional. The minimum value that the `value` property can be set to. Default is 0. Together with `maxvalue`, defines the scrolling range.
		    maxvalue: Optional. The maximum value that the `value` property can be set to. Default is 100. Together with `minvalue`, defines the scrolling range.

Type name	Class name	Description

slider	Slider	A slider with a moveable position indicator. All `slider` controls have a horizontal orientation. Calls the onChange (page 288) callback after the position of the indicator is changed or if its notify (page 287) method is called. Calls the onChanging (page 288) callback repeatedly while the user is moving the indicator.
		
		 The `value` property contains the current position of the indicator within the range of `minvalue` and `maxvalue`.
		
		 To add to a window w:
		
		 `w.add ("slider" [, bounds, value, minvalue, maxvalue]);`
		     bounds: Optional. The control's position and size.
		     value: Optional. The initial position of the indicator. Default is 0.
		     minvalue: Optional. The minimum value that the `value` property can be set to. Default is 0. Together with *maxvalue*, defines the range.
		     maxvalue: Optional. The maximum value that the `value` property can be set to. Default is 100. Together with *minvalue*, defines the range.

statictext	StaticText	A text field that the user cannot change.
		
		 To add to a window w:
		
		 `w.add ("statictext" [, bounds, text, {creation_properties}]);`
		     bounds: Optional. The control's position and size.
		     text: Optional. The text displayed in the control.
		     creation_properties: Optional. An object that contains any of the following properties:
		     multiline: When `false` (the default), the control displays a single line of text. When `true`, the control displays multiple lines, in which case the text wraps within the width of the control.
		     scrolling: When `false` (the default), the displayed text cannot be scrolled. When `true`, the displayed text can be vertically scrolled using the UP ARROW and DOWN ARROW; this case implies `multiline=true`.

Control object properties

The following table shows the properties of all ScriptUI elements. Some values apply only to controls of particular types, as indicated.

`active`	Boolean	When `true`, the object is active, `false` otherwise. Set to `true` to make a given control or dialog active. <ul><li>A modal dialog that is visible is by definition the active dialog.</li><li>An active palette is the front-most window.</li><li>An active control is the one with focus—that is, the one that accepts keystrokes, or in the case of a `Button`, be selected when the user types a Return.</li></ul>
| `alignment` | String | Applies to child elements of a container. If defined, this value overrides the `alignChildren` setting for the parent container. Allowed values depend on the `orientation` value of the parent container. For `orientation=row`:<br>```
top
bottom
center (default)
fill
```<br>For `orientation=column`:<br>```
left
right
center (default)
fill
```<br>For `orientation=stack`:<br>```
top
bottom
left
right
center (default)
fill
```<br>Values are not case sensitive. |
`bounds`	Bounds	A Bounds (page 290) object describing the boundaries of the element, in screen coordinates for `window` elements, and parent-relative coordinates for child elements. For windows, the bounds refer only to the window's content region. Setting an element's `size` or `location` changes its `bounds` property, and vice-versa.
`enabled`	Boolean	When `true`, the control is enabled, meaning that it accepts input. When `false`, control elements do not accept input, and all types of elements have a grayed-out appearance.
`helpTip`	String	A brief help message (also called a *tool tip*) that is displayed in a small floating window when the mouse cursor hovers over a UI control element. Set to an empty string or `null` to remove help text.
```

icon	String or File	The name of an icon resource or the pathname or File object (page 311) for a file that contains a platform-specific icon image in PNG format. ● For an `IconButton`, the icon appears as the content of the button. ● For a `ListItem`, the icon is displayed to the left of the text. ● For an `Image`, the icon is the entire content of the image element.
index	Number	For `ListItem` objects only. The index of this item in the `items` collection of its parent list control. Read-only.
items	Array of Object	For a list object (`listbox` or `dropdown` list), a collection of `ListItem` objects for the items in the list. Access by 0-based index. To obtain the number of items in the list, use `items.length`. Read-only.
itemSize	Dimension	For a list object (`listbox` or `dropdown` list), a Dimension (page 290) object describing the width and height in pixels of each item in the list. Used by auto-layout to determine the `preferredSize` of the list, if not otherwise specified. If not set explicitly, the size of each item is set to match the largest height and width among all items in the list
jumpdelta	Number	The amount to increment or decrement a `scrollbar` indicator's position when the user clicks ahead or behind the moveable element. Default is 20% of the range between the `maxvalue` and `minvalue` property values.

justify	String	The justification of text in static text and edit text controls. One of:
		`left (default)`
		`center`
		`right`
		Note: Justification only works if the value is set before the window containing the control is displayed for the first time.

location	Point	A Point (page 290) object describing the location of the element as an array, `[x, y]`, representing the coordinates of the upper left corner of the element. These are screen coordinates for `window` elements, and parent-relative coordinates for other elements. The `location` is defined as `[bounds.x, bounds.y]`. Setting an element's `location` changes its `bounds` property, and vice-versa. By default, `location` is `undefined`.

maxvalue	Number	The maximum value that the `value` property can have. If `maxvalue` is reset less than `value`, `value` is reset to `maxvalue`. If `maxvalue` is reset less than `minvalue`, `minvalue` is reset to `maxvalue`.
minvalue	Number	The minimum value that the `value` property can have. If `minvalue` is reset greater than `value`, `value` is reset to `minvalue`. If `minvalue` is reset greater than `maxvalue`, `maxvalue` is reset to `minvalue`.
parent	Object	The parent object of a UI object, a `window`, `panel` or `group`, or `null` for `window` objects. Read only.
preferredSize	Dimension	A Dimension (page 290) object used by layout managers to determine the best size for each element. If not explicitly set by a script, value is established by the UI framework in which ScriptUI is employed, and is based on such attributes of the element as its text, font, font size, icon size, and other UI framework-specific attributes. A script can explicitly set `preferredSize` before the layout manager is invoked in order to establish an element size other than the default.
properties	Object	An object that contains one or more creation properties of the element (properties used only when the element is created).
selected	Boolean	For `ListItem` objects only. When `true`, the item is part of the `selection` for its parent list. When `false`, the item is not selected. Set to true to select this item in a single-selection list, or to add it to the to the selection array for a multi-selection list.
selection	ListItem, Array of ListItem	For a list object (`listbox` or `dropdown` list), the currently selected `ListItem` object for a single-selection list, or an array of `ListItem` objects for current selection in a multi-selection list. Setting this value causes the selected item to be highlighted and to be scrolled into view if necessary. You can set the value using the index of an item or an array of indices, rather than object references. If set to an index value that is out of range, the operation is ignored. When set with index values, the property still returns object references. • If you set the value to an array for a single-selection list, only the first item in the array is selected. • If you set the value to a single item for a multi-selection list, that item is added to the current selection. If no items are selected, the value is `null`. Set to `null` to deselect all items.

`size`	Dimension	A Dimension (page 290) object that defines the actual dimensions of an element. Initially `undefined`, and unless explicitly set by a script, it is defined by a `LayoutManager`. A script can explicitly set size before the layout manager is invoked to establish an element size other than the `preferredSize` or the default size. Defined as `[bounds.width, bounds.height]`. Setting an element's `size` changes its `bounds` property, and vice versa.
`stepdelta`	Number	The amount by which to increment or decrement a `Scrollbar` element's position when the user clicks a stepper button.
`text`	String	The title, label, or displayed text. Ignored for certain window types. For controls, the meaning depends on the control type. Buttons use the `text` as a label, for example, while edit fields use the `text` to access the content. This is a localizable string; see "Localization in ScriptUI objects" on page 264.
`textselection`	String	The currently selected text in a control that displays text, or the empty string if there is no text selected. Setting the value replaces the current text selection and modifies the value of the `text` property. If there is no current selection, inserts the new value into the `text` string at the current insertion point. The `textselection` value is reset to an empty string after it modifies the `text` value. **Note:** Setting the `textselection` property before the `edittext` control's parent `Window` exists is an undefined operation.
`type`	String	Contains the type name of the element, as specified on creation. ● For `window` objects, one of the type names `window`, `palette`, or `dialog`. ● For controls, the type of the control, as specified in the `add` method that created it. Read only.
`value`	Boolean	For a checkbox or radiobutton, `true` if the control is in the selected or set state, `false` if it is not.
`value`	Number	For a scrollbar or slider, the current position of the indicator. If set to a value outside the range specified by `minvalue` and `maxvalue`, it is automatically reset to the closest boundary.
`visible`	Boolean	When `true`, the element is shown, when `false` it is hidden. When a container is hidden, its children are also hidden, but they retain their own visibility values, and are shown or hidden accordingly when the parent is next shown.

Control object functions

The following table shows the methods defined for each element type, and for specific control types as indicated.

add
`listObj.add`
`(type, text[, index])`
	For list objects (`listbox` or `dropdown` list) only. Adds an item to the `items` array at the given index. Returns the `item` control object for type=item, or null for type=separator.

type	The type of item to add. One of:
	    `item`: A basic, selectable item with a text label.
	    `separator`: A separator. For `dropdownlist` controls only. In this case, the *text* value is ignored, and the method returns `null`.

text	The localizable text label for the item.
index	Optional. The index into the current item list after which this item is inserted. If not supplied, or greater than the current list length, the new item is added at the end.
find `listObj.find(text)`	For list objects (`listbox` or `dropdown` list) only. Looks in this object's `items` array for an `item` object with the given `text` value. Returns the `item` object if found; otherwise, returns `null`.
text	The text of the item to find.
hide `controlObj.hide()`	Hides this container or control. When a window or container is hidden, its children are also hidden, but when it is shown again, the children retain their own visibility states.
notify `controlObj.notify([event])`	Sends a notification message, simulating the specified user interaction event.

event	Optional. The name of the control event handler to call. One of:
	    `onClick`
	    `onChange`
	    `onChanging`
	By default, simulates the `onChange` event for an `edittext` control, an `onClick` event for controls that support that event.

remove
`containerObj.remove(index)`
`containerObj.remove(text)`
`containerObj.remove(child)`
	For containers (`panel`, `group`), removes the specified child control from the container's `children` array.
	For list objects (`listbox` or `dropdown` list) only, removes the specified item from this object's `items` array. No error results if the item does not exist.

index *text* *child*	The item or child to remove, specified by 0-based index, `text` value, or as a `control` object.
removeAll `listObj.removeAll()`	For list objects (`listbox` or `dropdown` list) only. Removes all items from the object's `items` array.

show `controlObj.show()`	Shows this container or control. When a window or container is hidden, its children are also hidden, but when it is shown again, the children retain their own visibility states.
toString `listItemObj.toString()`	For `item` controls only. Returns the value of this item's `text` property as a string.
valueOf `listItemObj.valueOf()`	For `item` controls only. Returns the index number of this item in the parent list's `items` array.

Control event-handling callbacks

The following events are signalled in certain types of controls. To handle the event, define a function with the corresponding name in the control object.

onClick	Called when the user clicks one of the following control types:
	`button`
	`checkbox`
	`iconbutton`
	`radiobutton`

onChange	Called when the user finishes making a change in one of the following control types:
	`dropdownlist`
	`edittext`
	`listbox`
	`scrollbar`
	`slider`
	● For an `edittext` control, called only when the change is complete—that is, when focus moves to another control, or the user types ENTER. The exact behavior depends on the creation parameter `enterKeySignalsOnChange`; see the edittext (page 277) description.
	● For a `slider` or `scrollbar`, called when the user has finished dragging the position marker or has clicked the control.

onChanging	Called for each incremental change in one of the following control types:
	`edittext`
	`scrollbar`
	`slider`
	● For an `edittext` control, called for each keypress while the control has focus.
	● For a `slider` or `scrollbar`, called for any motion of the position marker.

Size and Location Objects

ScriptUI defines objects to represent the complex values of properties that place and size windows and UI elements. These objects cannot be created directly, but are created when you set the corresponding property. That property then returns that object. For example, the `bounds` property returns a `Bounds` object.

You can set these properties as objects, strings, or arrays.

- `e.prop = Object`: The object must contain the set of properties defined for this type, as shown in the table below. The properties have integer values.

- `e.prop = String`: The string must be an executable JavaScript inline object declaration, conforming to the same object description.

- `e.prop = Array`: The array must have integer coordinate values in the order defined for this type, as shown in the table below. For example:

The following examples show equivalent ways of placing a 380 by 390 pixel window near the upper left corner of the screen:

```
var dlg = new Window('dialog', 'Alert Box Builder');
dlg.bounds = {x:100, y:100, width:380, height:390};
//object
dlg.bounds = {left:100, top:100, right:480,
bottom:490}; //object
dlg.bounds = "x:100, y:100, width:380, height:390";
//string
dlg.bounds = "left:100, top:100, right:480,
bottom:490"; //string
dlg.bounds = [100,100,480,490]; //array
```

You can access the resulting object as an array with values in the order defined for the type, or as an object with the properties supported for the type.

The following table shows the property-value object types, the element properties that create and contain them, and their array and object-property formats.

Bounds	Defines the boundaries of a window within the screen's coordinate space, or of a UI element within the container's coordinate space. Contains an array, [left, top, right, bottom], that defines the coordinates of the upper left and lower right corners of the element. A Bounds object is created when you set an element's bounds property, and this property returns a Bounds object. • An object must contain properties named left, top, right, bottom, or x, y, width, height. • An array must have values in the order [left, top, right, bottom].
Dimension	Defines the size of a window or UI element. Contains an array, [width, height], that defines the element's size in pixels. A Dimension object is created when you set an element's size or preferredSize property. • An object must contain properties named width and height. • An array must have values in the order [width, height].
Margins	Defines the number of pixels between the edges of a container and its outermost child elements. Contains an array [left, top, right, bottom] whose elements define the margins between the left edge of a container and its leftmost child element, and so on. A Margins object is created when you set an element's margins property. • An object must contain properties named left, top, right, and bottom. • An array must have values in the order [left, top, right, bottom]. You can also set the margins property to a number; all of the array values are then set to this number.
Point	Defines the location of a window or UI element. Contains an array, [x, y], whose values represent the origin point of the element as horizontal and vertical pixel offsets from the origin of the element's coordinate space. A Point object is created when you set an element's location property. • An object must contain properties named x and y. • An array must have values in the order [x, y].

LayoutManager object

Controls the automatic layout behavior for a window or container. The subclass AutoLayoutManager implements the default automatic layout behavior.

AutoLayoutManager object constructor

Create an instance of the `AutoLayoutManager` class with the `new` operator:

```
myWin.layout = new AutoLayoutManager(myWin);
```

An instance is automatically created when you create a `window` or container (`group` or `panel`) object, and referenced by the container's layout (page 271) property. This instance implements the default layout behavior unless you override it.

AutoLayoutManager object properties

The default object has no predefined properties, but a script can assign arbitrary properties to an object it creates, to store data needed by the script-defined layout algorithm.

AutoLayoutManager object functions

layout *win*.layout.layout (*recalculate*)	Invokes the automatic layout behavior for the managed container. Adjusts sizes and positions of the child elements of this window or container according to the placement and alignment property values in the parent and children. Invoked automatically the first time the window is displayed. Thereafter, the script must invoke it explicitly to change the layout in case of changes in the size or position of the parent or children.
recalculate	Optional. When `true`, forces the layout manager to recalculate the container size for this and any child containers. Default is `false`.

MenuElement Object

The MenuElement class is used to represent application menu bars, their menus and submenus, and individual items or commands. Each application creates menuElement instances for each of the existing menu elements, and you can create additional instances to extend the existing menus.

Each menuElement object has unique identifier. Existing menu elements that can be extended have predefined identifiers, listed in Bridge menu and command identifiers (page 296). Not all existing menu elements can be extended. You can only add a new menu or command before or after an existing menu or command, which you must specify using the predefined unique identifier.

The menu, submenu, and command identifier names do not necessarily match the display names. Menu identifiers are case sensitive. They are not displayed and are never localized. When a script creates a new menu or command, you should assign a descriptive unique identifier. If you do not, one is generated using a numeric value.

The display text of a new menu element can be localized by specifying it with the Global localize function (page 372). See "Localizing ExtendScript Strings" on page 369.

Menu separators are not independent elements, but can be inserted before or after an element that you add to a menu. The separator is specified as part of the location string on creation; see "Creating new menu elements" on page 293.

MenuElement class functions

The MenuElement class defines these static functions that you can use to extend and work with existing menu elements.

create MenuElement.create (*type*, *text*, *location*[, *id*]);	Adds a new menu to a menu bar, a new submenu to an existing menu, or a new command to an existing menu or submenu. Returns the new menuElement object. See examples below.

type	The type of menu element, one of:
	    menu: a menu or submenu
	    command: a menu item

text	The localizable string that is displayed as the label text. Script-created menu and menu commands cannot have keyboard shortcuts or icons.

location	A string describing the location of the new menu element, with respect to existing menu elements. This can take one of the following forms:
	`before` *identifier*: Create the new element before the given menu element.
	`after` *identifier*: Create the new element before the given menu element.
	`at the end of` *identifier*: Append the new element to the given menu. The identifier must be for a menu, not a command item.
	To insert a separator before or after the new element, specify a dash (–) at the beginning or end of the location string.
	For example, this value draws separators before and after the new element, which is added after the Find submenu in the Edit menu:
	`-after /bridge/edit/find-`
	A string that does not conform to these rules causes a run-time error.
id	The unique identifier for this element. Optional.
	• If the ID of an existing menu or submenu is supplied, the call returns that menu or submenu object.
	• If the ID of an existing menu command is supplied, the call causes a JavaScript error.
	• If not supplied, the call generates a numeric value, which can be found in the id property of the returned menu object.

find MenuElement.find (*id*)	Finds and returns the menuElement object for the specified menu or menu item, or null if no such element is found.
id	String. The unique identifier for the menu element to find.

> ### Example

This example checks to see whether a specific menu item already exists to avoid an error if the script is executed a second time.

```
var menu = MenuElement.find ('myMenuId');
if (menu = null) //element does not yet exist
// add menu element
```

remove MenuElement.remove (*id*)	Removes a script-defined menu or menu item. Returns undefined.
id	String. The unique identifier for the menu element to remove.

Creating new menu elements

These examples illustrate the creation of new menus and menu items.

> ### Example: Adding a menu and command to the menu bar

This example adds a new menu to the menu bar, after the **Help** menu. It adds one command to that menu, labeled "Alert", and assigns it an onSelect callback that displays an alert dialog when the item is clicked.

```
newMenu = new MenuElement ( "menu", "MyMenu",
   "after Help", "myMenu" );
alertCommand = new MenuElement ( "command", "Alert",
   "at the end of myMenu",
   "myAlert" );
alertCommand.onSelect = function () {
Window.alert ("Hi."); }
```

➤ Example: Adding a command to a context menu

This example adds a "Count Children" command to the context menu for folder thumbnails, and assigns it an `onSelect` callback that counts and displays the number of child nodes in that folder.

The `onSelect` callback assumes that the thumbnail is for a folder, so the example makes sure it cannot be called for a thumbnail that does not represent a folder. To do this, the `onDisplay` callback of the new element (called each time the menu is displayed) enables the command only when the currently selected thumbnail is for a folder.

If multiple thumbnails are selected when the user invokes the context menu, the new command is enabled if the first one is a folder. In this case, selecting the command reports the number of items in that folder.

```
var cntCommand = new MenuElement ("command",
      "Count Children",
      "at the end of Thumbnail", "myCount");
cntCommand.onSelect = function (m) {
   try {
   // get the thumbnail associated with the context menu
      var tn = app.document.selections [0];
   // display the number of direct descendants
      Window.alert ("Number of direct descendants: " +
tn.children.length);
   } catch(error) { Window.alert (error); }
};
cntCommand.onDisplay = function (m) {
   try {
      var tn = app.document.selections [0];
                        //check the first selected node
      if (tn.container) //is it for a folder?
         m.enabled = true; // yes, enable the command
      else
         m.enabled = false; // no, disable the command
   } catch(error) { Window.alert (error); }
};
```

MenuElement object properties

`altDown`	Boolean	When true, the ALT modifier key was pressed when the item was selected. Read only.
`checked`	Boolean	When `true`, the command is selected. A check mark appears next to the label. When `false`, the item is not selected, and no check mark is shown. Read/write.
`cmdDown`	Boolean	When true, the COMMAND modifier key was pressed when the item was selected. Read only.
`ctrlDown`	Boolean	When true, the CONTROL modifier key was pressed when the item was selected. Read only.
`enabled`	Boolean	When `true`, the menu or command is selectable. When `false`, it is grayed out and cannot be selected. Read/write.
`id`	String	A unique identifier. Read only. Identifiers take the form: `/app/menu/submenu/command` They are not localized, and are case sensitive.
`onDisplay`	Function	The callback function that is called when the application is about to display this menu or menu item. The function takes no arguments, and returns nothing. It can change the `enabled` and `checked` properties according to the state of the application.
`optionDown`	Boolean	When true, the OPTION modifier key was pressed when the item was selected. Read only.

`onSelect`	Function	The callback function that is called when the user selects the menu or menu item. The function takes no arguments, and returns nothing. It implements the behavior of a menu item.
		
		The callback can check this object's properties to respond to the following modifier keys:
		<pre>if (this.ShiftDown)
		    // Shift key pressed
		if (this.altDown)
		    // Alt key pressed
		if (this.ctrlDown)
		    // Control key pressed
		if (this.cmdDown)
		    // Command key pressed
		if (this.optionDown)
		    // Option key pressed</pre>

`shiftDown`	Boolean	When true, the SHIFT modifier key was pressed when the item was selected. Read only.

text	String	The displayed label text, a localizable string. Read only.
type	String	The type of menu element, one of: menu: a menu or submenu command: a menu item Read only.

Bridge menu and command identifiers

These unique identifiers are predefined for Bridge menus that can be extended.

Bridge menu identifiers

These tables list unique identifiers for the top-level menus in Adobe Bridge

Menubar menus	Menu ID
Bridge (Mac OS only)	(not available)
File	File
Edit	Edit
Tools	Tools
Label	Labels
View	View
Window	Window
Help	Help
Context menus	**Menu ID**
thumbnail context	Thumbnail
Flyout menus	**Menu ID**
Folders tab flyout	FoldersTab
Keywords tab flyout	KeywordsTab
Metadata tab flyout	MetadataTab
Flyout menu submenus	**Menu ID**
Metadata flyout > AppendMetadata	Bridge/Submenu/AppendMetadata
Metadata flyout > ReplaceMetadata	Bridge/Submenu/ReplaceMetadata
Note: The commands in flyout menus are not available to scripts.	

Bridge submenu and command identifiers

These tables list unique identifiers for submenus and commands in the Adobe Bridge menus.

Bridge menu commands (Mac OS only)

Submenus/commands	Menu ID
About Bridge	mondo/command/about
Preferences	Prefs
Quit Bridge	mondo/command/quit

File menu commands

Submenus/commands	Menu ID
New Window	mondo/command/new
New Folder	NewFolder
Open	Open
Open with >	submenu/OpenWith
Open with > [installed application]	(not available)
Open in Camera Raw	OpenInCameraRaw
Eject	Eject
Close Window	mondo/command/close
Send to Recycle Bin	MoveToTrash
Return to	ReturnToApplication
Reveal in Explorer/Finder	Reveal
Reveal in Bridge	RevealInBridge
Place >	submenu/Place
Add To Favorites	AddToFavorites
File Info...	FileInfo
Versions...	Versions
Alternates...	Alternates
Exit	mondo/command/quit

Edit menu commands

Submenus/commands	Menu ID
Undo	mondo/command/undo
Cut	mondo/command/cut
Copy	mondo/command/copy
Paste	mondo/command/paste
Duplicate	Duplicate
Select All	mondo/command/selectAll
Select Labeled	SelectLabeled
Select Unlabeled	SelectUnlabeled
Invert Selection	InvertSelection
Deselect All	mondo/command/selectNone
Find...	Search
Camera Raw Settings...	submenu/CameraRaw
Apply Camera Raw Settings >	ApplyCameraRaw
Apply Camera Raw Settings > Camera Default	CRDefault
Apply Camera Raw Settings > Previous Conversion	CRPrevious
Apply Camera Raw Settings > Copy Camera Raw Settings	CRCopy
Apply Camera Raw Settings > Paste Camera Raw Settings	CRPaste
Apply Camera Raw Settings > Clear Settings	CRClear
Rotate 180°	Rotate180
Rotate 90° Clockwise	Rotate90CW
Rotate 90° Counterclockwise	Rotate90CCW
Creative Suite Color Settings...	SharedSettings
Camera Raw Preferences...	CRPreferences
Preferences...	Prefs

Tools menu commands

Submenus/commands	Menu ID
Batch Rename...	BatchRename
Version Cue >	submenu/VersionCue
Version Cue > Synchronize	Synchronize
Version Cue > Mark In Use	CheckOut
Version Cue > Save a Version	(not available)
Version Cue > Revert to Last Version	RevertToProject
Version Cue > Make Alternates	CreateAlternateGroup
Version Cue > New Project	NewProject
Version Cue > Connect to...	ConnectTo
Version Cue > Edit Properties...	EditProperties
Cache >	submenu/Cache
Cache > Build Cache for Subfolders	BuildSubCaches
Cache > Purge Cache for This Folder	PurgeCache
Cache > Purge Entire Cache	PurgeAllCaches
Cache > Export Cache	ExportCache
Append Metadata >	Bridge/Submenu/AppendMetadata
[templates]	(not available)
Replace Metadata >	Bridge/Submenu/ReplaceMetadata
[templates]	(not available)

Label menu commands

Submenus/commands	Menu ID
Rating	(not available)
No Rating	NoDot
*	OneDot
**	TwoDots
***	ThreeDots
****	FourDots
*****	FiveDots
Decrease Rating	RemoveDot

Increase Rating	AddDot
Label	(not available)
No Label	NoLabel
Red	Red
Yellow	Yellow
Green	Green
Blue	Blue
Purple	Purple

View menu commands

Submenus/commands	Menu ID
Compact Mode	ToggleCompactMode
Slide Show...	SlideShow
As Thumbnails	View/Thumbnail
As Details	View/Details
As Versions Alternates	View/Versions
As Filmstrip	View/Filmstrip
Favorites Panel	FavoritesTab
Folders Panel	FoldersTab
Preview Panel	PreviewTab
Metadata Panel	MetadataTab
Keywords Panel	KeywordsTab
Sort >	submenu/Sort
Sort > Ascending Order	Ascending
Sort > By File Name	SortFileName
Sort > By Document Kind	SortFileType
Sort > By Date Created	SortDateCreated
Sort > By Date File Modified	SortDateModified
Sort > By File Size	SortFileType
Sort > By Dimensions	SortDimensions
Sort > By Resolution	SortResolution
Sort > By Color Profile	SortColorProfile

Sort > By Copyright	SortCopyright
Sort > By Label	SortByLabel
Sort > By Rating	SortRating
Sort > By Purchase State	SortPurchaseState
Sort > By Version Cue Status	SortUseState
Sort > Manually	SortManually
Show Thumbnail Only	ShowThumbnailOnly
Show Hidden Files	ShowHidden
Show Folders	ShowFolders
Show All Files	FilterNoFiles
Show Graphic Files Only	FilterGraphicFiles
Show Camera Raw Files Only	FilterCameraRawFiles
Show Vector Files Only	FilterVectorFiles
Refresh	Refresh

Window menu commands

Submenus/commands	Menu ID
Workspace >	submenu/Workspace
Workspace > Save Workspace	SaveWorkspace
Workspace > Delete Workspace	DeleteWorkspace
Workspace > Reset to Default Workspace	(not available)
Workspace > Lightbox	(not available)
Workspace > File Navigator	(not available)
Workspace > Metadata Focus	(not available)
Workspace > Filmstrip Focus	(not available)

Help menu commands

Submenus/command	Menu ID
Bridge Help...	mondo/command/help
VersionCue Help...	VersionCueHelp
Updates...	Updates
About Bridge...	mondo/command/about

Context menu commands

Thumbnail context menu in Favorites tab commands	Menu ID
Remove From Favorites	Bridge/ContextMenu/Keyword/Delete
Thumbnail context menu in Folders tab commands	**Menu ID**
Send to Recycle Bin	Bridge/ContextMenu/Folders/Delete
Reveal in Explorer/Finder	Bridge/ContextMenu/Folders/Reveal
Add to Favorites	Bridge/ContextMenu/Folders/AddToFavorites
Thumbnail context menu in Content pane (folders) submenus/commands	**Menu ID**
Open	Thumbnail/Open
Open with >	submenu/OpenWith
Reveal in Explorer/Finder	Thumbnail/RevealLocation
Add to Favorites	Thumbnail/AddToFavorites
Send to Recycle Bin	Thumbnail/Remove
Label >	submenu/Label
Label > No Label	(not available)
Label > *label strings*	(not available)
Thumbnail context menu in Content pane (files) submenus/commands	**Menu ID**
Open	Thumbnail/Open
Open With >	subment/OpenWith
Reveal in Explorer/Finder	Thumbnail/RevealLocation
Send to Recycle Bin	Thumbnail/Remove
File Info...	Thumbnail/FileInfo
Label >	submenu/Label
Label > No Label	(not available)
Label > *label strings*	(not available)
Thumbnail context menu in Content pane (images) additional commands	**Menu ID**
Rotate 180°	Thumbnail/Rotate180
Rotate 90° Clockwise	Thumbnail/RotateCW

Rotate 90° Counterclockwise	Thumbnail/RotateCCW
Thumbnail context menu in Content pane (Version Cue nodes) additional command	**Menu ID**
Versions...	Thumbnail/Versions
Keywords context menu commands	**Menu ID**
New Keyword	Bridge/ContextMenu/Keyword/NewKey
New Keyword Set	Bridge/ContextMenu/Keyword/NewSet
Rename	Bridge/ContextMenu/Keyword/Rename
Delete	Bridge/ContextMenu/Keyword/DeleteNode
Find...	Bridge/ContextMenu/Keyword/Search

9 | Using File and Folder Objects

Overview

Because path name syntax is very different in Windows, Mac OS and UNIX®, Adobe ExendScript defines the `File` and `Folder` objects to provide platform-independent access to the underlying file system. A File object (page 311) represents a disk file, a Folder Object (page 320) represents a directory or folder.

- The `Folder` object supports file system functionality such as traversing the hierarchy; creating, renaming or removing files; or resolving file aliases.
- The `File` object supports input/output functions to read or write files.

There are several ways to distinguish between a `File` and a `Folder` object. For example:

```
if (f instanceof File) ...
if (typeof f.open == "undefined") ...
// Folders do not open
```

`File` and `Folder` objects can be used anywhere that a path name is required, such as in properties and arguments for files and folders. For details about the objects and their properties and methods, see Chapter 10, "File and Folder Object Reference."

Note: When you create two `File` objects that refer to the same disk file, they are treated as distinct objects. If you open one of them for I/O, the operating system may inhibit access from the other object, because the disk file already is open.

Specifying paths

When creating a `File` or `Folder` object, you can specify a platform-specific path name, or an absolute or relative path in a platform-independent format known as *universal resource identifier (URI)* notation. The path stored in the object is always an absolute, full path name that points to a fixed location on the disk.

- Use the `toString` method to obtain the name of the file or folder as string containing an absolute path name in URI notation.
- Use the fsName (page 315) property to obtain the platform-specific file name.

Absolute and relative path names

An absolute path name in URI notation describes the full path from a root directory down to a specific file or folder. It starts with one or two slashes (/), and a slash separates path elements. For example, the following describes an absolute location for the file myFile.jsx:

```
/dir1/dir2/mydir/myFile.jsx
```

A relative path name in URI notation is appended to the path of the current directory, as stored in the globally available current (page 320) property of the Folder class. It starts with a folder or file name, or with one of the special names dot (.) for the current directory, or dot dot (..) for the parent of the current directory. A slash (/) separates path elements. For example, the following paths describe various relative locations for the file myFile.jsx:

myFile.jsx ./myFile.jsx	In the current directory.
../myFile.jsx	In the parent of the current directory.
../../myFile.jsx	In the grandparent of the current directory.
../dir1/myFile.jsx	In dir1, which is parallel to the current directory.

Relative path names are independent of different volume names on different machines and operating systems, and therefore make your code considerably more portable. You can, for example, use an absolute path for a single operation, to set the current directory in the Folder.current property, and use relative paths for all other operations. You would then need only a single code change to update to a new platform or file location.

Character interpretation in paths

There are some platform differences in how pathnames are interpreted:

- In Windows and Mac OS, path names are not case sensitive. In UNIX, paths are case sensitive.
- In Windows, both the slash (/) and the backslash (\) are valid path element separators.
- In Mac OS, both the slash (/) and the colon (:) are valid path element separators.

If a path name starts with two slashes (or backslashes in Windows), the first element refers to a remote server. For example, //myhost/mydir/myfile refers to the path /mydir/myfile on the server myhost.

URI notation allows special characters in pathnames, but they must specified with an escape character (%) followed by a hexadecimal character code.

Special characters are those which are not alphanumeric and not one of the characters:

```
/ - _ . ! ~ * ' ( )
```

A space, for example, is encoded as `%20`, so the file name `"my file"` is specified as `"my%20file"`. Similarly, the character ä is encoded as `%E4`, so the file name `"Bräun"` is specified as `"Br%E4un"`.

This encoding scheme is compatible with the global JavaScript functions `encodeURI` and `decodeURI`.

The home directory

A path name can start with a tilde (~) to indicate the user's home directory. It corresponds to the platform's `HOME` environment variable.

UNIX and Mac OS assign the `HOME` environment variable according to the user login. In Mac OS, the default home directory is `/Users/username`. In UNIX, it is typically `/home/username` or `/users/username`. Extend Script assigns the home directory value directly from the platform value.

In Windows, the `HOME` environment variable is optional. If it is assigned, its value must be a Windows path name or a path name referring to a remote server (such as `\\myhost\mydir`). If the `HOME` environment variable is undefined, the Extend Script default is the user's home directory, usually the `C:\Documents and Settings\username` folder.

Note: A script can access many of the folders that are specified with platform-specific variables through static, globally available Folder class properties (page 320); for instance, appData (page 320) contains the folder that stores application data for all users.

Volume and drive names

A volume or drive name can be the first part of an absolute path in URI notation. The values are interpreted according to the platform.

Mac OS volumes

When Mac OS X starts, the startup volume is the root directory of the file system. All other volumes, including remote volumes, are part of the `/Volumes` directory. The `File` and `Folder` objects use these rules to interpret the first element of a path name:

- If the name is the name of the startup volume, discard it.
- If the name is a volume name, prepend `/Volumes`.
- Otherwise, leave the path as is.

Mac OS 9 is not supported as an operating system, but the use of the colon as a path separator is still supported and corresponds to URI and to Mac OS X paths as shown in the following table. These examples assume that the startup volume is `MacOSX`, and that there is a mounted volume `Remote`.

URI path name	Mac OS 9 path name	Mac OS X path name
/MacOSX/dir/file	MacOSX:dir:file	/dir/file
/Remote/dir/file	Remote:dir:file	/Volumes/Remote/dir/file
/root/dir/file	Root:dir:file	/root/dir/file
~/dir/file		/Users/jdoe/dir/file

Windows drives

In Windows, volume names correspond to drive letters. The URI path `/c/temp/file` normally translates to the Windows path `C:\temp\file`.

If a drive exists with a name matching the first part of the path, that part is always interpreted as that drive. It is possible for there to be a folder in the root that has the same name as the drive; imagine, for example, a folder `c:\c` in Windows. A path starting with `/c` always addresses the drive `c:`, so in this case, to access the folder by name, you must use both the drive name and the folder name, for example `/c/c` for `C:\C`.

If the current drive contains a root folder with the same name as another drive letter, that name is considered to be a folder. That is, if there is a folder `D:\C`, and if the current drive is `D:`, the URI path `/c/temp/file` translates to the Windows path `D:\c\temp\file`. In this case, to access drive C, you would have to use the Windows path name conventions.

To access a remote volume, use a uniform naming convention (UNC) path name of the form `//servername/sharename`. These path names are portable, because both Max OS X and UNIX ignore multiple slash characters. Note that in Windows, UNC names do *not* work for local volumes.

These examples assume that the current drive is `D:`

URI path name	Windows path name
/c/dir/file	c:\dir\file
/remote/dir/file	D:\remote\dir\file
/root/dir/file	D:\root\dir\file
~/dir/file	C:\Documents and Settings\jdoe\dir\file

Aliases

When you access an alias, the operation is transparently forwarded to the real file. The only operations that affect the alias are calls to `rename` and `remove`, and setting properties `readonly` and `hidden`. When a `File` object represents an alias, the `alias` property of the object returns `true`, and the `resolve` method returns the `File` or `Folder` object for the target of the alias.

In Windows, all file system aliases (called *shortcuts*) are actual files whose names end with the extension `.lnk`. Never use this extension directly; the `File` and `Folder` objects work without it.

For example, suppose there is a shortcut to the file `/folder1/some.txt` in the folder `/folder2`. The full Windows file name of the shortcut file is `\folder2\some.txt.lnk`.

To access the shortcut from a `File` object, specify the path `/folder2/some.txt`. Calling that `File` object's `open` method opens the linked file (in `/folder1`). Calling the `File` object's `rename` method renames the shortcut file itself (leaving the `.lnk` extension intact).

However, Windows permits a file and its shortcut to reside in the same folder. In this case, the `File` object always accesses the original file. You cannot create a `File` object to access the shortcut when it is in the same folder as its linked file.

A script can create a file alias by creating a `File` object for a file that does not yet exist on disk, and using its createAlias (page 316) method to specify the target of the alias.

Portability issues

If your application will run on multiple platforms, use relative path names, or try to originate path names from the home directory. If that is not possible, work with Mac OS X and UNIX aliases, and store your files on a machine that is remote to your Windows machine so that you can use UNC names.

As an example, suppose you use the UNIX machine `myServer` for data storage. If you set up an alias share in the root directory of `myServer`, and if you set up a Windows-accessible share at `share` pointing to the same data location, the path name `//myServer/share/file` would work for all three platforms.

Unicode I/O

When doing file I/O, Adobe applications convert 8-bit character encoding to Unicode. By default, this conversion process assumes that the system encoding is used (code page 1252 in Windows or Mac Roman in Mac OS). The encoding property of a File object returns the current encoding. You can set the encoding property to the name of the desired encoding. The File object looks for the corresponding encoder in the operating system to use for subsequent I/O. The name is one of the standard Internet names that are used to describe the encoding of HTML files, such as ASCII, X-SJIS, or ISO-8859-1. For a complete list, see "File and Folder Supported Encoding Names" on page 326.

A special encoder, BINARY, is provided for binary I/O. This encoder simply extends every 8-bit character it finds to a Unicode character between 0 and 255. When using this encoder to write binary files, the encoder writes the lower 8 bits of the Unicode character. For example, to write the Unicode character 1000, which is 0x3E8, the encoder actually writes the character 232 (0xE8).

The data of some of the common file formats (UCS-2, UCS-4, UTF-8, UTF-16) starts with a special byte order mark (BOM) character (\uFEFF). The File.open method reads a few bytes of a file looking for this character. If it is found, the corresponding encoding is set automatically and the character is skipped. If there is no BOM character at the beginning of the file, open() reads the first 2 KB of the file and checks whether the data might be valid UTF-8 encoded data, and if so, sets the encoding to UTF-8.

To write 16-bit Unicode files in UTF-16 format, use the encoding UCS-2. This encoding uses whatever byte-order format the host platform supports.

When using UTF-8 encoding or 16-bit Unicode, always write the BOM character "\uFEFF" as the first character of the file.

File Error Handling

Each object has an error property. If accessing a property or calling a method causes an error, this property contains a message describing the type of the error. On success, the property contains the empty string. You can set the property, but setting it only causes the error message to be cleared. If a file is open, assigning an arbitrary value to the property also resets its error flag.

For a complete list of supported error messages, see "File and Folder Error Messages" on page 325.

10 | File and Folder Object Reference

Overview

Because path name syntax is very different in Windows, Mac OS and UNIX, the `File` and `Folder` objects are defined to provide platform-independent access to the underlying file system. A `File` object is associated with a disk file, a `Folder` object with a directory or folder.

- The `Folder` object supports file-system functionality such as traversing the hierarchy, creating, renaming or removing files, or resolving file aliases.
- The `File` object supports I/O functions to read or write files.

`File` and `Folder` objects can be used anywhere a path name is required, such as in properties and arguments for files and folders.

For a description of the pathname syntax and object usage, see Chapter 9, "Using File and Folder Objects." This chapter provides detail about the classes and objects, their properties and methods, and the supported encoding names:

- File object
- Folder Object
- File and Folder Error Messages
- File and Folder Supported Encoding Names

File object

Represents a file in the local file system in an platform-independent manner. All properties and methods resolve file system aliases automatically and act on the original file unless otherwise noted.

File object constructors

To create a `File` object, use the `File` function or the `new` operator. The constructor accepts full or partial path names, and returns the new object. The CRLF sequence for the file is preset to the system default, and the encoding is preset to the default system encoding.

```
File ([path]); //can return a Folder object
new File ([path]); //always returns a File object
```

path	Optional. The absolute or relative path to the file associated with this object, specified in platform-specific or URI format; see "Specifying paths" on page 305. The value stored in the object is the absolute path.
	The path need not refer to an existing file. If not supplied, a temporary name is generated.
	If the path refers to an existing folder:
	● The `File` function returns a `Folder` object instead of a `File` object.
	● The `new` operator returns a `File` object for a nonexisting file with the same name.

File class properties

This property is available as a static property of the `File` class. It is not necessary to create an instance to access it.

`fs`	String	The name of the file system. Read-only. One of `Windows`, `Macintosh`, or `Unix`.

File class functions

These functions are available as static methods of the `File` class. It is not necessary to create an instance to call them.

decode `File.decode (what)`	Decodes the specified string as required by RFC 2396 and returns the decoded string.
what	String. The encoded string to decode.
	All special characters must be encoded in UTF-8 and stored as escaped characters starting with the percent sign followed by two hexadecimal digits. For example, the string `"my%20file"` is decoded as `"my file"`.
	Special characters are those with a numeric value greater than 127, except the following:
	`/ - _ . ! ~ * ' ( )`
encode `File.encode (what)`	Encodes the specified string as required by RFC 2396 and returns the encoded string.
	All special characters are encoded in UTF-8 and stored as escaped characters starting with the percent sign followed by two hexadecimal digits. For example, the string `"my file"` is encoded as `"my%20file"`.
	Special characters are those with a numeric value greater than 127, except the following:
	`/ - _ . ! ~ * ' ( )`
what	String. The string to encode.

isEncodingAvailable File.isEncodingAvailable (*name*)	Returns `true` if your system supports the specified encoding, `false` otherwise.
name	String. The encoding name.
openDialog File.openDialog ([*prompt*] [, *select*])	Opens the built-in platform-specific file-browsing dialog in which a user can select an existing file to open. If the user clicks **OK**, returns a `File` object for the selected file. If the user cancels, returns `null`.
prompt	Optional. A string containing the prompt text, if the dialog allows a prompt.
select	Optional. A file or files to be preselected when the dialog opens: • In Windows, a string containing a comma-separated list of file types with descriptive text, to be displayed in the bottom of the dialog as a drop-down list from which the user can select which types of files to display. Each element starts with the descriptive text, followed by a colon and the file search masks for this text, separated by semicolons. For example, to display two choices, one labeled **Text Files** that allows selection of text files with extensions .TXT and .DOC, and the other labeled **All files** that allows selection of all files: `Text Files:*.TXT;*.DOC,All files:*` • In Mac OS, a string containing the name of a function defined in the current JavaScript scope that takes a `File` object argument. The function is called for each file about to be displayed in the dialog, and the file is displayed only when the function returns `true`.
saveDialog File.saveDialog ([*prompt*] [, *select*])	Opens the built-in platform-specific file-browsing dialog in which a user can select an existing file location to which to save this file. If the user clicks **OK**, returns a `File` object for the selected file, and overwrites the existing file. If the user cancels, returns `null`.

prompt	Optional. A string containing the prompt text, if the dialog allows a prompt.
select	Optional. A file or files to be preselected when the dialog opens:

- In Windows, a string containing a comma-separated list of file types with descriptive text, to be displayed in the bottom of the dialog as a drop-down list from which the user can select which types of files to display.
- Each element starts with the descriptive text, followed by a colon and the file search masks for this text, separated by semicolons. For example, to display two choices, one labeled **Text Files** that allows selection of text files with extensions .TXT and .DOC, and the other labeled **All files** that allows selection of all files:

  ```
  Text Files:*.TXT;*.DOC,All files:*
  ```

- In Mac OS, a string containing the name of a function defined in the current JavaScript scope that takes a File object argument. The function is called for each file about to be displayed in the dialog, and the file is displayed only when the function returns true.

File object properties

These properties are available for File objects.

absoluteURI	String	The full path name for the referenced file in URI notation. Read-only.
alias	Boolean	When true, the object refers to a file system alias or shortcut. Read-only.
created	Date	The creation date of the referenced file, or null if the object does not refer to a file on disk. Read-only.
creator	String	The Mac OS file creator as a four-character string. In Windows or UNIX, value is "????". Read-only.
encoding	String	Gets or sets the encoding for subsequent read/write operations. One of the encoding constants listed in "File and Folder Supported Encoding Names" on page 326. If the value is not recognized, uses the system default encoding.

A special encoder, BINARY, is used to read binary files. It stores each byte of the file as one Unicode character regardless of any encoding. When writing, the lower byte of each Unicode character is treated as a single byte to write. |
eof	Boolean	When true, a read attempt caused the current position to be beyond the end of the file, or the file is not open. Read only
error	String	A message describing the last file system error; see "File and Folder Error Messages" on page 325. Setting this value clears any error message and resets the error bit for opened files.
exists	Boolean	When true, the path name of this object refers to an existing file. Read only.

`fsName`	String	The platform-specific name of the referenced file as a full path name. Read-only.
`hidden`	Boolean	When `true`, the file is not shown in the platform-specific file browser. Read/write. If the object references a file-system alias or shortcut, the flag is altered on the alias, not on the original file.
`length`	Number	The size of the file in bytes. Can be set only for a file that is not open, in which case it truncates or pads the file with 0-bytes to the new length.

`lineFeed`	String	How line feed characters are written. One of:
		    `windows`: Windows style
		    `mac`: Mac OS style
		    `unix`: UNIX style

`modified`	Date	The date of the referenced file's last modification, or `null` if the object does not refer to a file on disk. Read-only.
`name`	String	The name of the referenced file without the path specification. Read-only.
`parent`	Folder	The `Folder` object for the folder that contains this file. Read-only.
`path`	String	The path portion of the absolute URI, or the empty string If the name does not have a path. Read-only.
`readonly`	Boolean	When `true`, prevents the file from being altered or deleted. If the referenced file is a file-system alias or shortcut, the flag is altered on the alias, not on the original file.
`relativeURI`	String	The path name for the referenced file in URI notation, relative to the current folder. Read-only.
`type`	String	The Mac OS file type as a four-character string. In Windows and UNIX, the value is `"????"`. Read-only.

File object functions

These functions are available for `File` objects.

close `fileObj.close ()`	Closes this open file. Returns `true` on success, `false` if there are I/O errors.
copy `fileObj.copy (target)`	Copies this object's referenced file to the specified target location. Resolves any aliases to find the source file. If a file exists at the target location, it is overwritten. Returns `true` if the copy was successful, `false` otherwise.
target	A string with the URI path to the target location, or a `File` object that references the target location.

createAlias
`fileObj.createAlias`
`(toFile, [isFinderAlias])`
	Makes this file into a file-system alias or shortcut to the specified file. The referenced file for this object must exist on disk. Returns `true` if the operation was successful, `false` otherwise.

toFile	The `File` object for the target of the new alias.
isFinderAlias	Optional, Mac OS only. When `true`, the alias is created as a legacy Finder alias. When `false` (the default), the alias is created as a UNIX symlink.
execute `fileObj.execute ()`	Opens this file using the appropriate application (as if it had been double-clicked in a file browser). You can use this method to run scripts, launch applications, and so on. Returns `true` immediately if the application launch was successful.

getRelativeURI
`fileObj.getRelativeURI`
`([basePath])`
	Returns a string containing the URI for this file or folder relative to the specified base path, in URI notation. If no base path is supplied, returns the URI relative to the path of the current folder.

basePath	Optional. A string containing the base path for the relative URI. Default is the current folder.

open
`fileObj.open`
`(mode[, type] [, creator])`
	Open the file for subsequent read/write operations. The method resolves any aliases to find the file. Returns `true` if the file has been opened successfully, `false` otherwise.
	
	The method attempts to detect the encoding of the open file. It reads a few bytes at the current location and tries to detect the Byte Order Mark character `0xFFFE`. If found, the current position is advanced behind the detected character and the encoding property is set to one of the strings `UCS-2BE`, `UCS-2LE`, `UCS4-BE`, `UCS-4LE`, or `UTF-8`. If the marker character is not found, it checks for zero bytes at the current location and makes an assumption about one of the above formats (except UTF-8). If everything fails, the `encoding` property is set to the system encoding.
	
	Note: Be careful about opening a file more than once. The operating system usually permits you to do so, but if you start writing to the file using two different `File` objects, you can destroy your data.

mode	A string indicating the read/write mode. One of: `r`: (read) Opens for reading. If the file does not exist or cannot be found, the call fails. `w`: (write) Opens a file for writing. If the file exists, its contents are destroyed. If the file does not exist, creates a new, empty file. `e`: (edit) Opens an existing file for reading and writing.
type	Optional. In Mac OS, the type of a newly created file, a 4-character string. Ignored in Windows and UNIX.
creator	Optional. In Mac OS, the creator of a newly created file, a 4-character string. Ignored in Windows and UNIX.

openDlg fileObj.OpenDlg ([prompt][, select])	Opens the built-in platform-specific file-browsing dialog, in which the user can select an existing file to open. If the user clicks **OK**, returns a File or Folder object for the selected file or folder. If the user cancels, returns null. Differs from the class method openDialog() in that it presets the current folder to this File object's parent folder and the current file to this object's associated file.
prompt	Optional. A string containing the prompt text, if the dialog allows a prompt.

select	Optional. A file or files to be preselected when the dialog opens:
	
	• In Windows, a string containing a comma-separated list of file types with descriptive text, to be displayed in the bottom of the dialog as a drop-down list from which the user can select which types of files to display.
	
	  Each element starts with the descriptive text, followed by a colon and the file search masks for this text, separated by semicolons. For example, to display two choices, one labeled **Text Files** that allows selection of text files with extensions .TXT and .DOC, and the other labeled **All files** that allows selection of all files:
	
	    `Text Files:*.TXT;*.DOC,All files:*`
	• In Mac OS, a string containing the name of a function defined in the current JavaScript scope that takes a File object argument. The function is called for each file about to be displayed in the dialog, and the file is displayed only when the function returns true.

read fileObj.read ([chars])	Reads the contents of the file starting at the current position, and returns a string that contains up to the specified number of characters.
chars	Optional. An integer specifying the number of characters to read. By default, reads from the current position to the end of the file. If the file is encoded, multiple bytes might be read to create single Unicode characters.
readch fileObj.readch ()	Reads a single text character from the file at the current position, and returns it in a string. Line feeds are recognized as CR, LF, CRLF, or LFCR pairs. If the file is encoded, multiple bytes might be read to create single Unicode characters.
readln fileObj.readln ()	Reads a single line of text from the file at the current position, and returns it in a string. Line feeds are recognized as CR, LF, CRLF, or LFCR pairs. If the file is encoded, multiple bytes might be read to create single Unicode characters.
remove fileObj.remove ()	Deletes the file associated with this object from disk, immediately, without moving it to the system trash. Returns true if the file is deleted successfully. Does not resolve aliases; instead, deletes the referenced alias or shortcut file itself. **Note:** Cannot be undone. It is recommended that you prompt the user for permission before deleting.

rename *fileObj*.rename (*newName*)	Renames the associated file. Returns `true` on success. Does not resolve aliases, but renames the referenced alias or shortcut file itself.
newName	The new file or folder name, with no path.
resolve *fileObj*.resolve ()	If this object references an alias or shortcut, this method resolves that alias and returns a new `File` object that references the file-system element to which the alias resolves. Returns `null` if this object does not reference an alias, or if the alias cannot be resolved.
saveDlg *fileObj*.saveDlg ([*prompt*][,*preset*])	Opens the built-in platform-specific file-browsing dialog, in which the user can select an existing file location at which to save this file. If the user clicks **OK**, returns a `File` or `Folder` object for the selected file or folder. If the user cancels, returns `null`. Differs from the class method `saveDialog()` in that it presets the current folder to this `File` object's parent folder and the file to this object's associated file, and prompts the user to confirm before overwriting an existing file.
prompt	Optional. A string containing the prompt text, if the dialog allows a prompt.
preset	Optional. A file or files to be preselected when the dialog opens: • In Windows, a string containing a comma-separated list of file types with descriptive text, to be displayed in the bottom of the dialog as a drop-down list from which the user can select which types of files to display. Each element starts with the descriptive text, followed by a colon and the file search masks for this text, separated by semicolons. For example, to display two choices, one labeled **Text Files** that allows selection of text files with extensions `.TXT` and `.DOC`, and the other labeled **All files** that allows selection of all files: `    Text Files:*.TXT;*.DOC,All files:*` • In Mac OS, a string containing the name of a function defined in the current JavaScript scope that takes a `File` object argument. The function is called for each file about to be displayed in the dialog, and the file is displayed only when the function returns `true`.
seek *fileObj*.seek (*pos*, *mode*)	Seeks to the specified position in the file, and returns `true` if the position was changed. The new position cannot be less than 0 or greater than the current file size.
pos	The new current position in the file as an offset in bytes from the start, current position, or end, depending on the *mode*.
mode	The seek mode, one of: 0: Seek to absolute position, where `pos=0` is the first byte of the file. 1: Seek relative to the current position. 2. Seek backward from the end of the file.

tell *fileObj*.tell ()	Returns the current position as a byte offset from the start of the file.
write *fileObj*.write (*text*[, *text*...]...)	Writes the specified text to the file at the current position. Returns true on success. For encoded files, writing a single Unicode character may write multiple bytes. **Note:** Be careful not to write to a file that is open in another application or object, as this can overwrite existing data.
text	One or more strings to write, which are concatenated to form a single string.
writeln *fileObj*.writeln (*text*[, *text*...]...)	Writes the specified text to the file at the current position, and appends a Line Feed sequence in the style specified by the linefeed property. Returns true on success. For encoded files, writing a single Unicode character may write multiple bytes. **Note:** Be careful not to write to a file that is open in another application or object, as this can overwrite existing data.
text	One or more strings to write, which are concatenated to form a single string.

Folder Object

Represents a file-system folder or directory in a platform-independent manner. All properties and methods resolve file system aliases automatically and act on the original file unless otherwise noted.

Folder object constructors

To create a `Folder` object, use the `Folder` function or the `new` operator. The constructor accepts full or partial path names, and returns the new object.

```
Folder ([path]); //can return a File object
new Folder ([path]); //always returns a Folder object
```

path	Optional. The absolute or relative path to the folder associated with this object, specified in URI format; see "Specifying paths" on page 305. The value stored in the object is the absolute path. The path need not refer to an existing folder. If not supplied, a temporary name is generated. If the path refers to an existing file: ● The `Folder` function returns a `File` object instead of a `Folder` object. ● The `new` operator returns a `Folder` object for a nonexisting folder with the same name.

Folder class properties

These properties are available as static properties of the `Folder` class. It is not necessary to create an instance to access them.

appData	Folder	A `Folder` object for the folder that contains application data for all users. Read-only. ● In Windows, the value of `%APPDATA%` (by default, `C:\Documents and Settings\All Users\Application Data`) ● In Mac OS, `/Library/Application Support`
commonFiles	Folder	A `Folder` object for the folder that contains files common to all programs. Read-only. ● In Windows, the value of `%CommonProgramFiles%` (by default, `C:\Program Files\Common Files`) ● In Mac OS, `/Library/Application Support`
current	Folder	A `Folder` object for the current folder. Assign either a `Folder` object or a string containing the new path name to set the current folder.
fs	String	The name of the file system. Read-only. One of `Windows`, `Macintosh`, or `Unix`.

Adobe® Photoshop® CS2 Official JavaScript Reference

myDocuments	Folder	A `Folder` object for the default document folder. Read-only.
		• In Windows, `C:\Documents and Settings\`*username*`\My Documents`
		• In Mac OS, `~/Documents`
startup	Folder	A `Folder` object for the folder containing the executable image of the running application. Read-only.
system	Folder	A `Folder` object for the folder containing the operating system files. Read-only.
		• In Windows, the value of `%windir%` (by default, `C:\Windows`)
		• In Mac OS, `/System`
temp	Folder	A `Folder` object for the default folder for temporary files. Read-only.
trash	Folder	A `Folder` object for the folder containing deleted items. Read-only.
userData	Folder	A `Folder` object for the folder that contains application data for the current user. Read-only.
		• In Windows, the value of `%APPDATA%` (by default, `C:\Documents and Settings\`*username*`\Application Data`)
		• In Mac OS, `~/Library/Application Support`

Folder class functions

These functions are available as a static methods of the `Folder` class. It is not necessary to create an instance in order to call them.

decode `Folder.decode (what)`	Decodes the specified string as required by RFC 2396 and returns the decoded string.
what	String. The encoded string to decode.
	All special characters must be encoded in UTF-8 and stored as escaped characters starting with the percent sign followed by two hexadecimal digits. For example, the string `"my%20file"` is decoded as `"my file"`.
	Special characters are those with a numeric value greater than 127, except the following:
	`/ - _ . ! ~ * ' ( )`

encode `Folder.encode (what)`	Encodes the specified string as required by RFC 2396 and returns the encoded string.
	All special characters are encoded in UTF-8 and stored as escaped characters starting with the percent sign followed by two hexadecimal digits. For example, the string `"my file"` is encoded as `"my%20file"`.
	Special characters are those with a numeric value greater than 127, except the following:
	`/ - _ . ! ~ * ' ( )`
what	String. The string to encode.
isEncodingAvailable `File.isEncodingAvailable (name)`	Returns `true` if your system supports the specified encoding, `false` otherwise.
name	String. The encoding name.

selectDialog
`Folder.selectDialog`
  `([prompt][,preset])`
	Opens the built-in platform-specific file-browsing dialog. If the user clicks **OK**, returns a `Folder` object for the selected folder. If the user cancels, returns `null`.

	Differs from the object method `selectDlg()` in that it does not preselect a folder.
prompt	Optional. A string containing the prompt text, if the dialog allows a prompt.
preset	Optional. A `Folder` object for a folder to be preselected when the dialog opens.

Folder object properties

These properties are available for `Folder` objects.

absoluteURI	String	The full path name for the referenced folder in URI notation. Read-only.
alias	Boolean	When `true`, the object refers to a file system alias or shortcut. Read-only.
created	Date	The creation date of the referenced folder, or `null` if the object does not refer to a folder on disk. Read-only.
error	String	A message describing the last file system error; see "File and Folder Error Messages" on page 325. Setting this value clears any error message and resets the error bit for opened folders.
exists	Boolean	When `true`, the path name of this object refers to an existing folder. Read only.
fsName	String	The platform-specific name of the referenced folder as a full path name. Read-only.

modified	Date	The date of the referenced folder's last modification, or `null` if the object does not refer to a folder on disk. Read-only.
name	String	The name of the referenced folder without the path specification. Read-only.
parent	Folder	The `Folder` object for the folder that contains this folder, or `null` if this object refers to the root folder of a volume. Read-only.
path	String	The path portion of the absolute URI, or the empty string If the name does not have a path. Read-only.
relativeURI	String	The path name for the referenced folder in URI notation, relative to the current folder. Read-only.

Folder object functions

These functions are available for `Folder` objects.

create *folderObj*.create ()	Creates a folder at the location to which the path name points. Returns `true` if the folder was created successfully.
execute *folderObj*.execute ()	Opens this folder in the file browser (as if it had been double-clicked in a file browser). Returns `true` immediately if the folder was opened successfully.
getFiles *folderObj*.getFiles ([*mask*])	Returns an array of `File` and `Folder` objects for the contents of this folder, filtered by the supplied `mask`, or `null` if this object's referenced folder does not exist.
mask	Optional. A search mask for file names. A string that can contain question mark (?) and asterisk (*) wild cards. Default is "*", which matches all file names. Can also be the name of a function that takes a `File` or `Folder` object as its argument. It is called for each file or folder found in the search; if it returns `true`, the object is added to the return array. **Note:** In Windows, all aliases end with the extension `.lnk`, which is stripped from the file name when found to preserve compatibility with other operating systems. You can search for all aliases by supplying the search mask "`*.lnk`", but note that such code is not portable.
getRelativeURI *folderObj*.getRelativeURI ([*basePath*])	Returns a string containing the URI for this folder relative to the specified base path, in URI notation. If no base path is supplied, returns the URI relative to the path of the current folder.
basePath	Optional. A string containing the base path for the relative URI. Default is the current folder.

remove *folderObj*.remove ()	Deletes the empty folder associated with this object from disk, immediately, without moving it to the system trash. Returns `true` if the folder is deleted successfully. ● Folders must be empty before they can be deleted. ● Does not resolve aliases; instead, deletes the referenced alias or shortcut file itself. **Note:** Cannot be undone. It is recommended that you prompt the user for permission before deleting.
rename *folderObj*.rename (*newName*)	Renames the associated folder. Returns `true` on success. ● Does not resolve aliases; instead, renames the referenced alias or shortcut file itself.
newName	The new folder name, with no path.
resolve *folderObj*.resolve ()	If this object references an alias or shortcut, this method resolves that alias and returns a new `Folder` object that references the file-system element to which the alias resolves. Returns `null` if this object does not reference an alias, or if the alias cannot be resolved.
selectDlg *folderObj*.selectDlg ([*prompt*] [, *preset*])	Opens the built-in platform-specific file-browsing dialog. If the user clicks **OK**, returns a `File` or `Folder` object for the selected file or folder. If the user cancels, returns `null`. Differs from the class method `selectDialog()` in that it preselects this folder.
prompt	Optional. A string containing the prompt text, if the dialog allows a prompt.
preset	Optional. A `Folder` object for a folder to be preselected when the dialog opens.

File and Folder Error Messages

The following messages can be returned in the `error` property.

File or folder does not exist	The file or folder does not exist, but the parent folder exists.
File or folder already exists	The file or folder already exists.
I/O device is not open	An I/O operation was attempted on a file that was closed.
Read past EOF	Attempt to read beyond the end of a file.
Conversion error	The content of the file cannot be converted to Unicode.
Partial multibyte character found	The character encoding of the file data has errors.
Permission denied	The OS did not allow the attempted operation.
Cannot change directory	Cannot change the current folder.
Cannot create	Cannot create a folder.
Cannot rename	Cannot rename a file or folder.
Cannot delete	Cannot delete a file or folder.
I/O error	Unspecified I/O error.
Cannot set size	Setting the file size failed.
Cannot open	Opening of a file failed.
Cannot close	Closing a file failed.
Read error	Reading from a file failed.
Write error	Writing to a file failed.
Cannot seek	Seek failure.
Cannot execute	Unable to execute the specified file.

File and Folder Supported Encoding Names

The following list of names is a basic set of encoding names supported by the `File` object. Some of the character encoders are built in, while the operating system is queried for most of the other encoders. Depending on the language packs installed, some of the encodings may not be available. Names that refer to the same encoding are listed in one line. Underlines are replaced with dashes before matching an encoding name.

The `File` object processes an extended Unicode character with a value greater that 65535 as a Unicode surrogate pair (two characters in the range between 0xD700-0xDFFF).

Built-in encodings are:

```
US-ASCII, ASCII,ISO646-US,I SO-646.IRV:1991, ISO-IR-6,
ANSI-X3.4-1968,CP367,IBM367,US,ISO646.1991-IRV
UCS-2,UCS2, ISO-10646-UCS-2
UCS2LE,UCS-2LE,ISO-10646-UCS-2LE
UCS2BE,UCS-2BE,ISO-10646-UCS-2BE
UCS-4,UCS4, ISO-10646-UCS-4
UCS4LE,UCS-4LE,ISO-10646-UCS-4LE
UCS4BE,UCS-4BE,ISO-10646-UCS-4BE
UTF-8,UTF8,UNICODE-1-1-UTF-8,UNICODE-2-0-UTF-8,X-UNICODE-2-0-UTF-8
UTF16,UTF-16,ISO-10646-UTF-16
UTF16LE,UTF-16LE,ISO-10646-UTF-16LE
UTF16BE,UTF-16BE,ISO-10646-UTF-16BE
CP1252,WINDOWS-1252,MS-ANSI
ISO-8859-1,ISO-8859-1,ISO-8859-1:1987,ISO-IR-100,LATIN1
MACINTOSH,X-MAC-ROMAN
BINARY
```

The ASCII encoder raises errors for characters greater than 127, and the BINARY encoder simply converts between bytes and Unicode characters by using the lower 8 bits. The latter encoder is convenient for reading and writing binary data.

Additional encodings

In Windows, all encodings use code pages, which are assigned numeric values. The usual Western character set that Windows uses, for example, is the code page 1252. You can select Windows code pages by prepending the number of the code page with "CP" or "WINDOWS": for example, "CP1252" for the code page 1252. The `File` object has many other built-in encoding names that match predefined code page numbers. If a code page is not present, the encoding cannot be selected.

In Mac OS, you can select encoders by name rather than by code page number. The `File` object queries Mac OS directly for an encoder. As far as Mac OS character sets are identical with Windows code pages, Mac OS also knows the Windows code page numbers.

In UNIX, the number of available encoders depends on the installation of the `iconv` library.

Common encoding names

The following encoding names are implemented both in Windows and in Mac OS:

```
UTF-7,UTF7,UNICODE-1-1-UTF-7,X-UNICODE-2-0-UTF-7
ISO-8859-2,ISO-8859-2,ISO-8859-2:1987,ISO-IR-101,LATIN2
ISO-8859-3,ISO-8859-3,ISO-8859-3:1988,ISO-IR-109,LATIN3
ISO-8859-4,ISO-8859-4,ISO-8859-4:1988,ISO-IR-110,LATIN4,BALTIC
ISO-8859-5,ISO-8859-5,ISO-8859-5:1988,ISO-IR-144,CYRILLIC
ISO-8859-6,ISO-8859-6,ISO-8859-6:1987,ISO-IR-127,ECMA-114,ASMO-708,ARABIC
ISO-8859-7,ISO-8859-7,ISO-8859-7:1987,ISO-IR-126,ECMA-118,ELOT-928,
    GREEK8,GREEK
ISO-8859-8,ISO-8859-8,ISO-8859-8:1988,ISO-IR-138,HEBREW
ISO-8859-9,ISO-8859-9,ISO-8859-9:1989,ISO-IR-148,LATIN5,TURKISH
ISO-8859-10,ISO-8859-10,ISO-8859-10:1992,ISO-IR-157,LATIN6
ISO-8859-13,ISO-8859-13,ISO-IR-179,LATIN7
ISO-8859-14,ISO-8859-14,ISO-8859-14,ISO-8859-14:1998,ISO-IR-199,LATIN8
ISO-8859-15,ISO-8859-15,ISO-8859-15:1998,ISO-IR-203
ISO-8859-16,ISO-885,ISO-885,MS-EE
CP850,WINDOWS-850,IBM850
CP866,WINDOWS-866,IBM866
CP932,WINDOWS-932,SJIS,SHIFT-JIS,X-SJIS,X-MS-SJIS,MS-SJIS,MS-KANJI
CP936,WINDOWS-936,GBK,WINDOWS-936,GB2312,GB-2312-80,ISO-IR-58,CHINESE
CP949,WINDOWS-949,UHC,KSC-5601,KS-C-5601-1987,KS-C-5601-1989,ISO-IR-149,
    KOREAN
CP950,WINDOWS-950,BIG5,BIG-5,BIG-FIVE,BIGFIVE,CN-BIG5,X-X-BIG5
CP1251,WINDOWS-1251,MS-CYRL
CP1252,WINDOWS-1252,MS-ANSI
CP1253,WINDOWS-1253,MS-GREEK
CP1254,WINDOWS-1254,MS-TURK
CP1255,WINDOWS-1255,MS-HEBR
CP1256,WINDOWS-1256,MS-ARAB
CP1257,WINDOWS-1257,WINBALTRIM
CP1258,WINDOWS-1258
CP1361,WINDOWS-1361,JOHAB
EUC-JP,EUCJP,X-EUC-JP
EUC-KR,EUCKR,X-EUC-KR
HZ,HZ-GB-2312
X-MAC-JAPANESE
X-MAC-GREEK
X-MAC-CYRILLIC
X-MAC-LATIN
X-MAC-ICELANDIC
X-MAC-TURKISH
```

Additional Windows encoding names

```
CP437,IBM850,WINDOWS-437
CP709,WINDOWS-709,ASMO-449,BCONV4
EBCDIC
KOI-8R
KOI-8U
ISO-2022-JP
ISO-2022-KR
```

Additional Mac OS encoding names

These names are alias names for encodings that Mac OS might know.

```
TIS-620,TIS620,TIS620-0,TIS620.2529-1,TIS620.2533-0,TIS620.2533-1,
    ISO-IR-166
CP874,WINDOWS-874
JP,JIS-C6220-1969-RO,ISO646-JP,ISO-IR-14
JIS-X0201,JISX0201-1976,X0201
JIS-X0208,JIS-X0208-1983,JIS-X0208-1990,JIS0208,X0208,ISO-IR-87
JIS-X0212,JIS-X0212.1990-0,JIS-X0212-1990,X0212,ISO-IR-159
CN,GB-1988-80,ISO646-CN,ISO-IR-57
ISO-IR-16,CN-GB-ISOIR165
KSC-5601,KS-C-5601-1987,KS-C-5601-1989,ISO-IR-149
EUC-CN,EUCCN,GB2312,CN-GB
EUC-TW,EUCTW,X-EUC-TW
```

UNIX encodings

In UNIX, the `File` object looks for the presence of the `iconv` library, and uses whatever encoding it finds there. If you need a special encoding in UNIX, make sure that there is an `iconv` encoding module installed that converts between UTF-16 (the internal format that the `File` object uses) and the desired encoding.

11 | Scripting Constants

This section lists and describes the enumerations defined for use with Adobe Photoshop CS2 JavaScript properties and methods.

Constant type	Values	What it means
AdjustmentReference	ABSOLUTE RELATIVE	Method to use for interpreting selective color adjustment specifications: ABSOLUTE = % of the whole; RELATIVE = % of the existing color amount.
AnchorPosition	BOTTOMCENTER BOTTOMLEFT BOTTOMRIGHT MIDDLECENTER MIDDLELEFT MIDDLERIGHT TOPCENTER TOPLEFT TOPRIGHT	The point on the object that does not move when the object is rotated or resized.
AntiAlias	CRISP NONE SHARP SMOOTH STRONG	Method to use to smooth edges by softening the color transition between edge pixels and background pixels.
AutoKernType	MANUAL METRICS OPTICAL	The type of kerning to use for characters.
BatchDestinationType	FOLDER NODESTINATION SAVEANDCLOSE	The destination, if any, for batch-processed files: FOLDER: Save modified versions of the files to a new location (leaving the originals unchanged); NODESTINATIONTYPE: Leave all files open; SAVEANDCLOSE: Save changes and close the files.
BitmapConversionType	CUSTOMPATTERN DIFFUSIONDITHER HALFTHRESHOLD HALFTONESCREEN PATTERNDITHER	Specifies the quality of an image you are converting to bitmap mode.
BitmapHalfToneType	CROSS DIAMOND ELLIPSE LINE ROUND SQUARE	Specifies the shape of the dots (ink deposits) in the halftone screen.

Constant type	Values	What it means
`BitsPerChannelType`	EIGHT ONE SIXTEEN THIRTYTWO	The number of bits per color channel.
`BlendMode`	COLORBLEND COLORBURN COLORDODGE DARKEN DIFFERENCE DISSOLVE EXCLUSION HARDLIGHT HUE LIGHTEN LINEARBURN LINEARDODGE LINEARLIGHT LUMINOSITY MULTIPLY NORMAL OVERLAY PASSTHROUGH PINLIGHT SATURATION SCREEN SOFTLIGHT VIVIDLIGHT	Controls how pixels in the image are blended.
`BMPDepthType`	BMP_A1R5G5B5 BMP_A4R4G4B4 BMP_A8R8G8B8 BMP_R5G6B5 BMP_R8G8B8 BMP_X1R5G5B5 BMP_X4R4G4B4 BMP_X8R8G8B8 EIGHT FOUR ONE SIXTEEN THIRTYTWO TWENTYFOUR	The number of bits per channel (also called pixel depth or color depth). The number selected indicates the exponent of 2. For example, a pixel with a bit-depth of EIGHT has 2^8, or 256, possible color values.
`ByteOrder`	IBM MACOS	The order in which bytes will be read.
`CameraRAWSettingsType`	CAMERA CUSTOM SELECTEDIMAGE	The default CameraRaw settings to use: the camera settings, custom settings, or the settings of the selected image.

Constant type	Values	What it means
CameraRAWSize	EXTRALARGE LARGE MAXIMUM MEDIUM MINIMUM SMALL	The camera RAW size type options: EXTRALARGE=5120 x 1024 LARGE=4096 x 1024 MEDIUM=3072 x 1024 SMALL=2048 x 1024 MINIMUM=1536 x 1024
ChangeMode	BITMAP CMYK GRAYSCALE INDEXEDCOLOR LAB MULTICHANNEL RGB	The type of color mode to use. **Note:** Color images must be changed to GRAYSCALE mode before you can change them to BITMAP mode.
ChannelType	COMPONENT MASKEDAREA SELECTEDAREA SPOTCOLOR	The type of channel: COMPONENT: related to document color mode MASKEDAREA: Alpha channel where color indicates masked area SELECTEDAREA: Alpha channel where color indicates selected are SPOTCOLOR:
ColorBlendMode	BEHIND CLEAR COLOR COLORBURN COLORDODGE DARKEN DIFFERENCE DISSOLVE EXCLUSION HARDLIGHT HUE LIGHTEN LINEARBURN LINEARDODGE LINEARLIGHT LUMINOSITY MULTIPLY NORMAL OVERLAY PINLIGHT SATURATION SCREEN SOFTLIGHT VIVIDLIGHT	Color blend mode type.

Constant type	Values	What it means
ColorModel	CMYK GRAYSCALE HSB LAB NONE RGB	The color model to use.
ColorPicker	ADOBE APPLE PLUGIN WINDOWS	The color picker to use.
ColorProfile	CUSTOM NONE WORKING	The color profile type to use to manage this document.
ColorReductionType	ADAPTIVE BLACKWHITE CUSTOM GRAYSCALE MACINTOSH PERCEPTUAL RESTRICTIVE SELECTIVE WINDOWS	The color reduction algorithm option to use.
ColorSpaceType	ADOBERGB COLORMATCHRGB PROPHOTORGB SRGB	The type of color space to use.
CopyrightedType	COPYRIGHTEDWORK PUBLICDOMAIN UNMARKED	The copyright status of the document.
CreateFields	DUPLICATION INTERPOLATION	The method to use for creating fields.
CropToType	ARTBOX BLEEDBOX BOUNDINGBOX CROPBOX MEDIABOX TRIMBOX	The style to use when cropping a page.
DCSType	COLORCOMPOSITE GRAYSCALECOMPOSITE NOCOMPOSITE	The DCS format to use: COLORCOMPOSITE: Creates a color composite file in addition to DCS files; GRAYSCALECOMPOSITE: Creates a grayscale composite file in addition to DCS files; NOCOMPOSITE: Does not create a composite file.
DepthMapSource	IMAGEHIGHLIGHT LAYERMASK NONE TRANSPARENCYCHANNEL	What to use for the depth map.

Adobe® Photoshop® CS2 Official JavaScript Reference

Constant type	Values	What it means
DescValueType	ALIASTYPE BOOLEANTYPE CLASSTYPE DOUBLETYPE ENUMERATEDTYPE INTEGERTYPE LISTTYPE OBJECTTYPE RAWTYPE REFERENCETYPE STRINGTYPE UNITDOUBLE	The value type of an object.
DialogModes	ALL ERROR NO	Controls the type (mode) of dialogs Photoshop displays when running scripts.
Direction	HORIZONTAL VERTICAL	The orientation of the object.
DisplacementMapType	STRETCHTOFIT TILE	Describes how the displacement map fits the image if the image is not the same size as the map.
Dither	DIFFUSION NOISE NONE PATTERN	The default type of dithering to use.
DocumentFill	BACKGROUNDCOLOR TRANSPARENT WHITE	The fill of the document.
DocumentMode	BITMAP CMYK DUOTONE GRAYSCALE INDEXEDCOLOR LAB MULTICHANNEL RGB	The color mode of the open document.
EditLogItemsType	CONCISE DETAILED SESSIONONLY	The history log edit options: CONCISE: Save a concise history log. DETAILED: Save a detailed history log. SESSIONONLY: Save history log only for the session.

Constant type	Values	What it means
ElementPlacement	INSIDE PLACEATBEGINNING PLACEATEND PLACEBEFORE PLACEAFTER	The object's position in the Layers palette. **Note:** Not all values are valid for all object types. Please refer to the object property definition in JavaScript Object Reference (page 65) to make sure you are using a valid value.
EliminateFields	EVENFIELDS ODDFIELDS	The type of fields to eliminate.
ExportType	ILLUSTRATORPATHS SAVEFORWEB	The export options to use.
Extension	LOWERCASE NONE UPPERCASE	The formatting of the extension in the filename.
FileNamingType	DDMM DDMMYY DOCUMENTNAMELOWER DOCUMENTNAMEMIXED DOCUMENTNAMEUPPER EXTENSIONLOWER EXTENSIONUPPER MMDD MMDDYY SERIALLETTERLOWER SERIALLETTERUPPER SERIALNUMBER1 SERIALNUMBER2 SERIALNUMBER3 SERIALNUMBER4 YYDDMM YYMMDD YYYYMMDD	File naming options for the batch command.
FontPreviewType	LARGE MEDIUM NONE SMALL	The type size to use for font previews in the type tool font menus.
ForcedColors	BLACKWHITE NONE PRIMARIES WEB	The type of colors to be forced (included) into the color table: BLACKWHITE: Pure black and pure white, NONE, PRIMARIES: Red, green, blue, cyan, magenta, yellow, black, and white; WEB: the 216 web-safe colors.

Constant type	Values	What it means
FormatOptions	OPTIMIZEDBASELINE PROGRESSIVE STANDARDBASELINE	The option with which to save a JPEG file: OPTIMIZEDBASELINE: Optimized color and a slightly reduced file size; PROGRESSIVE: Displays a series of increasingly detailed scans as the image downloads; STANDARDBASELINE: Format recognized by most web browsers.
GalleryConstrainType	CONSTRAINBOTH CONSTRAINHEIGHT CONSTRAINWIDTH	The type of proportions to constrain for images.
GalleryFontType	ARIAL COURIERNEW HELVETICA TIMESNEWROMAN	The fonts to use for the Web photo gallery captions and other text.
GallerySecurityTextColorType	BLACK CUSTOM WHITE	The color to use for text displayed over gallery images as an antitheft deterrent.
GallerySecurityTextPositionType	CENTERED LOWERLEFT LOWERRIGHT UPPERLEFT UPPERRIGHT	The position of the text displayed over gallery images as an antitheft deterrent.
GallerySecurityTextRotateType	CLOCKWISE45 CLOCKWISE90 COUNTERCLOCKWISE45 COUNTERCLOCKWISE90 ZERO	The orientation of the text displayed over gallery images as an antitheft deterrent.
GallerySecurityType	CAPTION COPYRIGHT CREDIT CUSTOMTEXT FILENAME NONE TITLE	The content to use for text displayed over gallery images as an antitheft deterrent. **Note:** All types draw from the image's file information except CUSTOMTEXT.
GalleryThumbSizeType	CUSTOM LARGE MEDIUM SMALL	The size of thumbnail images in the web photo gallery.
Geometry	HEPTAGON HEXAGON OCTAGON PENTAGON SQUARE TRIANGLE	Geometric options for shapes, such as the iris shape in the Lens Blur Filter.

Constant type	Values	What it means
GridLineStyle	DASHED DOTTED SOLID	The line style for the nonprinting grid displayed over images.
GridSize	LARGE MEDIUM NONE SMALL	The value of grid line spacing.
GuideLineStyle	DASHED SOLID	The line style for nonprinting guides displayed over images.
IllustratorPathType	ALLPATHS DOCUMENTBOUNDS NAMEDPATH	The paths to export.
Intent	ABSOLUTECOLORIMETRIC PERCEPTUAL RELATIVECOLORIMETRIC SATURATION	The rendering intent to use when converting from one color space to another.
JavaScriptExecutionMode	BEFORERUNNING NEVER ONRUNTIMEERROR	The debugger mode to use.
Justification	CENTER CENTERJUSTIFIED FULLYJUSTIFIED LEFT LEFTJUSTIFIED RIGHT RIGHTJUSTIFIED	The placement of paragraph text within the bounding box.
Language	BRAZILLIANPORTUGUESE CANADIANFRENCH DANISH DUTCH ENGLISHUK ENGLISHUSA FINNISH FRENCH GERMAN ITALIAN NORWEGIAN NYNORSKNORWEGIAN OLDGERMAN PORTUGUESE SPANISH SWEDISH SWISSGERMAN	The language to use.
LayerCompression	RLE ZIP	Compression methods for data for pixels in layers.

Constant type	Values	What it means
LayerKind	BRIGHTNESSCONTRAST CHANNELMIXER COLORBALANCE CURVES GRADIENTFILL GRADIENTMAP HUESATURATION INVERSION LEVELS NORMAL PATTERNFILL POSTERIZE SELECTIVECOLOR SMARTOBJECT SOLIDFILL TEXT THRESHOLD	The kind of artLayer object. **Note:** You can create a text layer only from an empty art layer.
LensType	MOVIEPRIME PRIME105 PRIME35 ZOOMLENS	The type of lens to use.
MagnificationType	ACTUALSIZE FITPAGE	The type of magnification to use when viewing an image.
MatteType	BACKGROUND BLACK FOREGROUND NETSCAPE NONE SEMIGRAY WHITE	The color to use for matting.
NewDocumentMode	BITMAP CMYK GRAYSCALE LAB RGB	The color profile to use for the document.
NoiseDistribution	GAUSSIAN UNIFORM	Distribution method to use when applying an Add Noise filter.
OffsetUndefinedAreas	REPEATEDGEPIXELS SETTOBACKGROUND WRAPAROUND	Method to use to fill the empty space left by offsetting a an image or selection.
OpenDocumentMode	CMYK GRAYSCALE LAB RGB	The color profile to use.

Constant type	Values	What it means
OpenDocumentType	ACROBATTOUCHUPIMAGE ALIASPIX BMP CAMERARAW COMPUSERVEGIF ELECTRICIMAGE EPS EPSPICTPREVIEW EPSTIFFPREVIEW FILMSTRIP JPEG PCX PDF PHOTOCD PHOTOSHOP PHOTOSHOPDCS_1 PHOTOSHOPDCS_2 PHOTOSHOPEPS PHOTOSHOPPDF PICTFILEFORMAT PICTRESOURCEFORMAT PIXAR PNG PORTABLEBITMAP RAW SCITEXCT SGIRGB SOFTIMAGE TARGA TIFF WAVEFRONTRLA WIRELESSBITMAP	The format in which to open the document.
OperatingSystem	OS2 WINDOWS	The operating system.
Orientation	LANDSCAPE PORTRAIT	The page orientation.
OtherPaintingCursors	PRECISEOTHER STANDARDOTHER	The pointer for the following tools: Eraser, Pencil, Paintbrush, Healing Brush, Rubber Stamp, Pattern Stamp, Smudge, Blur, Sharpen, Dodge, Burn, Sponge.
PaintingCursors	BRUSHSIZE PRECISE STANDARD	The pointer for the following tools: Marquee, Lasso, Polygonal Lasso, Magic Wand, Crop, Slice, Patch Eyedropper, Pen, Gradient, Line, Paint Bucket, Magnetic Lasso, Magnetic Pen, Freeform Pen, Measure, Color Sampler.

Constant type	Values	What it means
`Palette`	EXACT LOCALADAPTIVE LOCALPERCEPTUAL LOCALSELECTIVE MACOSPALETTE MASTERADAPTIVE MASTERPERCEPTUAL MASTERSELECTIVE PREVIOUSPALETTE UNIFORM WEBPALETTE WINDOWSPALETTE	The palette type to use.
`PathKind`	CLIPPINGPATH NORMALPATH TEXTMASK VECTORMASK WORKPATH	The type of path.
`PDFCompatibility`	PDF13 PDF14 PDF15 PDF16	The PDF version to make the document compatible with.
`PDFEncoding`	JPEG JPEG2000HIGH JPEG2000LOSSLESS JPEG2000LOW JPEG2000MED JPEG2000MEDHIGH JPEG2000MEDLOW JPEGHIGH JPEGLOW JPEGMED JPEGMEDHIGH JPEGMEDLOW NONE PDFZIP PDFZIP4BIT	The type of compression to use when saving a document in PDF format.
`PDFResample`	NONE PDFAVERAGE PDFBICUBIC PDFSUBSAMPLE	The down sample method to use.
`PDFStandard`	NONE PDFX1A2001 PDFX1A2003 PDFX32002 PDFX32003	The PDF standard to make the document compatible with.
`PhotoCDColorSpace`	LAB16 LAB8 RGB16 RGB8	The color space to use when creating a Photo CD.

Constant type	Values	What it means
PhotoCDSize	EXTRALARGE LARGE MAXIMUM MEDIUM MINIMUM SMALL	The pixel dimensions of the image.
PICTBitsPerPixels	EIGHT FOUR SIXTEEN THIRTYTWO TWO	The number of bits per pixel to use when compression a PICT file. **Note:** Use 16 or 32 for RGB images; use 2, 4, or 8 for bitmap and grayscale images.
PICTCompression	JPEGHIGHPICT JPEGLOWPICT JPEGMAXIMUMPICT JPEGMEDIUMPICT NONE	The type of compression to use when saving an image as a PICT file.
PicturePackageTextType	CAPTION COPYRIGHT CREDIT FILENAME NONE ORIGIN USER	The function or meaning of text in a Picture Package.
PointKind	CORNERPOINT SMOOTHPOINT	The role a `pathPoint` plays in a `pathItem`.
PointType	POSTSCRIPT TRADITIONAL	The kind of measurement to use for type points: POSTSCRIPT = 72 points/inch; TRADITIONAL = 72.27 points/inch.
PolarConversionType	POLARTORECTANGULAR RECTANGULARTOPOLAR	The method of polar distortion to use.
Preview	EIGHTBITTIFF MACOSEIGHTBIT MACOSJPEG MACOSMONOCHROME MONOCHROMETIFF NONE	The type of image to use as a low-resolution preview in the destination application.
PrintEncoding	ASCII BINARY JPEG	The type of encoding to use.
PurgeTarget	ALLCACHES CLIPBOARDCACHE HISTORYCACHES UNDOCACHES	Cache to be targeted in a purge operation.

Adobe® Photoshop® CS2 Official JavaScript Reference

Constant type	Values	What it means
QueryStateType	ALWAYS ASK NEVER	Permission state for queries.
RadialBlurMethod	SPIN ZOOM	The blur method to use.
RadialBlurQuality	BEST DRAFT GOOD	The smoothness or graininess of the blurred image.
RasterizeType	ENTIRELAYER FILLCONTENT LAYERCLIPPINGPATH LINKEDLAYERS SHAPE TEXTCONTENTS	The layer element to rasterize.
ReferenceFormType	CLASSTYPE ENUMERATED IDENTIFIER INDEX NAME OFFSET PROPERTY	The type of an ActionReference (page 73) object.
ResampleMethod	BICUBIC BICUBICSHARPER BICUBICSMOOTHER BILINEAR NEARESTNEIGHBOR NONE	The method to use for image interpolation.
ResetTarget	ALLTOOLS ALLWARNINGS EVERYTHING	The type of object or objects to reset to default settings.
RippleSize	LARGE MEDIUM SMALL	The size of undulations to use.
SaveBehavior	ALWAYSSAVE ASKWHENSAVING NEVERSAVE	The application's behavior when a save() method is called.

Constant type	Values	What it means
`SaveDocumentType`	ALIASPIX BMP COMPUSERVEGIF ELECTRICIMAGE JPEG PCX PHOTOSHOP PHOTOSHOPDCS_1 PHOTOSHOPDCS_2 PHOTOSHOPEPS PHOTOSHOPPDF PICTFileFORMAT PICTRESOURCEFORMAT PIXAR PNG PORTABLEBITMAP RAW SCITEXCT SGIRGB SOFTIMAGE TARGA TIFF WAVEFRONTRLA WIRELESSBITMAP	The format in which to save a document. **Note:** The `format` property of the `ExportOptionsSaveForWeb` class uses only the following values: COMPUSERVEGIF, JPEG, PNG-8, PNG-24, and BMP. See "ExportOptionsSaveForWeb" on page 133.
`SaveEncoding`	ASCII BINARY JPEGHIGH JPEGLOW JPEGMAXIMUM JPEGMEDIUM	The type of encoding to use when saving a file.
`SaveLogItemsType`	LOGFILE LOGFILEANDMETADATA METADATA	The location of history log data.
`SaveOptions`	DONOTSAVECHANGES PROMPTTOSAVECHANGES SAVECHANGES	The "save" method to use when closing a document.
`SelectionType`	DIMINISH EXTEND INTERSECT REPLACE	The selection behavior when a selection already exists: DIMINISH: Remove the selection from the already selected area; EXTEND: Add the selection to an already selected area; INTERSECT: Make the selection only the area where the new selection intersects the already selected area; REPLACE: Replace the selected area.
`ShapeOperation`	SHAPEADD SHAPEINTERSECT SHAPESUBTRACT SHAPEXOR	A `subPathItem` object's behavior when it intersects another `subPathItem` object.

Constant type	Values	What it means
SmartBlurMode	EDGEONLY NORMAL OVERLAYEDGE	The method to use for smart blurring: EDGEONLY, OVERLAYEDGES: Apply blur only to edges of color transitions; NORMAL: Apply blur to entire image.
SmartBlurQuality	HIGH LOW MEDIUM	The blur quality to use.
SourceSpaceType	DOCUMENT PROOF	
SpherizeMode	HORIZONTAL NORMAL VERTICAL	The curve (or stretch shape) to use for the distortion.
StrikeThruType	STRIKEBOX STRIKEHEIGHT STRIKEOFF	The style of strikethrough to use.
StrokeLocation	CENTER INSIDE OUTSIDE	The placement of path or selection boundary strokes.
TargaBitsPerPixels	SIXTEEN THIRTYTWO TWENTYFOUR	The resolution to use when saving an image in Targa format.
TextCase	ALLCAPS NORMAL SMALLCAPS	The case usage for type.
TextComposer	ADOBEEVERYLINE ADOBESINGLELINE	The composition method to use to optimize the specified hyphenation and justification options.
TextType	PARAGRAPHTEXT POINTTEXT	The type of text: PARAGRAPHTEXT: Text that wraps within a bounding box; POINTTEXT: Text that does not wrap.
TextureType	BLOCKS CANVAS FILE FROSTED TINYLENS	The type of texture or glass surface image to load for a texturizer or glass filter.
TIFFEncoding	JPEG NONE TIFFLZW TIFFZIP	The encoding to use for TIFF files.

Constant type	Values	What it means
ToolType	ARTHISTORYBRUSH BACKGROUNDERASER BLUR BRUSH BURN CLONESTAMP COLORREPLACEMENTTOOL DODGE ERASER HEALINGBRUSH HISTORYBRUSH PATTERNSTAMP PENCIL SHARPEN SMUDGE SPONGE	The tool selection.
TransitionType	BLINDSHORIZONTAL BLINDSVERTICAL BOXIN BOXOUT DISSOLVE GLITTERDOWN GLITTERRIGHT GLITTERRIGHTDOWN NONE RANDOM SPLITHORIZONTALIN SPLITHORIZONTALOUT SPLITVERTICALIN SPLITVERTICALOUT WIPEDOWN WIPELEFT WIPERIGHT WIPEUP	The method to use to transition from one image to the next in a PDF presentation.
TrimType	BOTTOMRIGHT TOPLEFT TRANSPARENT	Type of pixels to trim around an image: BOTTOMRIGHT = bottom right pixel color; TOPLEFT = top left pixel color.
TypeUnits	MM PIXELS POINTS	The unit to use for measuring text characters.
UndefinedAreas	REPEATEDGEPIXELS WRAPAROUND	The method to use to treat undistorted areas or areas left blank in an image to which the a filter in the Distort category has been applied.

Constant type	Values	What it means

UnderlineType	UNDERLINELEFT
	UNDERLINEOFF
	UNDERLINERIGHT
		The placement of text underlining.
		Note: `UnderlineType.`
		`UNDELINELEFT` and
		`UnderlineType.`
		`UNDELINERIGHT` are valid
		only when `direction =`
		`Direction.VERTICAL.`

Units	CM INCHES MM PERCENT PICAS PIXELS POINTS	The measurement unit for type and ruler increments.
Urgency	FOUR HIGH LOW NONE NORMAL SEVEN SIX THREE TWO	The editorial urgency of the artwork.
WarpStyle	ARC ARCH ARCLOWER ARCUPPER BULGE FISH FISHEYE FLAG INFLATE NONE RISE SHELLLOWER SHELLUPPER SQUEEZE TWIST WAVE	The warp style to use.
WaveType	SINE SQUARE TRIANGULAR	The type of wave to use.

Constant type	Values	What it means
WhiteBalanceType	ASSHOT AUTO CLOUDY CUSTOM DAYLIGHT FLASH FLUORESCENT SHADE TUNGSTEN	The lighting conditions to use (affects color balance).
ZigZagType	AROUNDCENTER OUTFROMCENTER PONDRIPPLES	The method of zigzagging to use.

12 | ExtendScript Tools and Features

ExtendScript is Adobe's extended implementation of JavaScript, and is used by all Adobe Creative Suite 2 applications that provide a scripting interface. In addition to implementing the JavaScript language according to the W3C specification, ExtendScript provides certain additional features and utilities.

- For help in developing, debugging, and testing scripts, ExtendScript provides:
  - The ExtendScript Toolkit (page 348), an interactive development and testing environment for ExtendScript.
  - A global debugging object, the Dollar ($) Object (page 362).
  - A reporting utility for ExtendScript elements, the ExtendScript Reflection Interface (page 366).
- In addition, ExtendScript provides these tools and features:
  - A localization utility for providing user-interface string values in different languages. See "Localizing ExtendScript Strings" on page 369.
  - Global functions for displaying short messages in dialog boxes. See "User Notification Helper Functions" on page 373.
  - An object type for specifying measurement values together with their units. See "Specifying Measurement Values" on page 376.
  - Tools for combining scripts, such as a `#include` directive, and `import` and `export` statements. See "Modular Programming Support" on page 381.
  - Support for extending or overriding math and logical operator behavior on a class-by-class basis. See "Operator Overloading" on page 384.
- ExtendScript provides a common scripting environment for all Adobe Creative Suite 2 applications, and allows interapplication communication through scripts.
  - To identify specific Adobe Creative Suite 2 applications, scripts must use Application and Namespace Specifiers (page 385).
  - Applications can run scripts automatically on startup. See "Script Locations and Checking Application Installation" on page 387.

The ExtendScript Toolkit

The ExtendScript Toolkit provides an interactive development and testing environment for ExtendScript in all Adobe Creative Suite 2 applications. The Toolkit includes a full-featured, syntax-highlighting editor with Unicode capabilities and multiple undo/redo support. The Toolkit allows you to:

- Single-step through JavaScripts inside a CS2 application.
- Inspect all data for a running script.
- Set and execute breakpoints.

The Toolkit is the default editor for ExtendScript files, which use the extension .jsx. You can use the Toolkit to edit or debug scripts in JS or JSX files.

When you double-click a JSX file in the platform's windowing environment, the script runs in the Toolkit, unless it specifies a particular target application using the #target directive. For more information, see "Selecting a debugging target" on page 350 and "Preprocessor directives" on page 381.

Configuring the Toolkit window

The ExtendScript Toolkit initially appears with a default arrangement of panes, containing a default configuration of tabs. You can adjust the relative sizes of the panes by dragging the separators up or down, or right or left. You can regroup the tabs. To move a tab, drag the label into another pane.

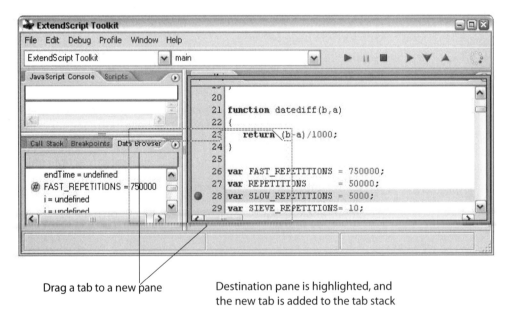

Drag a tab to a new pane

Destination pane is highlighted, and the new tab is added to the tab stack

---

If you drag a tab so that the entire destination pane is highlighted, it becomes another stacked tab in that pane. If you drag a tab to the top or bottom of a pane (so that only the top or bottom bar of the destination pane is highlighted), that pane splits to show the tabs in a tiled format.

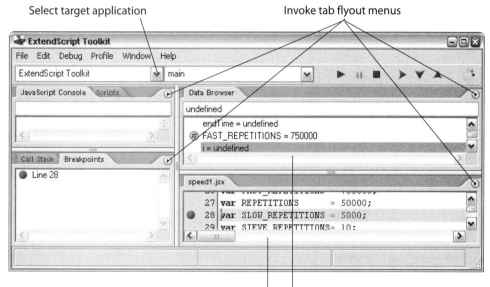

Split pane shows Browser and Editor tabs

Each tab has a flyout menu, accessed through the triangle icon in the upper right corner. The same menu is available as a context menu, which you invoke with a right-click in the tab. This menu always includes a **Hide Pane** command to hide that pane. Use the **Window** menu to show a hidden pane, or to bring it to the front.

The Editor, which has a tab for each script, has an additional context menu for debugging, which appears when you right-click in the line numbers area.

The Toolkit saves the current layout when you exit, and restores it at the next startup. It also saves and restores the open documents, the current positions within the documents, and any breakpoints that have been set.

- If you do not want to restore all settings on startup, hold SHIFT while the Toolkit loads to restore default settings. This reconnects to the last application and engine that was selected.

- If you want to restore the layout settings on startup, but not load the previously open documents, choose **Start with a clean workspace** in the Preferences dialog.

Selecting a debugging target

The Toolkit can debug multiple applications at one time. If you have more than one Adobe Creative Suite 2 application installed, use the drop-down list at the upper left under the menu bar to select the target application. All installed applications that use ExtendScript are shown in this list. If you select an application that is not running, the Toolkit prompts for permission to run it.

All available engines in the selected target application are shown in a drop-down list to the right of the application list, with an icon that shows the current debugging status of that engine. A target application can have more than one ExtendScript engine, and more than one engine can be *active*, although only one is *current*. An active engine is one that is currently executing code, is halted at a breakpoint, or, having executed all scripts, is waiting to receive events. An icon by each engine name indicates whether it is *running*, *halted*, or *waiting* for input:

▶	**running**
■	**halted**
▷	**waiting**

The current engine is the one whose data and state is displayed in the Toolkit's panes. If an application has only one engine, its engine becomes current when you select the application as the target. If there is more than one engine available in the target application, you can select an engine in the list to make it current.

When you open the Toolkit, it attempts to reconnect to the same target and engine that was set last time it closed. If that target application is not running, the Toolkit prompts for permission to launch it. If permission is refused, the Toolkit itself becomes the target application.

If the target application that you select is not running, the Toolkit prompts for permission and launches the application. Similarly, if you run a script that specifies a target application that is not running (using the #target directive), the Toolkit prompts for permission to launch it. If the application is running but not selected as the current target, the Toolkit prompts you to switch to it.

If you select an application that cannot be debugged in the Toolkit (such as Adobe Help), an error dialog reports that the Toolkit cannot connect to the selected application.

The ExtendScript Toolkit is the default editor for JSX files. If you double-click a JSX file in a file browser, the Toolkit looks for a `#target` directive in the file and launches that application to run the script; however, it first checks for syntax errors in the script. If any are found, the Toolkit displays the error in a message box and quits silently, rather than launching the target application. For example:

Selecting scripts

The Scripts tab offers a list of debuggable scripts for the target application, which can be JS or JSX files or (for some applications) HTML files that contain embedded scripts.

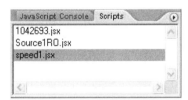

Select a script in this tab to load it and display its contents in the editor pane, where you can modify it, save it, or run it within the target application.

Tracking data

The Data Browser tab is your window into the JavaScript engine. This tab displays all live data defined in the current context, as a list of variables with their current values. If execution has stopped at a breakpoint, it shows variables that have been defined using `var` in the current function, and the function arguments. To show variables defined in the global or calling scope, use the call stack to change the context (see "The call stack" on page 353).

You can use the Data Browser to examine and set variable values.

- Click a variable name to show its current value in the edit field at the top of the tab.
- To change the value, enter a new value and press ENTER. If a variable is read-only, the edit field is disabled.

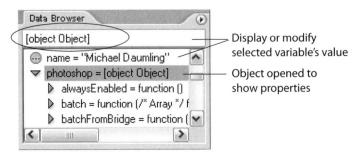

Display or modify selected variable's value

Object opened to show properties

The flyout menu for this tab lets you control the amount of data displayed:

- **Show Global Functions** toggles the display of all global function definitions.
- **Show Object Methods** toggles the display of all functions that are attached to objects. Most often, the interesting data in an object are its callable methods.
- **Show JavaScript Language Elements** toggles the display of all data that is part of the JavaScript language standard, such as the Array constructor or the Math object. An interesting property is the __proto__ property, which reveals the JavaScript object prototype chain.

Each variable has a small icon that indicates the data type. An invalid object is a reference to an object that has been deleted. If a variable is undefined, it does not have an icon.

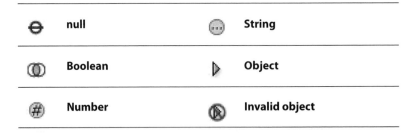

	null		String
	Boolean		Object
	Number		Invalid object

You can inspect the contents of an object by clicking its icon. The list expands to show the object's properties (and methods, if **Show Object Methods** is enabled), and the triangle points down to indicate that the object is open.

Note: In Photoshop CS2 the Data Browser pane is populated only during the debugging of a JavaScript program within Photoshop.

The JavaScript console

The JavaScript console is a command shell and output window for the currently selected JavaScript engine. The console connects you to the global namespace of that engine.

The command line entry field accepts any JavaScript code, and you can use it to evaluate expressions or call functions. Enter any JavaScript statement on the command line and execute it by pressing ENTER. The statement executes within the stack scope of the line highlighted in the Call Stack tab, and the result appears in the output field.

- The command-line input field keeps a command history of 32 lines. Use the Up and Down Arrow keys to scroll through the previous entries.
- Commands entered in this field execute with a timeout of one second. If a command takes longer than one second to execute, the Toolkit generates a timeout error and terminates the attempt.

The output field is standard output for JavaScript execution. If any script generates a syntax error, the error is displayed here along with the file name and the line number. The Toolkit displays errors here during its own startup phase. The tab's flyout menu allows you to clear the contents of the output field and change the size of the font used for output.

The call stack

The Call Stack tab is active while debugging a program. When an executing program stops because of a breakpoint or run-time error, the tab displays the sequence of function calls that led to the current execution point. The Call Stack tab shows the names of the active functions, along with the actual arguments passed in to that function.

For example, this stack pane shows a break occurring at a breakpoint in a function dayOfWeek:

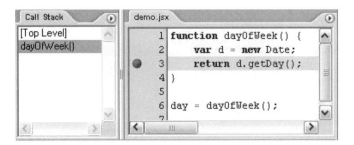

The function containing the breakpoint is highlighted in both the Call Stack and the Editor tabs.

You can click any function in the call hierarchy to inspect it. In the Editor, the line containing the function call that led to that point of execution is marked with a green background. In the example, when you select the line [Top Level] in the call stack, the Editor highlights the line where the dayOfWeek function was called.

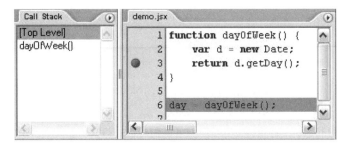

Switching between the functions in the call hierarchy allows you to trace how the current function was called. The Console and Data Browser tabs coordinate with the Call Stack pane. When you select a function in the call stack:

- The Console pane switches its scope to the execution context of that function, so you can inspect and modify its local variables. These would otherwise be inaccessible to the running JavaScript program from within a called function.

- The Data Browser pane displays all data defined in the selected context.

The Script Editor

You can open any number of Script Editor tabs; each displays one Unicode source code document. The editor supports JavaScript syntax highlighting, JavaScript syntax checking, multiple undo and redo operations, and advanced search and replace functionality.

You can use the mouse or special keyboard shortcuts to move the insertion point or to select text in the editor.

Mouse navigation and selection

Click the left mouse button in the editor to move the position caret.

To select text with the mouse, click in unselected text, then drag over the text to be selected. If you drag above or below the currently displayed text, the text scrolls, continuing to select while scrolling. You can also double-click to select a word, or triple-click to select a line.

To initiate a drag-and-drop of selected text, click in the block of selected text, then drag to the destination. You can drag text from one editor pane to another. You can also drag text out of the Toolkit into another application that accepts dragged text, and drag text from another application into a Toolkit editor.

You can drop files from the Explorer or the Finder onto the Toolkit to open them in an editor.

Keyboard navigation and selection

In addition to the usual keyboard input, the editor accepts these special movement keys. You can also select text by using a movement key while pressing SHIFT.

Enter	Insert a Line Feed character
Backspace	Delete character to the left
Delete	Delete character to the right
Left arrow	Move insertion point left one character
Right arrow	Move insertion point right one character
Up arrow	Move insertion point up one line; stay in column if possible
Down arrow	Move insertion point down one line; stay in column if possible
Page up	Move insertion point one page up
Page down	Move insertion point one page down
CTRL + up arrow	Scroll up one line without moving the insertion point

CTRL + down arrow	Scroll down one line without moving the insertion point
CTRL + page up	Scroll one page up without moving the insertion point
CTRL + page down	Scroll one page down without moving the insertion point
CTRL + left arrow	Move insertion point one word to the left
CTRL + right arrow	Move insertion point one word to the right
Home	Move insertion point to start of line
End	Move insertion point to end of line
CTRL + Home	Move insertion point to start of text
CTRL + End	Move insertion point to end of text

The editor supports extended keyboard input via IME (Windows®) or TMS (Mac OS®). This is especially important for Far Eastern characters.

Syntax checking

Before running the new script or saving the text as a script file, you can check whether the text contains JavaScript syntax errors. Choose **Check Syntax** from the **Edit** menu or from the Editor's right-click context menu.

- If the script is syntactically correct, the status line shows "No syntax errors."
- If the Toolkit finds a syntax error, such as a missing quote, it highlights the affected text, plays a sound, and shows the error message in the status line so you can fix the error.

Debugging in the Toolkit

You can debug the code in the currently active Editor tab. Select one of the debugging commands to either run or to single-step through the program.

When you run code from the Editor, it runs in the current target application's selected JavaScript engine. The Toolkit itself runs an independent JavaScript engine, so you can quickly edit and run a script without connecting to a target application.

Evaluation in help tips

If you let your mouse pointer rest over a variable or function in an Editor tab, the result of evaluating that variable or function is displayed as a help tip. When you are not debugging the program, this is helpful only if the variables and functions are already known to the JavaScript engine. During debugging, however, this is an extremely useful way to display the current value of a variable, along with its current data type.

You can turn off the display of help tips using the **Display JavaScript variables** and **Enable UI help tips** options on the Help Options page of the Preferences dialog.

Controlling code execution

The debugging commands are available from the **Debug** menu, from the Editor's right-click context menu, through keyboard shortcuts, and from the toolbar buttons. Use these menu commands and buttons to control the execution of code when the JavaScript Debugger is active.

▶	**Run Continue**	**F5** (Windows) **Control R** (Mac OS)	Starts or resumes execution of a script. Disabled when script is executing.
❚❚	**Break**	**Ctrl F5** (Windows) **Cmd .** (Mac OS)	Halts the currently executing script temporarily and reactivates the JavaScript Debugger. Enabled when a script is executing.
■	**Stop**	**Shift F5** (Windows) **Control K** (Mac OS)	Stops execution of the script and generates a run-time error. Enabled when a script is executing.
▶	**Step Over**	**F10** (Windows) **Control S** (Mac OS)	Halts after executing a single JavaScript line in the script. If the statement calls a JavaScript function, executes the function in its entirety before stopping (do not step into the function).
▼	**Step Into**	**F11** (Windows) **Control T** (Mac OS)	Halts after executing a single JavaScript line statement in the script or after executing a single statement in any JavaScript function that the script calls.
▲	**Step Out**	**Shift F11** (Windows) **Control U** (Mac OS)	When paused within the body of a JavaScript function, resumes script execution until the function returns. When paused outside the body of a function, resumes script execution until the script terminates.

Visual indication of execution states

While the engine is running, an icon ⟳ in the upper right corner of the Toolkit window indicates that the script is active.

When the execution of a script halts because the script reaches a breakpoint, or when the script reaches the next line when stepping line by line, the Editor displays the current script with the current line highlighted in yellow.

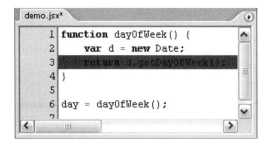

```
demo.jsx
  1  function dayOfWeek() {
  2      var d = new Date;
  3      var day;
  4      try { // test dayOfWeek
  5          day = d.getDayOfWeek();
  6      }
  7      catch (error) { // no dayOfWeek
  8          day = -1;
  9      }
 10      return day;
 11  }
```

If the script encounters a run-time error, the Toolkit halts the execution of the script, displays the current script with the current line highlighted in red, displays the error message in the status line, and plays a sound.

```
demo.jsx*
  1  function dayOfWeek() {
  2      var d = new Date;
  3      return d.getDayOfWeek();
  4  }
  5
  6  day = dayOfWeek();
  7
```

Scripts often use a try/catch clause to execute code that might cause a run-time error, to catch the error programmatically rather than have the script terminate. You can choose to allow regular processing of such errors using the catch clause, rather than breaking into the debugger. To set this behavior, choose **Debug > Don't Break On Guarded Exceptions**. Some run-time errors, such as Out Of Memory, always cause the termination of the script, regardless of this setting.

Setting breakpoints

When debugging a script, it is often helpful to make it stop at certain lines so that you can inspect the state of the environment, whether function calls are nested properly, or whether all variables contain the expected data.

- To stop execution of a script at a given line, click to the left of the line number to set a breakpoint. A filled dot indicates the breakpoint.
- Click a second time to temporarily disable the breakpoint; the icon changes to an outline.
- Click a third time to delete the breakpoint. The icon is removed.

Adobe® Photoshop® CS2 Official JavaScript Reference

Some breakpoints need to be conditional. For example, if you set a breakpoint in a loop that is executed several thousand times, you would not want to have the program stop each time through the loop, but only on each 1000th iteration.

You can attach a condition to a breakpoint, in the form of a JavaScript expression. Every time execution reaches the breakpoint, it runs the JavaScript expression. If the expression evaluates to a nonzero number or `true`, execution stops.

To set a conditional breakpoint in a loop, for example, the conditional expression could be `"i >= 1000"`, which means that the program execution halts if the value of the iteration variable `i` is equal to or greater than 1000.

You can set breakpoints on lines that do not contain any code, such as comment lines. When the Toolkit runs the program, it automatically moves such a breakpoint down to the next line that actually contains code.

Breakpoint icons

Each breakpoint is indicated by an icon to the left of the line number. The icon for a conditional breakpoint is a diamond, while the icon for an unconditional breakpoint is round. Disabled breakpoints are indicated by an outline icon, while active ones are filled.

 Unconditional breakpoint. Execution stops here.

 Unconditional breakpoint, disabled. Execution does not stop.

 Conditional breakpoint. Execution stops if the attached JavaScript expression evaluates to `true`.

 Conditional breakpoint, disabled. Execution does not stop.

The Breakpoints tab

The Breakpoints tab displays all breakpoints set in the current Editor tab. You can use the tab's flyout menu to add, change, or remove a breakpoint.

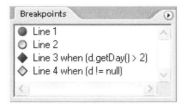

You can edit a breakpoint by double-clicking it, or by selecting it and choosing **Add** or **Change** from the context menu. A dialog allows you to change the line number, the breakpoint's enabled state, and the condition statement.

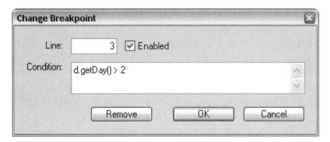

Whenever execution reaches this breakpoint, the debugger evaluates this condition. If it does not evaluate to `true`, the breakpoint is ignored and execution continues. This allows you to break only when certain conditions are met, such as a variable having a particular value.

Profiling

The Profiling tool helps you to optimize program execution. When you turn profiling on, the JavaScript engine collects information about a program while it is running. The tool counts how often the program executes a line or function, or how long it takes to execute a line or function. You can choose exactly which profiling data to display.

Because profiling significantly slows execution time, the **Profile** menu offers these profiling options.

Off	Profiling turned off. This is the default.
Functions	The profiler counts each function call. At the end of execution, displays the total to the left of the line number where the function header is defined.
Lines	The profiler counts each time each line is executed. At the end of execution, displays the total to the left of the line number. Consumes more execution time, but delivers more detailed information.
Add Timing Info	Instead of counting the functions or lines, records the time taken to execute each function or line. At the end of execution, displays the total number of microseconds spent in the function or line, to the left of the line number. This is the most time-consuming form of profiling.
No Profiler Data	When selected, do not display profiler data.
Show Hit Count	When selected, display hit counts.
Show Timing	When selected, display timing data.

Adobe® Photoshop® CS2 Official JavaScript Reference

Erase Profiler Data	Clear all profiling data.
Save Data As	Save profiling data as comma-separated values in a CSV file that can be loaded into a spreadsheet program such as Excel.

When execution halts (at termination, at a breakpoint, or due to a run-time error), the Toolkit displays this information in the Editor, line by line. The profiling data is color coded:

- Green indicates the lowest number of hits, or the fastest execution time.
- Red indicates trouble spots, such as a line that has been executed many times, or which line took the most time to execute.

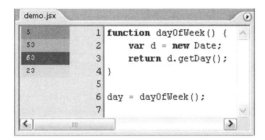

```
demo.jsx

5      1  function dayOfWeek() {
53     2      var d = new Date;
53     3      return d.getDay();
23     4  }
       5
       6  day = dayOfWeek();
       7
```

This example displays timing information for the program, where the fastest line took 4 microseconds to execute, and the slowest line took 29 microseconds. The timing might not be accurate down to the microsecond; it depends on the resolution and accuracy of the hardware timers built into your computer.

Dollar ($) Object

This global ExtendScript object provides a number of debugging facilities and informational methods. The properties of the $ object allow you to get global information such as the most recent run-time error, and set flags that control debugging and localization behavior. The methods allow you to output text to the JavaScript Console during script execution, control execution and other ExtendScript behavior programmatically, and gather statistics on object use.

Dollar ($) object properties

`build`	Number	The ExtendScript build number. Read only.
`buildDate`	Date	The date ExtendScript was built. Read only.
`error`	Error String	The most recent run-time error information, contained in a JavaScript `Error` object. Assigning error text to this property generates a run-time error; however, the preferred way to generate a run-time error is to throw an `Error` object.
`flags`	Number	Gets or sets low-level debug output flags. A logical AND of the following bit flag values: 0x0002 (2): Displays each line with its line number as it is executed. 0x0040 (64): Enables excessive garbage collection. Usually, garbage collection starts when the number of objects has increased by a certain amount since the last garbage collection. This flag causes ExtendScript to garbage collect after almost every statement. This impairs performance severely, but is useful when you suspect that an object gets released too soon. 0x0080 (128): Displays all calls with their arguments and the return value. 0x0100 (256): Enables extended error handling. See "strict" on page 363. 0x0200 (512): Enables the localization feature of the `toString` method. Equivalent to the localize property (page 363).
`global`	Object	Provides access to the global object, which contains the JavaScript global namespace.
`level`	Number	Enables or disables the JavaScript debugger. One of: 0: No debugging 1: Break on run-time errors 2: Full debug mode

locale	String	Gets or sets the current locale. The string contains five characters in the form *LL_RR*, where *LL* is an ISO 639 language specifier, and *RR* is an ISO 3166 region specifier. Initially, this is the value that the application or the platform returns for the current user. You can set it to temporarily change the locale for testing. To return to the application or platform setting, set to `undefined`, `null`, or the empty string.
localize	Boolean	Enable or disable the extended localization features of the built-in `toString` method. See "Localizing ExtendScript Strings" on page 369.
memCache	Number	Gets or sets the ExtendScript memory cache size in bytes.
objects	Number	The total count of all JavaScript objects defined so far. Read only.
os	String	The current operating system version. Read only.
screens	Array	An array of objects containing information about the display screens attached to your computer. Each object has the properties `left`, `top`, `right`, and `bottom`, which contain the four corners of each screen in global coordinates. A property `primary` is `true` if that object describes the primary display.
strict	Boolean	When `true`, any attempt to write to a read-only property causes a run-time error. Some objects do not permit the creation of new properties when `true`.
version	String	The version number of the ExtendScript engine as a three-part number and description; for example: "3.6.5 (debug)" Read only.

Dollar ($) object functions

about $.about ()	Displays the About box for the ExtendScript component, and returns the text of the About box as a string.
bp $.bp ([*condition*])	Executes a breakpoint at the current position. Returns `undefined`. If no condition is needed, it is recommended that you use the JavaScript `debugger` statement in the script, rather than this method.
condition	Optional. A string containing a JavaScript statement to be used as a condition. If the statement evaluates to `true` or nonzero when this point is reached, execution stops.
clearbp $.clearbp ([*line*])	Removes a breakpoint from the current script. Returns `undefined`.
line	Optional. The line at which to clear the breakpoint. If 0 or not supplied, clears breakpoint at the current line number.
gc $.gc ()	Initiates garbage collection. Returns `undefined`.

getenv $.getenv (*envname*)	Returns the value of the specified environment variable, or `null` if no such variable is defined.
envname	The name of the environment variable.

list $.list ([*classname*])	Collects object information into a table and returns this table as a string. See "Object statistics" on page 365.
classname	Optional. The type of object about which to collect information. If not supplied, collects information about all objects currently defined.

setbp $.setbp ([*line, condition*])	Sets a breakpoint in the current script. Returns `undefined`. If no arguments are needed, it is recommended that you use the JavaScript `debugger` statement in the script, rather than this method.
line	Optional. The line at which to stop execution. If 0 or not supplied, sets the breakpoint at the current line number.
condition	Optional. A string containing a JavaScript statement to be used for a conditional breakpoint. If the statement evaluates to `true` or nonzero when the line is reached, execution stops.

sleep $.sleep (*milliseconds*)	Suspends the calling thread for the given number of milliseconds. Returns `undefined`. During a sleep period, checks at 100 millisecond intervals to see whether the sleep should be terminated. This can happen if there is a break request, or if the script timeout has expired.
milliseconds	The number of milliseconds to wait.

summary
$.summary ([*classname*])
	Collects a summary of object counts into a table and returns this table as a string. The table shows the number of objects in each specified class. For example:
	
	  3 Array
	  5 String

classname	Optional. The type of object to count. If not supplied, counts all objects currently defined.

write $.write (*text*[, *text*...]...)	Writes the specified text to the JavaScript Console. Returns `undefined`.
text	One or more strings to write, which are concatenated to form a single string.

writeln $.writeln (*text*[, *text*...]...)	Writes the specified text to the JavaScript Console and appends a linefeed sequence. Returns `undefined`.
text	One or more strings to write, which are concatenated to form a single string.

Object statistics

The output from $.list() is formatted as in the following example.

Address	L	Refs	Prop	Class	Name
0092196c	4	0	Function	[toplevel]	
00976c8c	2	1	Object	Object	
00991bc4L	1	1	LOTest	LOTest	
0099142cL	2	2	Function	LOTest	
00991294	1	0	Object	Object	workspace

The columns show the following object information.

Address	The physical address of the object in memory.
L	This column contains the letter "L" if the object is a LiveObject (which is an internal data type).
Refs	The reference count of the object.
Prop	A second reference count for the number of properties that reference the object. The garbage collector uses this count to break circular references. If the reference count is not equal to the number of JavaScript properties that reference it, the object is considered to be used elsewhere and is not garbage collected.
Class	The class name of the object.
Name	The name of the object. This name does not reflect the name of the property the object has been stored into. The name is mostly relevant to Function objects, where it is the name of the function or method. Names in brackets are internal names of scripts. If the object has an ID, the last column displays that ID.

ExtendScript Reflection Interface

ExtendScript provides a reflection interface that allows you to find out everything about an object, including its name, a description, the expected data type for properties, the arguments and return value for methods, and any default values or limitations to the input values.

Reflection Object

Every object has a `reflect` property that returns a `reflection` object that reports the contents of the object. For example, you can show the values of all the properties of an object with code like this:

```
var f= new File ("myfile");
var props = f.reflect.properties;
for (var i = 0; i < props.length; i++) {
    $.writeln('this property ' + props[i].name + ' is ' +
f[props[i].name]);
}
```

Reflection object properties

All properties are read only.

description	String	Short text describing the reflected object, or undefined if no description is available.
help	String	Longer text describing the reflected object more completely, or undefined if no description is available.
methods	Array of ReflectionInfo	An Array of ReflectionInfo Objects (page 367) containing all methods of the reflected object, defined in the class or in the specific instance.
name	String	The class name of the reflected object.
properties	Array of ReflectionInfo	An Array of ReflectionInfo Objects (page 367) containing all properties of the reflected object, defined in the class or in the specific instance. For objects with dynamic properties (defined at runtime) the list contains only those dynamic properties that have already been accessed by the script. For example, in an object wrapping an HTML tag, the names of the HTML attributes are determined at run time.

Reflection object functions

find *reflectionObj*.find (*name*)	Returns the ReflectionInfo Object (page 367) for the named property of the reflected object, or `null` if no such property exists. Use this method to get information about dynamic properties that have not yet been accessed, but that are known to exist.
name	The property for which to retrieve information.

➤ Examples

This code determines the class name of an object:

```
obj = new String ("hi");
obj.reflect.name; // => String
```

This code gets a list of all methods:

```
obj = new String ("hi");
obj.reflect.methods; //=> indexOf,slice,...
obj.reflect.find ("indexOf"); // => the method info
```

This code gets a list of properties:

```
Math.reflect.properties; //=> PI,LOG10,...
```

This code gets the data type of a property:

```
Math.reflect.find ("PI").type; // => number
```

ReflectionInfo Object

This object contains information about a property, a method, or a method argument.

- You can access `ReflectionInfo` objects in a Reflection Object's `properties` and `methods` arrays (page 366), by name or index:

```
obj = new String ("hi");
obj.reflect.methods[0];
obj.reflect.methods ["indexOf"];
```

- You can access the `ReflectionInfo` objects for the arguments of a method in the `arguments` array of the `ReflectionInfo` object for the method, by index:

```
obj.reflect.methods ["indexOf"].arguments[0];
```

ReflectionInfo object properties

arguments	Array of ReflectionInfo	For a reflected method, an array of ReflectionInfo Objects (page 367) describing each method argument.

dataType	String	The data type of the reflected element. One of:
		`boolean`
		`number`
		`string`
		Classname: The class name of an object.
		Note: Class names start with a capital letter. Thus, the value `string` stands for a JavaScript string, while `String` is a JavaScript `String` wrapper object.
		`*`: Any type. This is the default.
		`null`
		`undefined`: Return data type for a function that does not return any value.
		`unknown`

defaultValue	any	The default value for a reflected property or method argument, or `undefined` if there is no default value, if the property is undefined, or if the element is a method.
description	String	Short text describing the reflected object, or `undefined` if no description is available.
help	String	Longer text describing the reflected object more completely, or `undefined` if no description is available.
isCollection	Boolean	When `true`, the reflected property or method returns a collection; otherwise, `false`.
max	Number	The maximum numeric value for the reflected element, or `undefined` if there is no maximum or if the element is a method.
min	Number	The minimum numeric value for the reflected element, or `undefined` if there is no minimum or if the element is a method.
name	String Number	The name of the reflected element. A string, or a number for an array index.
type	String	The type of the reflected element. One of: `readonly`: A read-only property. `readwrite`: A read-write property. `createonly`: A property that is valid only during creation of an object. `method`: A method.

Localizing ExtendScript Strings

Localization is the process of translating and otherwise manipulating an interface so that it looks as if it had been originally designed for a particular language. ExtendScript gives you the ability to localize the strings in your script's user interface. The language is chosen by the application at startup, according to the current locale provided by the operating system.

For portions of your user interface that are displayed on the screen, you might want to localize the displayed text. You can localize any string explicitly using the Global localize function (page 372), which takes as its argument a *localization object* containing the localized versions of a string.

A localization object is a JavaScript object literal whose property names are locale names, and whose property values are the localized text strings. The locale name is a standard language code with an optional region identifier. For details of the syntax, see "Locale names" on page 370.

In this example, a `msg` object contains localized text strings for two locales. This object supplies the text for an alert dialog.

```
msg = { en: "Hello, world", de: "Hallo Welt" };
alert (msg);
```

ExtendScript matches the current locale and platform to one of the object's properties and uses the associated string. On a German system, for example, the property `de: "Hallo Welt"` is converted to the string `"Hallo Welt"`.

Variable values in localized strings

Some localization strings need to contain additional data whose position and order might change according to the language used.

You can include variables in the string values of the localization object, in the form `%n`. The variables are replaced in the returned string with the results of JavaScript expressions, supplied as additional arguments to the `localize` function. The variable `%1` corresponds to the first additional argument, `%2` to the second, and so on.

Because the replacement occurs after the localized string is chosen, the variable values are inserted in the correct position. For example:

```
today = {
   en: "Today is %1/%2.",
   de: "Heute ist der %2.%1."
   };
d = new Date();
alert (localize (today, d.getMonth()+1, d.getDate()));
```

Enabling automatic localization

ExtendScript offers an automatic localization feature. When it is enabled, you can specify a localization object directly as the value of any property that takes a localizable string, without using the `localize` function. For example:

```
msg = { en: "Yes", de: "Ja", fr: "Oui" };
alert (msg);
```

To use automatic translation of localization objects, you must enable localization in your script with this statement:

```
$.localize = true;
```

The `localize` function always performs its translation, regardless of the setting of the `$.localize` variable. For example:

```
msg = { en: "Yes", de: "Ja", fr: "Oui" };
//Only works if the $.localize=true
alert (msg);
//Always works, regardless of $.localize value
alert ( localize (msg));
```

If you need to include variables in the localized strings, use the `localize` function.

Locale names

A locale name is an identifier string in that contains an ISO 639 language specifier, and optionally an ISO 3166 region specifier, separated from the language specifier by an underscore.

- The ISO 639 standard defines a set of two-letter language abbreviations, such as `en` for English and `de` for German.
- The ISO 3166 standard defines a region code, another two-letter identifier, which you can optionally append to the language identifier with an underscore. For example, `en_US` identifies U.S. English, while `en_GB` identifies British English.

This object defines one message for British English, another for all other flavors of English, and another for all flavors of German:

```
message = {
    en_GB: "Please select a colour."
    en: "Please select a color."
    de: "Bitte wählen Sie eine Farbe."
};
```

If you need to specify different messages for different platforms, you can append another underline character and the name of the platform, one of `Win`, `Mac`, or `Unix`. For example, this object defines one message in British

English to be displayed in Mac OS, one for all other flavors of English in Mac OS, and one for all other flavors of English on all other platforms:

```
pressMsg = {
    en_GB_Mac: "Press Cmd-S to select a colour.",
    en_Mac: "Press Cmd-S to select a color.",
    en: "Press Ctrl-S to select a color."
};
```

All of these identifiers are case sensitive. For example, EN_US is not valid.

➤ **How locale names are resolved**

1. ExtendScript gets the hosting application's locale; for example, en_US.

2. It appends the platform identifier; for example, en_US_Win.

3. It looks for a matching property, and if found, returns the value string.

4. If not found, it removes the platform identifier (for example, en_US) and retries.

5. If not found, it removes the region identifier (for example, en) and retries.

6. If not found, it tries the identifier en (that is, the default language is English).

7. If not found, it returns the entire localizer object.

Testing localization

ExtendScript stores the current locale in the variable $.locale. This variable is updated whenever the locale of the hosting application changes.

To test your localized strings, you can temporarily reset the locale. To restore the original behavior, set the variable to null, false, 0, or the empty string. An example:

```
$.locale = "ru"; // try your Russian messages
$.locale = null; // restore to the locale of the app
```

Global localize function

The globally available `localize` function can be used to provide localized strings anywhere a displayed text value is specified.

localize
`localize (localization_obj[, args])`
`localize (ZString)`
	Returns the localized string for the current locale.

`localization_obj`	A JavaScript object literal whose property names are locale names, and whose property values are the localized text strings. The locale name is an identifier as specified in the ISO 3166 standard, a set of two-letter language abbreviations, such as "en" for English and "de" for German.
	
	For example:
	<pre>btnText = { en: "Yes", de: "Ja", fr: "Oui" };
	b1 = w.add ("button", undefined, localize (btnText));</pre>The string value of each property can contain variables in the form %1, %2, and so on, corresponding to additional arguments. The variable is replaced with the result of evaluating the corresponding argument in the returned string.

`args`	Optional. Additional JavaScript expressions matching variables in the string values supplied in the localization object. The first argument corresponds to the variable %1, the second to %2, and so on. Each expression is evaluated and the result inserted in the variable's position in the returned string.

➤ Example

```
today = {
   en: "Today is %1/%2",
   de: "Heute ist der %2.%1."
   };
d = new Date();
alert (localize (today, d.getMonth()+1, d.getDate()));
```

`ZString`	Internal use only. A ZString is an internal Adobe format for localized strings, which you might see in Adobe scripts. A ZString begins with $$$ and contains a path to the localized string in an installed ZString dictionary. For example: w = new Window ("dialog", localize ("$$$/UI/title1=Sample"));

User Notification Helper Functions

ExtendScript provides a set of globally available functions that allow you to display short messages to the user in platform-standard dialog boxes. There are three types of message dialogs:

- **Alert**: Displays a dialog containing a short message and an **OK** button.
- **Confirm**: Displays a dialog containing a short message and two buttons, **Yes** and **No**, allowing the user to accept or reject an action.
- **Prompt**: Displays a dialog containing a short message, a text entry field, and **OK** and **Cancel** buttons, allowing the user to supply a value to the script.

These dialogs are customizable to a small degree. The appearance is platform specific.

Global alert function

`alert`
`alert (message[, title,`
`errorIcon]);`
	Displays a platform-standard dialog containing a short message and an **OK** button. Returns `undefined`.

`message`	The string for the displayed message.
`title`	Optional. A string to appear as the title of the dialog, if the platform supports a title. Mac OS does not support titles for alert dialogs. The default title string is "Script Alert".
`errorIcon`	Optional. When `true`, the platform-standard alert icon is replaced by the platform-standard error icon in the dialog. Default is `false`.

➤ **Examples**

This figure shows simple alert dialogs in Windows and Mac OS.

This figure shows alert dialogs with error icons.

Global confirm function

confirm confirm (message[,noAsDflt ,title]);	Displays a platform-standard dialog containing a short message and two buttons labeled **Yes** and **No**. Returns `true` if the user clicked **Yes**, `false` if the user clicked **No**.
message	The string for the displayed message.
noAsDflt	Optional. When `true`, the **No** button is the default choice, selected when the user types ENTER. Default is `false`, meaning that **Yes** is the default choice.
title	Optional. A string to appear as the title of the dialog, if the platform supports a title. Mac OS does not support titles for confirmation dialogs. The default title string is "Script Alert".

> **Examples**

This figure shows simple confirmation dialogs in Windows and Mac OS.

This figure shows confirmation dialogs with **No** as the default button.

Global prompt function

prompt prompt (*message*, *preset*[, *title*]);	Displays a platform-standard dialog containing a short message, a text edit field, and two buttons labeled **OK** and **Cancel**. Returns the value of the text edit field if the user clicked **OK**, null if the user clicked **Cancel**.
message	The string for the displayed message.
preset	The initial value to be displayed in the text edit field.
title	Optional. A string to appear as the title of the dialog. In Windows, this appears in the window's frame, while in Mac OS it appears above the message. The default title string is "Script Prompt".

➤ **Examples**

This figure shows simple prompt dialogs in Windows and Mac OS.

This figure shows confirmation dialogs with a `title` value specified.

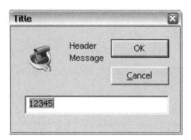

Specifying Measurement Values

ExtendScript provides the UnitValue Object (page 376) to represent measurement values. The properties and methods of the `UnitValue` object make it easy to change the value, the unit, or both, or to perform conversions from one unit to another.

UnitValue Object

Represents measurement values that contain both the numeric magnitude and the unit of measurement.

UnitValue object constructor

The `UnitValue` constructor creates a new `UnitValue` object. The keyword `new` is optional:

```
myVal = new UnitValue (value, unit);
myVal = new UnitValue ("value unit");
myVal = new UnitValue (value, "unit");
```

The *value* is a number, and the *unit* is specified with a string in abbreviated, singular, or plural form, as shown in the following table.

Abbreviation	Singular	Plural	Comments
in	inch	inches	2.54 cm
ft	foot	feet	30.48 cm
yd	yard	yards	91.44 cm
mi	mile	miles	1609.344 m
mm	millimeter	millimeters	
cm	centimeter	centimeters	
m	meter	meters	

Abbreviation	Singular	Plural	Comments
km	kilometer	kilometers	
pt	point	points	inches / 72
pc	pica	picas	points * 12
tpt	traditional point	traditional points	inches / 72.27
tpc	traditional pica	traditional picas	12 tpt
ci	cicero	ciceros	12.7872 pt
px	pixel	pixels	baseless (see below)
%	percent	percent	baseless (see below)

If an unknown unit type is supplied, the type is set to "?", and the UnitValue object prints as "UnitValue 0.00000".

For example, all of the following formats are equivalent:

```
myVal = new UnitValue (12, "cm");
myVal = new UnitValue ("12 cm");
myVal = UnitValue ("12 centimeters");
```

UnitValue object properties

baseUnit	UnitValue	A UnitValue Object (page 376) that defines the size of one pixel, or a total size to use as a base for percentage values. This is used as the base conversion unit for pixels and percentages; see "Converting pixel and percentage values" on page 378.
		Default is 0.013889 inches (1/72 in), which is the base conversion unit for pixels at 72 dpi. Set to null to restore the default.
type	String	The unit type in abbreviated form; for example, "cm" or "in".
value	Number	The numeric measurement value.

UnitValue object functions

as	Returns the numeric value of this object in the given unit.
unitValueObj.as (*unit*)	If the unit is unknown or cannot be computed, generates a run-time error.
unit	The unit type in abbreviated form; for example, "cm" or "in".

convert *unitValueObj*.convert (*unit*)	Converts this object to the given unit, resetting the `type` and `value` accordingly. Returns `true` if the conversion is successful. If the unit is unknown or the object cannot be converted, generates a run-time error and returns `false`.
unit	The unit type in abbreviated form; for example, "cm" or "in".

Converting pixel and percentage values

Converting measurements among different units requires a common base unit. For example, for length, the meter is the base unit. All length units can be converted into meters, which makes it possible to convert any length unit into any other length unit.

Pixels and percentages do not have a standard common base unit. Pixel measurements are relative to display resolution, and percentages are relative to an absolute total size.

- To convert pixels into length units, you must know the size of a single pixel. The size of a pixel depends on the display resolution. A common resolution measurement is 72 dpi, which means that there are 72 pixels to the inch. The conversion base for pixels at 72 dpi is 0.013889 inches (1/72 inch).

- Percentage values are relative to a total measurement. For example, 10% of 100 inches is 10 inches, while 10% of 1 meter is 0.1 meters. The conversion base of a percentage is the unit value corresponding to 100%.

The default `baseUnit` of a `unitValue` object is 0.013889 inches, the base for pixels at 72 dpi. If the `unitValue` is for pixels at any other dpi, or for a percentage value, you must set the `baseUnit` value accordingly. The `baseUnit` value is itself a `unitValue` object, containing both a magnitude and a unit.

For a system using a different dpi, you can change the `baseUnit` value in the `UnitValue` class, thus changing the default for all new `unitValue` objects. For example, to double the resolution of pixels:

```
UnitValue.baseUnit = UnitValue (1/144, "in"); //144 dpi
```

To restore the default, assign `null` to the class property:

```
UnitValue.baseUnit = null; //restore default
```

You can override the default value for any particular `unitValue` object by setting the property in that object. For example, to create a unitValue object for pixels with 96 dpi:

```
pixels = UnitValue (10, "px");
myPixBase = UnitValue (1/96, "in");
pixels.baseUnit = myPixBase;
```

For percentage measurements, set the `baseUnit` property to the measurement value for 100%. For example, to create a `unitValue` object for 40% of 10 feet:

```
myPctVal = UnitValue (40, "%");
myBase = UnitValue (10, "ft")
myPctVal.baseUnit = myBase;
```

Use the `as` method (page 377) to get to a percentage value as a unit value:

```
myFootVal = myPctVal.as ("ft"); // => 4
myInchVal = myPctVal.as ("in"); // => 36
```

You can convert a `unitValue` from an absolute measurement to pixels or percents in the same way:

```
myMeterVal = UnitValue (10, "m"); // 10 meters
myBase = UnitValue (1, "km");
myMeterVal.baseUnit = myBase;
                      //as a percentage of 1 kilometer
pctOfKm = myMeterVal.as ('%'); // => 1

myVal = UnitValue ("1 in");
                      // Define measurement in inches
// convert to pixels using default base
myVal.convert ("px"); // => value=72 type=px
```

Computing with unit values

`UnitValue` objects can be used in computational JavaScript expressions. The way the value is used depends on the type of operator.

- Unary operators (~, !, +, -)

~*unitValue*	The numeric value is converted to a 32-bit integer with inverted bits.
!*unitValue*	Result is `true` if the numeric value is nonzero, `false` if it is not.
+*unitValue*	Result is the numeric value.
-*unitValue*	Result is the negated numeric value.

- Binary operators (+, -, *, /, %)

  If one operand is `unitValue` object and the other is a number, the operation is applied to the number and the numeric value of the object.

The expression returns a new `unitValue` object with the result as its value. For example:

```
val = new UnitValue ("10 cm");
res = val * 20;
// res is a UnitValue (200, "cm");
```

If both operands are `unitValue` objects, JavaScript converts the right operand to the same unit as the left operand and applies the operation to the resulting values. The expression returns a new `unitValue` object with the unit of the left operand, and the result `value`. For example:

```
a = new UnitValue ("1 m");
b = new UnitValue ("10 cm");
a + b;
// res is a UnitValue (1.1, "m");
b + a;
// res is a UnitValue (110, "cm");
```

- Comparisons (=, ==, <, >, <=, >=)

  If one operand is a `unitValue` object and the other is a number, JavaScript compares the number with the `unitValue`'s numeric value.

  If both operands are `unitValue` objects, JavaScript converts both objects to the same unit, and compares the converted numeric values.

  For example:

```
a = new UnitValue ("98 cm");
b = new UnitValue ("1 m");
a < b;    // => true
a < 1;    // => false
a == 98; // => true
```

Modular Programming Support

ExtendScript provides support for a modular approach to scripting by allowing you to include one script in another as a resource, and allowing a script to export definitions that can be imported and used in another script.

Preprocessor directives

ExtendScript provides preprocessor directives for including external scripts, naming scripts, specifying an ExtendScript engine, and setting certain flags. You can specify these in two ways:

- With a C-style statement starting with the # character:

      #include "file.jsxinc"

- In a comment whose text starts with the @ character:

      // @include "file.jsxinc"

When a directive takes one or more arguments, and an argument contains any nonalphanumeric characters, the argument must be enclosed in single or double quotes. This is generally the case with paths and file names, for example, which contain dots and slashes.

`#engine name`	Identifies the ExtendScript engine that runs this script. This allows other engines to refer to the scripts in this engine by importing the exported functions and variables. See "Importing and exporting between scripts" on page 382.

	Use JavaScript identifier syntax for the name. Enclosing quotes are optional. For example:
	
	`#engine library`
	`#engine "$lib"`

`#include file`	Includes a JavaScript source file from another location. Inserts the contents of the named file into this file at the location of this statement. The `file` argument is an Adobe portable file specification. See "Application and Namespace Specifiers" on page 385.
	As a convention, use the file extension `.jsxinc` for JavaScript include files. For example: `#include "../include/lib.jsxinc"` To set one or more paths for the `#include` statement to scan, use the `#includepath` preprocessor directive.
	If the file to be included cannot be found, ExtendScript throws a run-time error.
	Included source code is not shown in the debugger, so you cannot set breakpoints in it.

`#includepath path`	One or more paths that the `#include` statement should use to locate the files to be included. The semicolon (;) separates path names.
	
	If a `#include` file name starts with a slash (/), it is an absolute path name, and the include paths are ignored. Otherwise, ExtendScript attempts to find the file by prefixing the file with each path set by the `#includepath` statement.
	
	For example:
	
	    `#includepath "include;../include"`
	    `#include "file.jsxinc"`
	Multiple `#includepath` statements are allowed; the list of paths changes each time an `#includepath` statement is executed.
	
	As a fallback, ExtendScript also uses the contents of the environment variable JSINCLUDE as a list of include paths.
	
	Some engines can have a predefined set of include paths. If so, the path provided by `#includepath` is tried before the predefined paths. If, for example, the engine has a predefined path set to `predef;predef/include`, the preceding example causes the following lookup sequence:
	
	    `file.jsxinc`: literal lookup
	    `include/file.jsxinc`: first `#includepath` path
	    `../include/file.jsxinc`: second `#includepath` path
	    `predef/file.jsxinc`: first predefined engine path
	    `predef/include/file.jsxinc`: second predefined engine path

`#script name`	Names a script. Enclosing quotes are optional, but required for names that include spaces or special characters. For example:
	
	    `#script SetupPalette`
	    `#script "Load image file"`
	The *name* value is displayed in the Toolkit Editor tab. An unnamed script is assigned a unique name generated from a number.

`#strict on`	Turns on strict error checking. See the Dollar ($) Object's strict property (page 363).
`#target name`	Defines the target application of this JSX file. The *name* value is an application specifier; see "Application and Namespace Specifiers" on page 385. Enclosing quotes are optional. If the Toolkit is registered as the handler for files with the `.jsx` extension (as it is by default), opening the file opens the target application to run the script. If this directive is not present, the Toolkit loads and displays the script. A user can open a file by double-clicking it in a file browser, and a script can open a file using a `File` object's `execute` method.

Importing and exporting between scripts

The ExtendScript JavaScript language has been extended to support function calls and variable access across various source code modules and ExtendScript engines. A script can use the `export` statement to make its

---

                      Adobe® Photoshop® CS2 Official JavaScript Reference

definitions available to other scripts, which use the `import` statement to access those definitions.

To use this feature, the exporting script must name its ExtendScript engine using the `#engine` preprocessor statement. The name must follow JavaScript naming syntax; it cannot be an expression.

For example, the following script could serve as a library or resource file. It defines and exports a constant and a function:

```
#engine library
export random, libVersion;
const libVersion = "Library 1.0";
function random (max) {
    return Math.floor (Math.random() * max);
}
```

A script running in a different engine can import the exported elements. The import statement identifies the resource script that exported the variables using the engine name:

```
import library.random, library.libVersion;
print (random (100));
```

You can use the asterisk wildcard (*) to import all symbols exported by a library:

```
import library.*
```

Objects cannot be transferred between engines. You cannot retrieve or store objects, and you cannot call functions with objects as arguments. However, you can use the JavaScript `toSource` function to serialize objects into strings before passing them. You can then use the JavaScript `eval` function to reconstruct the object from the string.

For example, this function takes as its argument a serialized string and constructs an object from it:

```
function myFn (serialized) {
    var obj = eval (serialized);
    // continue working...
}
```

In calling the function, you deconstruct the object you want to pass into a serialized string:

```
myFn (myObject.toSource ()); // pass a serialized object
```

Operator Overloading

ExtendScript allows you to extend or override the behavior of a math or a Boolean operator for a specific class by defining a method in that class with same name as the operator. For example, this code defines the addition (+) operator for the class `MyClass`. In this case, the addition operator simply adds the operand to the property value:

```
// define the constructor method
function MyClass (initialValue) {
   this.value = initialValue;
}
// define the addition operator
MyClass.prototype ["+"] = function (operand) {
   return this.value + operand;
}
```

This allows you to perform the "+" operation with any object of this class:

```
var obj = new MyClass (5);
Result: [object Object]
obj + 10;
Result: 15
```

You can override the following operators:

Unary	+, - ~
Binary	+, - *, /, %, ^ <, <=, == <<, >>, >>> &, |, ===

- The operators > and >= are implemented by executing NOT operator <= and NOT operator <.
- Combined assignment operators such as *= are not supported.

All operator overload implementations must return the result of the operation. To perform the default operation, return `undefined`.

Unary operator functions work on the `this` object, while binary operators work on the `this` object and the first argument. The + and - operators have both unary and binary implementations. If the first argument is undefined, the operator is unary; if it is supplied, the operator is binary.

For binary operators, a second argument indicates the order of operands. For noncommutative operators, either implement both order variants in your

function or return `undefined` for combinations that you do not support. For
example:

```
this ["/"] = function (operand, rev) {
    if (rev) {
        // do not resolve operand / this
        return;
    } else {
        // resolve this / operand
        return this.value / operand;
    }
}
```

Application and Namespace Specifiers

All forms of interapplication communication use *Application specifiers*
(page 386) to identify Adobe applications.

- In all ExtendScript scripts, the `#target` directive can use an specifier to
  identify the application that should run that script. See "Preprocessor
  directives" on page 381.

- In interapplication messages, the specifier is used as the value of the
  `target` property of the message object, to identify the target application
  for the message.

- Bridge (which is integrated with all Adobe Creative Suite 2 applications)
  uses an application specifier as the value of the `document.owner`
  property, to identify another Creative Suite 2 application that created or
  opened a Bridge browser window.

When a script for one application invokes Cross-DOM or exported functions,
it identifies the exporting application using Namespace specifiers
(page 386).

Application specifiers

Application specifiers are strings that encode the application name, a version number and a language code. They take the following form:

```
appname[-version[-locale]]
```

appname	An Adobe application name. One of:
	
	`acrobat`
	`aftereffects`
	`atmosphere`
	`audition`
	`bridge`
	`encore`
	`golive`
	`illustrator`
	`incopy`
	`indesign`
	`photoshop`
	`premiere`

version	Optional. A number indicating at least a major version. If not supplied, the most recent version is assumed. The number can include a minor version separated from the major version number by a dot; for example, `1.5`.
locale	Optional. An Adobe locale code, consisting of a 2-letter ISO-639 language code and an optional 2-letter ISO 3166 country code separated by an underscore. Case is significant. For example, `en_US`, `en_UK`, `ja_JP`, `de_DE`, `fr_FR`. If not supplied, ExtendScript uses the current platform locale. Do not specify a locale for a multilingual application, such as Bridge, that has all locale versions included in a single installation.

The following are examples of legal specifiers:

```
photoshop
bridge-1
bridge-1.0
illustrator-12.2
bridge-1-en_us
golive-8-de_de
```

Namespace specifiers

When calling Cross-DOM and exported functions from other applications, a namespace specifier qualifies the function call, directing it to the appropriate application

Namespace specifiers consist of an application name, as used in an application specifier, with an optional major version number. Use it as a prefix to an exported function name, with the JavaScript dot notation.

```
appname[majorVersion].functionName(args)
```

For example:

- To call the Cross-DOM function `quit` in Photoshop CS2, use `photoshop.quit()`, and to call it in GoLive CS2, use `golive.quit()`.
- To call the exported function `place`, defined for Illustrator® CS2 (version 12), call `illustrator12.place(myFiles)`.

Script Locations and Checking Application Installation

On startup, all Adobe Creative Suite 2 applications execute all JSX files that they find in the user startup folder:

- In Windows®, the startup folder is:

```
%APPDATA%\Adobe\StartupScripts
```

- In Mac OS®, the startup folder is

```
~/Library/Application
Support/Adobe/StartupScripts/
```

A script in the startup directory is executed on startup by all applications. If you place a script here, it must contain code to check whether it is being run by the intended application. You can do this using the `appName` static property of the `BridgeTalk` class. For example:

```
if( BridgeTalk.appName == "bridge" ) {
      //continue executing script
}
```

In addition, individual applications might look for application-specific scripts in a subfolder named with that application's specifier and version, in the form:

```
%APPDATA%\Adobe\StartupScripts\appname\version
~/Library/Application Support/Adobe/StartupScripts/
      appname/version/
```

The name and version in these folder names are specified in the form required for Application specifiers (page 386). For example, in Windows, GoLive CS2 version 8.2 would look for scripts in the directory:

```
%APPDATA%\Adobe\StartupScripts\golive\8.2
```

The *version* portion of the Bridge-specific folder path is an exact version number. That is, scripts in the folder `bridge/1.5` are executed only by Bridge version 1.5, and so on.

Individual applications might also implement a path in the installation directory for application-specific startup scripts. For example:

```
IllustratorCS2_install_dir\Startup Scripts
IllustratorCS2_install_dir/Startup Scripts/
```

If a script that is run by one application communicates with another application, or adds functionality that depends on another application, it must first check whether that application and version is installed. You can do this using the BridgeTalk.getSpecifier static function. For example:

```
if( BridgeTalk.appName == "bridge" ) {
// Check that PS CS2 is installed
   if( BridgeTalk.getSpecifier("photoshop",9)){
       // add PS automate menu to Bridge UI
   }
}
```

Appendix A: Event ID Codes

The following table lists events and their four-character ID codes or string identifiers for use with the `notifier` object.

Note: **Do not include single quotes (') with four-character IDs in your code.** The single quotes are used in this table to illustrate the placement of required spaces in codes that do not contain four letters. However, string identifiers, which are longer than four characters, require double quotes in the code.

Event	4-char ID or String
3DTransform	'TdT '
Average	'Avrg'
ApplyStyle	'ASty'
Assert	'Asrt'
AccentedEdges	'AccE'
Add	'Add '
AddNoise	'AdNs'
AddTo	'AddT'
Align	'Algn'
All	'All '
AngledStrokes	'AngS'
ApplyImage	'AppI'
BasRelief	'BsRl'
Batch	'Btch'
BatchFromDroplet	'BtcF'
Blur	'Blr '
BlurMore	'BlrM'
Border	'Brdr'
Brightness	'BrgC'
CanvasSize	'CnvS'
ChalkCharcoal	'ChlC'
ChannelMixer	'ChnM'
Charcoal	'Chrc'

Event	4-char ID or String
Chrome	'Chrm'
Clear	'Cler'
Close	'Cls '
Clouds	'Clds'
ColorBalance	'ClrB'
ColorHalftone	'ClrH'
ColorRange	'ClrR'
ColoredPencil	'ClrP'
ContactSheet	"0B71D221-F8CE-11d2-B21B-0008C75B322C"
ConteCrayon	'CntC'
Contract	'Cntc'
ConvertMode	'CnvM'
Copy	'copy'
CopyEffects	'CpFX'
CopyMerged	'CpyM'
CopyToLayer	'CpTL'
Craquelure	'Crql'
CreateDroplet	'CrtD'
Crop	'Crop'
Crosshatch	'Crsh'
Crystallize	'Crst'
Curves	'Crvs'
Custom	'Cstm'
Cut	'cut '
CutToLayer	'CtTL'
Cutout	'Ct '
DarkStrokes	'DrkS'
DeInterlace	'Dntr'
DefinePattern	'DfnP'
Defringe	'Dfrg'
Delete	'Dlt '
Desaturate	'Dstt'

Event	4-char ID or String
Deselect	'Dslc'
Despeckle	'Dspc'
DifferenceClouds	'DrfC'
Diffuse	'Dfs '
DiffuseGlow	'DfsG'
DisableLayerFX	'dlfx'
Displace	'Dspl'
Distribute	'Dstr'
Draw	'Draw'
DryBrush	'DryB'
Duplicate	'Dplc'
DustAndScratches	'DstS'
Emboss	'Embs'
Equalize	'Eqlz'
Exchange	'Exch'
Expand	'Expn'
Export	'Expr'
Jumpto	'Jpto'
ExportTransparentImage	"02879e00-cb66-11d1-bc43-0060b0a13dc4"
Extrude	'Extr'
Facet	'Fct '
Fade	'Fade'
Feather	'Fthr'
Fibers	'Fbrs'
Fill	'Fl '
FilmGrain	'FlmG'
Filter	'Fltr'
FindEdges	'FndE'
FitImage	"3caa3434-cb67-11d1-bc43-0060b0a13dc4"
FlattenImage	'FltI'
Flip	'Flip'
Fragment	'Frgm'

Event	4-char ID or String
Fresco	'Frsc'
GaussianBlur	'GsnB'
Get	'getd'
Glass	'Gls '
GlowingEdges	'GlwE'
Gradient	'Grdn'
GradientMap	'GrMp'
Grain	'Grn '
GraphicPen	'GraP'
Group	'GrpL'
Grow	'Grow'
HalftoneScreen	'HlfS'
Hide	'Hd '
HighPass	'HghP'
HSBHSL	'HsbP'
HueSaturation	'HStr'
ImageSize	'ImgS'
Import	'Impr'
InkOutlines	'InkO'
Intersect	'Intr'
IntersectWith	'IntW'
Inverse	'Invs'
Invert	'Invr'
LensFlare	'LnsF'
Levels	'Lvls'
LightingEffects	'LghE'
Link	'Lnk '
Make	'Mk '
Maximum	'Mxm '
Median	'Mdn '
MergeLayers	'Mrg2'
MergeLayersOld	'MrgL'

Event	4-char ID or String
MergeSpotChannel	'MSpt'
MergeVisible	'MrgV'
Mezzotint	'Mztn'
Minimum	'Mnm '
ModeChange	"8cba8cd6-cb66-11d1-bc43-0060b0a13dc4"
Mosaic	'Msc '
Mosaic_PLUGIN	'MscT'
MotionBlur	'MtnB'
Move	'move'
NTSCColors	'NTSC'
NeonGlow	'NGlw'
Next	'Nxt '
NotePaper	'NtPr'
Notify	'Ntfy'
Null	typeNull
OceanRipple	'OcnR'
Offset	'Ofst'
Open	'Opn '
Paint	'Pnt '
PaintDaubs	'PntD'
PaletteKnife	'PltK'
Paste	'past'
PasteEffects	'PaFX'
PasteInto	'PstI'
PasteOutside	'PstO'
Patchwork	'Ptch'
Photocopy	'Phtc'
PicturePackage	"4C1ABF40-DD82-11d2-B20F-0008C75B322C"
Pinch	'Pnch'
Place	'Plc '
Plaster	'Plst'
PlasticWrap	'PlsW'

Event	4-char ID or String
Play	'Ply '
Pointillize	'Pntl'
Polar	'Plr '
PosterEdges	'PstE'
Posterize	'Pstr'
Previous	'Prvs'
Print	'Prnt'
ProfileToProfile	'PrfT'
Purge	'Prge'
Quit	'quit'
RadialBlur	'RdlB'
Rasterize	'Rstr'
RasterizeTypeSheet	'RstT'
RemoveBlackMatte	'RmvB'
RemoveLayerMask	'RmvL'
RemoveWhiteMatte	'RmvW'
Rename	'Rnm '
ReplaceColor	'RplC'
Reset	'Rset'
ResizeImage	"1333cf0c-cb67-11d1-bc43-0060b0a13dc4"
Reticulation	'Rtcl'
Revert	'Rvrt'
Ripple	'Rple'
Rotate	'Rtte'
RoughPastels	'RghP'
Save	'save'
Select	'slct'
SelectiveColor	'SlcC'
Set	'setd'
SharpenEdges	'ShrE'
Sharpen	'Shrp'
SharpenMore	'ShrM'

Adobe® Photoshop® CS2 Official JavaScript Reference

Event	4-char ID or String
Shear	'Shr '
Show	'Shw '
Similar	'Smlr'
SmartBlur	'SmrB'
Smooth	'Smth'
SmudgeStick	'SmdS'
Solarize	'Slrz'
Spatter	'Spt '
Spherize	'Sphr'
SplitChannels	'SplC'
Sponge	'Spng'
SprayedStrokes	'SprS'
StainedGlass	'StnG'
Stamp	'Stmp'
Stop	'Stop'
Stroke	'Strk'
Subtract	'Sbtr'
SubtractFrom	'SbtF'
Sumie	'Smie'
TakeMergedSnapshot	'TkMr'
TakeSnapshot	'TkSn'
TextureFill	'TxtF'
Texturizer	'Txtz'
Threshold	'Thrs'
Tiles	'Tls '
TornEdges	'TrnE'
TraceContour	'TrcC'
Transform	'Trnf'
Trap	'Trap'
Twirl	'Twrl'
Underpainting	'Undr'
Undo	'undo'

Event	4-char ID or String
Ungroup	'Ungr'
Unlink	'Unlk'
UnsharpMask	'UnsM'
Variations	'Vrtn'
Wait	'Wait'
WaterPaper	'WtrP'
Watercolor	'Wtrc'
Wave	'Wave'
Wind	'Wnd '
ZigZag	'ZgZg'
BackLight	'BacL'
FillFlash	'FilE'
ColorCast	'ColE'

Index

A

absolute pathnames 306
Action Manager 222
actions
    command lists 70
    creating and running 221
    descriptions 73
    descriptors 67
    playing 77
    vs. scripting 6
Actions, palette 221
active document 75
Add Noise filter
adjustments
    brightness 84
    color 329
    color balance 84, 90
    contrast 84, 88
    curves 84
    highlights 91
    levels 84, 88
    shadows 91
    temperature 90
Adobe Illustrator, exporting paths to 132
Adobe Photoshop CS2 object model 9, 33
alerts 236, 268, 373
aliases, referencing 309
alpha channels
    defined 102
    from transparency (TIFF documents) 219
    opacity 102
    saving
        in BMP documents 99
        in PDF documents 177
        in PICT documents 182
        in PICT resources 183
        in Pixar documents 185
        in PSD documents 181
        in RAW documents 194
        in SGIRGB documents 202
        in Targa documents 207
        in TIFF documents 219
anchor points
    adding 173

    specifying position of 329
annotations 119
anti aliasing
    options 329
    text 210
Application object
    defined 9
    display dialogs 33
    using 34
applications
    activating 77
    as script execution targets 382
    calling exported functions 386
    communication between 385
    debugging 350
    defaults 187
    location 76
    preferences 187
    specifiers 386
arguments, using 13
arrays 17
Art Layer object
    applying styles to 37
    creating 36
    defined 10
    making text layer 38
    referencing 36
    working with 35
artLayers, *See* layers
Asian text 190
authors 124
auto kerning 210, 329
auto leading 217
auto spacing, contact sheets 111
automatic layout of UI controls 243, 291
available memory 76
Average filter 84

B

background color
    application 75
    galleries 136
background layers 82
backslashes in pathnames 306

paths 132
scripts 382
ExtendScript
command line 353
Dollar ($) object 362
engines 381
multiple engines 350
operator overloading 384
preprocessor directives 381
Reflection object 366
ScriptUI module 225, 267
ExtendScript Toolkit 348
configuring window 348
debugging 356
editing scripts 355
optimization tools 360
setting breakpoints 358

F

file extensions
format 190
including 187
File object 311
files
extensions for valid scripts 61
info 124
merging 78
name and path specifications 305
platform-independent reference objects
305
filesystem
aliases 309
error handling 310, 325
object references 305, 311
filetypes
Mac OS 76
Windows 76
filling
paths 168
selections 197
filters
MotionBlur, applying 56
See also individual filter names
Wave, applying 54
working with 46
Folder object 320
folders
distinguishing from files 305

platform-independent reference objects
305
fonts
detecting 75
determining family of 208
determining style of 208
PostScript name of 208
formats
See individual document formats
frames for UI controls 226, 231
functions
call stack for debugging 353
using 25

G

galleries
background color 136
banners 135
captions 137
color options 136
credits 137
custom settings 139
dimensions 137
filenames 137
link colors 136
making 77, 78
metadata 139
photographer 135
security text 141
thumbnail images 142
GalleryBannerOptions 135
GalleryCustomColorOptions 136
GalleryImagesOptions 137, 138
GalleryOptions 139
GallerySecurityOptions 141
GalleryThumbnailOptions 142, 143
Gaussian Blur filter 85
GIF documents
See Compuserve GIF documents
GIFSaveOptions 145
Glass Effect filter 85
global dialogs 236, 268, 373
global localize function 372
global object 362
glyph scaling 211–215
GrayColor 146
grids 188
grouped layers 82

---

var 14
variables
    assigning values to 14
    creating 14–15
    defined 13
    naming 15
    reasons for using 13
    values 14
    values during execution 351
version
    application 76
    scripting interface 76
video alpha 191
video filters
    De-Interlace 85
    NTSC 86
visibility
    channels 103
    layer comps 153
    layer sets 397
    layers 83
volumes, specifying in paths 307

W

warp 218
Wave filter, applying 54, 88
Web photo galleries
    See galleries.
Web Safe color 46
webSnap 134

Window class 268
windows
    accessing child controls 229
    adding controls 272
    automatic layout 243
    controlling 270
    creating 225, 269
    creation properties 229
    grouping controls 226, 271
    layout 227
    placing 289
    removing child controls 230
    responding to user interaction 274
    reusing 268
Windows filetypes 76
word spacing 212–216
work paths
    designating 339
    from selected area 197
wrapping, text 213

X

xml 220
xmp metadata 117, 220

Z

Zigzag filter 88
zoom 189